Making Witches

Making Witches

Newfoundland Traditions of Spells and Counterspells

BARBARA RIETI

McGill-Queen's University Press
Montreal & Kingston · London · Ithaca

© Barbara Rieti 2008
ISBN 978-0-7735-3360-8 (cloth)
ISBN 978-0-7735-4105-4 (paper)

Legal deposit second quarter 2008
Bibliothèque nationale du Québec
First paperback edition 2012

This book has been published with the help of a grant from the Canadian Federation for the Humanities and Social Sciences, through the Aid to Scholarly Publications Programme, using funds provided by the Social Sciences and Humanities Research Council of Canada. Funding has also been provided by the Memorial University of Newfoundland.

McGill-Queen's University Press acknowledges the support of the Canada Council for the Arts for our publishing program. We also acknowledge the financial support of the Government of Canada through the Book Publishing Industry Development Program (BPIDP) for our publishing activities.

Library and Archives Canada Cataloguing in Publication

Rieti, Barbara
    Making witches: Newfoundland traditions
    of spells and counterspells / Barbara Rieti.
    Includes bibliographical references.
    ISBN 978-0-7735-3360-8 (bound).
    ISBN 978-0-7735-4105-4 (pbk).
    1. Witchcraft – Newfoundland and Labrador – History. 2. Witches – Newfoundland and Labrador – History. 3. Witches – Newfoundland and Labrador – Biography. 4. Incantations – Newfoundland and Labrador – History. I. Title.
    BF1584.C3R53 2008   133.4'309718   C2007-907610-6

Typeset in Minion 11/13
by Infoscan Collette, Quebec City

For Martin and John

Contents

Acknowledgments

It seems strange to begin a list of acknowledgments with people who cannot be named, but it is my "informants" who made this book possible. To everyone who let me into their homes and lives, patiently answered questions, and helped me find other people to pester: you all have my deepest gratitude, not only for the information but for the chance to spend time as one should in Newfoundland, that is, in the kitchen telling stories.

I was lucky to have as my companion on many of these occasions Martin Lovelace, who has been unflagging in support of this project – and twenty-plus years is a long time not to flag. During those early field trips he was busy tending to small John Rieti-Lovelace; now John is a journalist and editor whose energy was an inspiration to take the manuscript off the shelf. During its long incubation, portions of it benefited greatly from being read by Marianne Stopp and Philip Hiscock. I have had helpful discussions with almost all my friends but must particularly mention Janet McNaughton, Diane Tye, and Pauline Greenhill. I could always depend on encouragement from the crowd in California: weird sisters Janet Rieti Johnson and Nancy Rieti, and old friends Peter Maund, Monique Young (fellow students at Berkeley), and William Gross.

At Memorial University, I am indebted to the contributors to the Folklore and Language Archive, on whose work I have so heavily drawn. In the Folklore department office, Sharon Cochrane and Cindy Turpin are ever resourceful, whether it's a printer problem or a sudden need for tea; the archivist, Patricia Fulton, and staff were unfailingly helpful. Generous postdoctoral support from the Institute for Social and Economic Research and from the Social Sciences and

Humanities Research Council of Canada made the field research possible. Subventions from the Memorial University Publications Subvention Program and the Aid to Scholarly Publications Programme made this publication possible.

At McGill-Queen's University Press, Philip Cercone's optimism and advice were much appreciated at a critical stage, and Joan McGilvray has been patient with plaintive e-mails over minute matters. Claire K. Gigantes's editing helped enormously with form and detail.

It is a pleasure to list a fraction of my debts here, and to think of the many people who have helped me over two decades, even if it was not in direct connection with the book. One cannot work on the subject too long without an appreciation of the bonds of affection and exchange.

Introduction

In 1729 "all Witchcrafts, Inchantments, Sorceries, Magick-Arts" were among the possible offences listed in a document for the appointment of justices of the peace throughout "the Island of Newfoundland in America."[1] Six years later, official belief in witchcraft was discarded by English law, but witch lore flourished for centuries more and continued to be imported as vigorously as salt or twine. It was baggage from the earliest days: in 1609 Basque women accused in a massive witch trial confessed to having travelled through the air to attend satanic assemblies in Terre-Neuve, perching atop ships' masts, poisoning the catch as it dried on the shore, and sinking ships.[2] All the Europeans who came to exploit the fisheries – the English and Irish, who made up the majority of settlers, as well as the French, Channel Islanders, Basques, Portuguese, and Scots – brought witch tales (if not witches) that proved to be hardy transplants. Stories of spells became staples of oral tradition in outport societies, where a great many women – and some men, too – acquired the epithet "witch." Their names, unlike those of their counterparts in Europe or early America, appear in no court records; until university-based ethnographic research began in the 1960s, only a handful of written references noted their existence. Professional scholars broke the ground, but the best reports came from students in folklore classes who interviewed family and friends or drew on their own experience. Over the next three decades, their contributions to the Memorial University of Newfoundland Folklore and Language Archive (MUNFLA) mounted to hundreds of accounts of "witching," as the matter is commonly called when someone puts a spell, or "wish," on someone else. I have combined some of this material (which I cite by the year in which it was recorded) with my own interviews, conducted mostly in the early 1990s, to consider how some people came to believe that others could influence their fortunes through sheer force of will.

Some people, not all: the first thing to know is that witch lore is not common knowledge in Newfoundland but is stronger in some places than in others. Even where it is well known, it is not necessarily taken as true; not everyone is like William Heywood, a fisherman in his seventies who told me, "We've been plagued with witches all our lives. There were thousands around here!" He was using a traditional exaggeration – one can speak of "thousands of money" – for there are only several thousand people altogether in his town, which at that is one of the biggest in the province. The island of Newfoundland is huge, about half the size of the United Kingdom, or just a little bigger than Cuba or Ohio, and its population small, just over half a million at present, including Labrador on the mainland (which adds another 294,330 square kilometres). "Newfoundland and Labrador" is the official name of the province, but I will refer to "Newfoundland" throughout this study for the sake of brevity, and since most of the examples come from the island. Communities on the island are studded along 9,656 kilometres (about six thousand miles) of jagged glaciated coast – headlands, islands, peninsulas, bays within bays. Archival data clearly show which places harbour the most witch lore; Mr Heywood's town, for instance, stands out as a veritable hotbed. "It was incredible the number of people who believed in witches," wrote a student who grew up there in the 1940s and 1950s, "and the number of events, both major and minor, that were blamed on witchcraft, everything from difficulty in starting a motor to lingering illnesses" (79/1). In contrast, there are places where it is hard to find a single story.

The reason has partly to do with ethnicity. "The English have the witches and the Irish have the fairies," Earle Mackay told me. This was an overgeneralization (Earle himself had been both fairy-led and cursed by an angry landlady)[3] but it is true enough that predominantly English and Protestant areas, such as Bonavista or Notre Dame Bays, have more witch lore than predominantly Irish and Catholic areas, such as the Southern Shore or Cape Shore. Moreover, comparison of material from the witch-rich English counties of Dorset, Devon, and Somerset readily shows that they are the parent stock of the Newfoundland strain. National origin, however, only partly explains the problem of uneven distribution; some English communities, for instance, have relatively little witch lore. This is especially true of the

Avalon Peninsula, which as the oldest settled part of the province might be expected to have the most, yet has the least. Why witchcraft gripped the imagination of some but not others is a complex question at the heart of this study; I raise it here to emphasize that many Newfoundlanders are as surprised as anyone else to learn of its existence.

For some it is an unpleasant discovery. "How fascinating!" is a typical response at, say, a dinner party, from someone hearing of my research. They are soon disenchanted, if I start telling how to break a spell by boiling a bottle of urine so that the witch will swell up and burst. Witch stories are not pretty things, dealing as they do in envy, rancour, and revenge; they are chronicles of hard looks, hard words, hard luck. They *are* dramatic, however, pitting "witch" against "bewitched" in a covert struggle for control. Rage as they might largely in the mind of the "victim," these battles arise from situations in the everyday world and feature real enough protagonists. The narratives bring colour and mystery to the quotidian round, suggesting subterranean currents fed by emotion and will. They draw tellers and audience into a negotiation of reality: what really happened? What *could* really happen? It doesn't take a lot of "believers" to keep witch tradition alive, only the circulation of gossip and tales. Occasionally someone will be inspired by what they have heard to create their own witchcraft scenario and thus infuse new blood into the repertoire. But anyone can maintain it by repeating any story, old or new. I know I've done my part, with my unsavoury dinner party conversation.

Abroad, I am more circumspect. As a resident of Newfoundland for twenty-five years, I know too well the stereotypes Newfoundlanders have had to endure, and few words are more synonymous with backwardness than "witchcraft." So I seldom mention it among people who are unfamiliar with Newfoundland unless I feel up to a long discussion of history and context; of how witch tradition grew out of the intense interdependence that made outport life possible; and of how, for all its grotesquerie, it reflects a deep-seated cultural ethic of cooperation and fair play. It is important to know, for example, that with a few official exceptions, permanent settlement was discouraged by colonial government into the nineteenth century; those determined to stay were left largely to their own devices, with results as described by George Story:

Throughout most of their history these villages existed without many of the institutions which, in other parts of the overseas

English-speaking world, shaped the development of organized societies. Their "laws," were those of a different pattern of custom, unenforced by magistrate, constable, or town council and with their own rationale for the maintenance of harmony within the community. Their people ... achieved a virtuosity in technical accomplishments which enabled them to construct their own houses, build their own boats, and conduct a fishing operation requiring judgement, skill, and daring.[4]

Astoundingly independent but also interdependent: in this setting, mutual aid was essential – it is impossible to fish alone, or birth a baby, or cut enough wood for fuel and shelter, or do almost anything else necessary to survive. Everything was cooperative, everyone was in the same boat in pursuit of a living. Given the precariousness of most endeavours, people could not always expect an immediate return for assistance rendered but they could hope for help in turn as needed. The perils of seafaring life and a harsh environment meant intimate familiarity with hardship and disaster, and the proverbial generosity of Newfoundlanders is, in my opinion, that of people who recognize the good fortune of being in a position to help, rather than being helped.

The impulse to share is no airy abstraction but a fact of culture, as attested to by the Methodist missionary William Wilson in 1865:

Here let me bear my sincere and unreserved testimony to the universal kindness and hospitality of the Newfoundlanders. I never heard of the Newfoundlander closing his door to the stranger, refusing the contents of his larder to the hungry, or tying his purse-strings when the calls of religion and humanity were made upon him. He is liberal according to his means, and I have seen in a case of famine ... a poor man and a poor widow sharing their last morsel with their necessitous and starving neighbors.[5]

Today, the province of Newfoundland and Labrador is a national leader in charitable donations, despite having the lowest per capita income; fundraisers of every description abound, for causes both local and abroad.[6] The inhabitants' hospitality came to international notice after September 11, 2001, when seventy-five flights to the United States were diverted to the province for almost a week, and stranded travellers were taken into local homes, fed, clothed, and entertained. An

American journalist billeted in Gander wrote, "Their willingness to help others is arguably the single most important trait that defines them as Newfoundlanders."[7]

All this is not to say that everyone in Newfoundland is, or was, charitable or kind: witch tales amply demonstrate otherwise. But the tales do turn endlessly on themes of giving and taking – of goods and services, offence and revenge – thus revealing an abiding cultural concern. Reciprocity in all its permutations is the lynchpin of witch lore; the narratives posit that everyone is connected whether they like it or not. One student made explicit the karmic sense of interlaced fate (as I have emphasized below):

> Old Skipper Enoch was the first to tell me that Aunt Polly Light was a witch, but everybody in the whole of the Bay knew that she was one. Everybody would try to please her, because to offend her would surely invite trouble. If she visited your house, you were expected to give her a cup of tea, because *not to do so would mean a scarcity of food in your household* during the coming year … I remember her well. She was a little old wrinkled woman and she and her husband, Lawrence, lived in a small two-room house on the outskirts of Victory Cove. They received government relief until they qualified for the Federal old-age pension. (70/2/FSC)

Since there were no federal pensions before confederation with Canada in 1949, people like Polly and her husband depended on scant public aid and whatever anyone chose to give them. Fear of spells encouraged people to oblige.

Even the most uncharitable "victims," alive to the possibilities, evince a kind of paranoid empathy in their obsession with what the witch must be thinking, doing, feeling. "I remember one incident which happened when I was in the Bay," continued the chronicler of Aunt Polly:

> A friend of mine, Ted Burton, who lived several hundred yards from Aunt Polly, was building a new house, and it seemed as if Aunt Polly for some reason or another resented it. When Ted was ready to put on the roofing material, he asked me to give him a hand. It was during the summer holidays and I went along. We had almost completed the work when Ted said, "Just look at old Poll peeping out around the corner of her house. I wouldn't be

surprised if she's up to something." Just as we were placing the last strip of roofing in place the wind suddenly changed, lifted the roofing, and away it went off the roof into the woods nearby. "Now," said Ted, "what did I say about that old bitch?" And there was no doubt that he believed it was Aunt Polly's doing.

If tradition provides the recipe and ingredients for witch episodes, the individual psyche is the cauldron wherein they are brewed. Stewing over their suspicions, the bewitched work them into a recognizable dysphoria for which there is social support and simple prescriptions for relief.

Old Caroline Bennett about 1900 put a spell on Tom Melton. Apparently Tom was so sick in the stomach that he had to stay in bed. His brother John boiled a half dollar and soon old Mr Bennett came to the house and told him that he should take the kettle off the stove, and he did. Next day he heard Mrs Bennett was in bed with a bad stomach, but Tom was well again. (69/3/FSC)

Clearly, psychological mechanisms such as displacement and projection are mainsprings of witch belief, but they intercoil so closely with social circumstance that it is impossible to say which is the more impelling force. The long habit of lending a hand or almost anything else that was needed made it hard to refuse a request; and it is around such refusals that most witch incidents revolve.

This was true in England, too. Keith Thomas wrote in *Religion and the Decline of Magic* (1971), "The overwhelming majority of fully documented witch cases fall into this simple pattern. The witch is sent away empty-handed, perhaps mumbling a malediction; and in due course something goes wrong with the household, for which she is immediately held responsible."[8] As a new student at Memorial in 1982, I was reading *Decline* as well as Alan Macfarlane's *Witchcraft in Tudor and Stuart England* (1970), landmark works that sparked the current boom in witchcraft studies, even as I was reading accounts of living tradition in the archive. I was surprised to find that only two published papers from Newfoundland[9] dealt with this fixture of anthropological research that was newly attracting feminist and social historians. I got excited at the prospect of doing fieldwork, as Jeanne Favret-Saada did for *Deadly Words: Witchcraft in the Bocage* (1980), and decided that when I had finished my research on the fairies,[10] I would move on to witches. I saw that Newfoundland promised tremendous insights into "a problem of transcultural significance," as John Demos calls witchcraft.[11]

Of course, the Newfoundland tradition is fascinating in its own right. Intensely evocative of time, place, and character, the narratives are the magic realism of folk literature, with their casual mix of ordinary and extraordinary affairs. An old woman controls the newly built boats of a town: "They found if they didn't give this woman a present, they wouldn't be able to launch the boat" (63/4/FSC). Jerseymen cross the Atlantic overnight to visit their homeland aboard coal grates or brooms, or turn themselves into loons or seals. A group of fishermen, nets empty day after day, go to the witch's tilt (temporary house) at dawn and lift the sod roof by all four corners, thus breaking the spell (64/5/FSC). Like the latter, some stories come from long ago, "when they used to have sand on the floor of their houses and burn cod oil in their lamps" (68/6/FSC), while others are set in the present day, like that of the witch who would appear in her neighbours' television screen (95/7). They etch scenes of everyday lives, especially those of women, with trenchant detail. Among the peculiarities of the "witch" Agnes Chatwin, for instance, was that she wore no underwear; people knew this because she would relieve herself in the street, something normally only men would do. Fred Earle, who told me about her, said that his mother would give her things because she was poor, and she would try to return the favour in some immaterial way, such as by prescribing a cow manure plaster as a "sure cure" for pneumonia.[12]

Although such graphic details hook the imagination, the stories, as they pass en masse from first to second to third hand and beyond, tend to streamline into shapes that make one much like another, at least from an outsider's perspective. These forms, otherwise known as folklore, are highly significant: people create and recreate narratives along certain lines because they find something meaningful or satisfying in them; these narrative structures are therefore very revealing. At the same time their formulaic, almost artifactual quality can obscure the fact that emotion is the essential fuel of witch episodes: anxiety, anger, suspicion, hate. I was sometimes surprised, in the course of my interviews, by the strength of feeling expressed by some narrators, even toward long-ago events or ones in which they were not personally involved. Describing or interpreting emotion is a tricky business, however, ethnographically speaking. The days are gone when fieldworkers tried to present their data as if they were nowhere in the vicinity when it was recorded, but personal impressions are still suspect. Looking backward through texts is even worse, trying to guess what might have gone on in someone's mind. Does a person who is bewitched after refusing a request, for instance, feel guilty, or is he simply worried because he knows from the tales what to expect? Was the man in the following story stalked by his conscience, or by the spectre of tradition?

> This man was very tight and would not give away anything. One day a woman came to his door and asked him for some meat and the man refused. Later this man went to the woods to hunt deer [caribou]. He had not gone far when he saw a deer. He put up a rifle to fire but when he took sight he saw the woman who had asked for the meat. He took down the gun and saw that the deer was still there. He did this a couple of times and the same thing happened. Finally he put a chew of tobacco in the gun with powder and shot and fired at the old lady which was a deer before he put up the gun. When he fired the deer fell down. He skinned it and took it home. When he got home he found that the old lady had been hurt and was in bed nearly dead. (68/8/FSC)

Like the man peering down his gun barrel, we – that is, we hearers and readers of Newfoundland witch tales – see events through the eyes of the bewitched: every tale in the archive is told from their perspective. They are the ones who construe certain events as witchcraft, and who, insofar as any "craft" is involved, practise magic rituals with intent to harm. Yet the stories accumulate not around *them* but around the witch. During my research I sometimes felt an unsettling sense of collusion in joining the direction of that gaze, in focusing on that figure when it is the "victims" who are the main makers and purveyors of witch lore. This is not to say that "witches" were never deliberate actors in witch dramas, only that there is little information from people who cultivated the role. And almost certainly some did: potential witches knew the tradition as well as anyone else and would be just as aware of the impact of certain words in certain situations. If the shoe fit, why not wear it? I did interview a woman who applied the word "witch" to herself (Frances Long of Part Three) and who told a chilling tale of how she had predicted death by cancer for a man who offended her. But whether she truly believed that she had done this, I cannot say. Probably no one will ever know whether *anyone* really believes that he or she can cast spells: the silence from that quarter is profound. We never hear the witches' side of the story because, unlike their unfortunate predecessors, they were not arrested or tortured into "confessing" and they never had to defend themselves in court, trying to escape being burnt or hanged.

The witch lore of Newfoundland, grown outside the purview of law, literature, and official history, has been haphazardly and belatedly documented and is still little known. In the wake of the disastrous collapse of the northern cod stocks, many communities are renovating old fishing properties and grand houses as museums where visitors can learn about former ways of life. But one could visit every heritage site in the province or read a hundred histories and never have a clue that witching existed. This study will fill that gap in the record. Perhaps it will do more, beyond the shores of Newfoundland; for all individuals and societies have their "endopsychic demons" (to borrow Norman Cohn's phrase),[13] and the anatomy of witch lore can hand us a mirror.

A NOTE ON SOURCES

For obvious reasons, a promise not to use the real names of people or places was essential to my field research. I also changed names in the archival data, which unless otherwise noted is all housed in the Memorial University of Newfoundland Folklore and Language Archive. As already mentioned, the first number in the citation shows the year in which the material was recorded (unless otherwise noted). The whole number is keyed to a list of real accession numbers to be held in confidence by MUNFLA. This is necessary to preserve confidentiality, but anyone wishing to check authenticity can do so by arrangement with the archivist or the Department of Folklore. A "C" suffix indicates a transcription of a tape recording, and "FSC" means a Folklore Survey Card, or short self-contained account on a five-by-eight-inch card. Copies of my own field tapes and notes are in the archive under restricted access.

In some instances I do use the real name of a collector, if she or he is a folklorist or other professional researcher who would expect to be recognized by myself and by other scholars who might read this work. It is not that I think their contributions are any better than those of regular students: on the contrary, the student reports are often the most valuable, coming from insiders speaking to family, friends, and people they know – which is precisely why I cannot identify them and do not think they would appreciate it if I did. Names of people and places in quotations from published sources have not been changed.

Finally, the reader will notice more citations from the 1960s than from subsequent years. This does not indicate a precipitous decline in tradition so much as changes in teaching practice. Early folklore courses were taken on a year-long basis using a survey approach that required students to investigate many areas of folklore and to submit their reports to the archive. In later years, classes became shorter (with no Christmas break during which to do research at home); the focus changed to single-topic essays and the requirement to deposit them in the archive was dropped.

Making Witches

Perry told me his father was having a real bad summer one year. He couldn't get a fish. There was always a black crow following the boat. One day he said to himself, "I'll finish her." He grabbed his gun that he had aboard the boat and shot the crow in the wing. He meant to kill her but he didn't. When they came ashore he met this woman with her arm up in a sling. When he asked her what had happened, she said that she had fallen down and hurt her arm. But he knew damn well what had happened.

Recorded by a Barrenville student from her father in 1976 and deposited in the Memorial University of Newfoundland Folklore and Language Archive

PART ONE

Witchful Thinking: An Overview of Patterns and Themes

Witchcraft is all about power, imagined and real. The existence of the proposed preternatural power is debatable – some believe in it, others do not. But it is indisputable that the *idea* has allowed its possessors to influence the behaviour, thought, and emotions of others. It gives great strength to narrative, too. "Victims" fall under the spell of a story constructed from coincidental events and based on similar tales; "witches" can be inspired by traditional scripts to act a role, to speak lines that they know will be taken as a "wish" for another's misfortune. Typically, both parties are interlocutors in some kind of conflict, but equally the victim may deduce a spell without the witch's having said a word. It seems odd to think of this quintessentially dyadic scenario as a one-person affair, but then witch tradition is suffused with irony and inversion, from the vast power assigned to obvious underdogs to the victims' self-imposed psychodramas that are blamed on the malice of others. An even larger paradox is how something so utterly intangible could have such practical effects, how tales that stand reality on its head do so to unethereal ends. Witch lore is like a hammer or knife, a simple tool with many uses. Numbingly monotonous in plot and motif, the tales open out into manifold channels of meaning, depending on who is talking, or listening, or just thinking of spells. Sometimes the dynamics are plain, sometimes subtle; often we can only speculate as to what was really going on. The patterns matter or they wouldn't recur, but their apparent uniformity can belie the diverse involvement of individuals in the life of a tale, from the original protagonists and their contemporaries to the people who pass it across time. From the tradition's protean ability to be many things to many people comes its tremendous power to persist.

Enemies and Economies

Elements of exchange permeate every aspect of witch lore. Individuals trade words, looks, insults and injury; some obtain goods or services while others acquire scapegoats for all occasions. On the south coast in the 1920s,

> Old Mrs Parot was very poor and used to go around to people's houses begging for food. People always gave her something supposing they had to do without it themselves, because if they didn't she would put a spell on them. Once she went to this door and the man of the house told her to go to hell. She went on her way but didn't forget to put a spell on him. The next day the man went into the woods to haul some wood for the winter. He had a fine strong horse and was very proud of him. All day he hauled wood. At evening he noticed his horse wasn't himself (feeling well) and that night his horse died. He said after, "She put the spell on me alright, the old witch." (74/9/FSC)

There was no surer route to witchhood than itinerant questing like that of Mrs Parot. She didn't even have to say anything when turned away: the man simply knew what he had brought upon himself. Should the refused party utter a veiled threat, all doubt is removed. Willy Dray, Mrs Parot's contemporary in the same town, perambulated twice a year collecting money for his daughter's birthday. One day, looking for breakfast, he went aboard a Lunenburg schooner tied at the wharf, but the cook refused him. "You'll be looking for someone to give you your breakfast tomorrow morning," Willy said. The schooner sank in the harbour that night. "And did people feel that Willy had something to do with it?" asked Herbert Halpert, the folklorist who recorded this story (and who always believed in asking the obvious). "Well, they felt that they wouldn't want to cross Willy," was the cautious reply (65/10/C).[1]

Since the destitute were forced to ask outright for help, it was easy for them to become witches through habitual requests. The marginally poor, like Willy, courted the same reputation as they negotiated the small exchanges that kept them afloat, for the line between charity and what was rightfully owed to them could become blurred. Halpert's informant recalled a skipper exclaiming, just as the ship left port, "Oh my, I forgot to pay Willy Dray for some rod brooms I had from him, I won't have any luck on this trip, I'll have to send him some money."

Anyone tempted to leave debts in his wake might be checked by the prospect of "supernatural" retribution, which was thus a protection for creditors, especially women who were left ashore. In the 1920s, for instance, George Allan England noted that it was dangerous to sail with someone who had not paid his washerwoman.[2] Social pressure on the would-be deadbeat is increased if the entire vessel stands to suffer, as all have a stake in seeing that he pays up. Not that everyone knows everyone else's business (though often they did), but the tales hold up cautionary cases in which dishonourable conduct spelt disaster. They also redress social inequities, if only symbolically or temporarily, as in the case of the north coast merchant who tried to dismiss a reputed witch to whom he owed money. She had rowed out to his vessel where it was moored in the harbour:

> She could man a boat as good as any man. She went aboard to get the money he owed her but he couldn't see her right now, there was someone in his office. So she got mad of course and told him before the boat leaves the harbour it will go upon a rock. Sure enough it went upon a rock, and it was a harbour that the captain had been in hundreds of times, and he knew the harbour. This is a true story. (66/11)

The narrator of this story had reason to believe – he had once promised the same woman a goose from a new brood but changed his mind when they arrived. She informed him that all his geese would die, and so they began to, one by one, until he delivered on his promise.

Outport culture was filled with such informal exchange and expectations, underwritten by tacit codes of conduct. There was no letter of the law, only spirit, and violating the spirit could cause corrosive unease. Tension ran especially high if money was involved. There was little cash in most households. Through the 1930s the fishery operated on a barter, or "truck," system whereby fishers got only credit and supplies in return for their product (a system banned a century earlier in Britain because it ensured the economic servitude of the producer);[3]

some lived in permanent debt to the merchants. The collapse of the salt fish markets and the Depression racked Newfoundland to the point where in 1933 it traded the status of self-governing dominion for government by a six-man commission appointed in London (a fateful political step backward).[4] Mining and logging offered some paying jobs, but it was not until the Second World War and the construction of American military bases that a cash economy really began.

Lack of cash did not mean that people went hungry, for it was possible to make a good subsistence living from water and land (especially after several centuries of practice). Fishing, growing, gathering, hunting, cooking, building, tending, and mending revolved in daily and seasonal cycles that many people recall as deeply satisfying, not just materially but emotionally; for all these things took cooperation and everyone had a place. But disaster was never remote, and hard-won prosperity could quickly be lost through accident or disease. Tuberculosis was rampant; women died in childbirth; men drowned at sea or died in foreign wars. Even for the thriving, resources were limited and became the bare bones of contention when deals (or ideals) went awry.

The flashpoint embedded in issues of neighbourly aid was first described to me by May and Douglas Nolan of the north shore of Conception Bay.[5] In their seventies in 1985, they were typical of the modestly successful fishing family, having raised a dozen children; Mr Nolan still went to the wharf each day to observe and advise. Less fortunate was Mrs Franklin, a veritable spectre of poverty past. In the 1930s she lived in a little house with "neither window in it nor pane of glass" and would canvass her neighbours in search of things she could use.

MR N: Now there was another old lady here, she'd go around the houses looking for something, you know, perhaps clothes, something like this, perhaps boots or something. No one would refuse her, because she'd put a wish on you …

MRS N: That was Mrs Franklin. She was – my dear, she was as tall as that door, every bit of it … And you know, she was just like a witch … And she was in the midst of poverty. Really poor off. And what she wore for stockings, she'd tie old clothes around her legs and everything; and what she wore for a cap, she'd take a man's cap, these old-fashioned caps, and she'd cut the bib off,

you know, and she'd just put it on her head. And everyone was
scared to death of her, you know. She was really bad, too.

So one time she went to a woman's house, and the woman was
picking some turrs [cleaning seabirds] that her husband was just
after coming in, he'd just gone down to Back Island and got
some turrs … So she [Mrs Franklin] asked her for one. She [the
woman] said, "I couldn't give you one without my husband was
here," she said, "because I don't like to."

"That's all right," [Mrs Franklin] said, "my dear. You won't
have none to pick after today."

So the next morning her husband went out shooting birds
again. And he lost his gun. So now, that was one wish, wasn't it?
That's very true, that's as true as the sun, my dear.

Although the drama in all its detail and dialogue is played out between
the women, the denouement is with the man who suffers the "result,"
and who therefore must have been the originator of the tale, or at
least a collaborator with his wife. He saves face after the loss of his
gun by blaming Mrs Franklin (and his wife for having refused her).
Yet Mrs Franklin probably gained most by the tale by its encouragement for others to oblige her at all costs. Mrs Nolan's mother was one
who did so.

So she [Mrs Franklin] used to come up to my house, too, when
we were growing up … So my father went away one summer, to
Boston. 'Twas no work, and no fish, so he went away. And times
wasn't very good then, you know? So, her husband used to mend
boots, you know, put the leather on the boots and mend them.
So my mother brought down a few pair of boots for him to
mend, and he mended them, and she brought them up. And she
charged a lot for them, and at that time I suppose, anyone didn't
have much money, and my mother happened to say to her, "My,"
she says, "that's awful expensive," she said.

"That's all right," [Mrs Franklin] said, "You won't be getting no
boots to have next summer." And no more she didn't. No, she
must have put a wish on my mother, too, then. So then she came
up again, two or three years after, then, she came back again. She
says, "I come in now," she says, "to see did you have a pair of
stockings to give me." And me mother said, "Yes, my dear, indeed
I have."

Her mother went upstairs and brought down the only pair of stockings she had.

For all this, Mrs Nolan stopped short of calling Mrs Franklin a witch straight out (as I've emphasized here): "She was really a bad woman, you know, really a bad woman. Oh, my, you ever see her, she'd frighten you … *just like an old witch,* my darling … You wouldn't pass along the road if she were there, you'd try to get away, you know, where you wouldn't meet her." Mrs Franklin was the only woman to elicit the "witch" word at all, although the Nolans described two others who were surely contenders. (Intent on fairy lore at the time, I didn't press the matter as I might have done later.) A Mrs Cotter didn't hold the same menace as Mrs Franklin despite her mendicant ways; a single sentence in Mrs Nolan's account (emphasis mine) suggests that she was handled with care: "And this old lady I was telling you about, she'd go around to the houses – a Mrs Cotter, she was a real old woman. She'd go around every day, now, she'd visit so many houses a day, and ask you for cookies, or a piece of bread, or a sandwich. *Well, everywhere she went, everybody gave her what she asked for.*" With her apron full of food, she would disappear each day into the hills where she said that she talked to her deceased husband Mike, although everyone else said she was talking to the fairies. Her modest requirements, spread over time ("so many houses a day"), seemed not to engender resentment; only when requests became onerous did the possibility of witching arise.

As eccentric as Mrs Cotter but much more capable was Mrs Travis of nearby Red Cove. "They said she could do anything," said Mr Nolan, "she'd cure people and she could put a wish on you." He didn't call her a witch, though. He was drawing on his mother's recollections of her rather than his own, but even his brief description conveys a person of exceptional energy and independence. Mrs Travis told fortunes by reading palms, and every October she would disappear for two weeks and claim to have been with the fairies. She would warn people, "My darlings, I'll soon be going away, now, you won't be able to visit me no more for a little while," so she must have been accustomed to company; still, "she always kept herself to herself," most notably when she would depart from Red Cove unseen, no small feat in this tiny community on a wide plain above the sea. No boat would have come or gone unmonitored, but the barrens stretched for miles behind the clutch of houses and a determined walker could reach several larger communities within a day. No wonder she was always "right thin" when she returned – but "'I was with the fairies,' that's all they'd get out of her." Clearly she was a woman who used folklore to her advantage.

Many people did, or so I was told when I asked whether reputed witches exploited or encouraged their reputation. Enoch Riall, a man in his seventies on the north coast, recalled Polly Mason, who lived near his family when he was growing up.[6] "She liked for people to call her a witch," he said, "if she didn't, she wouldn't have done so much of it, you know, because she'd say to you today, 'Well, you're going to go up in boat tomorrow,' you'd say yeah, she'd say, 'Well, my dear, you won't get nar [no] seal tomorrow.' You'd come back and you didn't get nar seal; well, you'd say Aunt Polly witched you." He thinks that she played on the beliefs of tiny Port Antler, to which she had moved from a larger town when she married. If she wanted to keep a good berry-picking spot for herself, for instance, she would try to keep others away by saying that she saw the fairies there. Her husband was "the finest kind of man" and well able to support the family, but Polly was "a kind of contrary person" – "she didn't like nobody," and nobody liked her, least of all Mr Riall's family. When anyone in his house saw her approach, they would put a broom in the doorway because "a witch would never step over a broom," but "she was too smart for that" and always picked it up. Once his brother had a litter of puppies and Polly wanted one for her children, but he refused to give it to her. "You won't get no good of them, your pups will die," she told him. When they did die, the family suspected that she had poisoned them. Although he and other boys (including her own son) shot her in effigy many times, he insists that he was always sceptical: "I don't think she was any more a witch than I was."

Martin Everly used exactly the same words about Margaret Hines, whom he called "a professional witch" who "used it to good advantage."[7] Like Mr Riall, Mr Everly was in his seventies when I interviewed him on the northeast coast, and like Aunt Polly, Mrs Hines had been a contemporary of his parents. She too "made out she could witch" and once even told his parents how to do it: "She said you had to wash your hands and say they were clear of Jesus Christ the Saviour ... That's what you had to do, but she never said she did it." What she did do was go collecting. "She'd go around, she'd get flowers; and everybody, wherever she'd go, they'd give her something, for to keep on the good side of her." Dressed all in black, she was attended on her rounds by a black crackie, a little dog which no one would touch even though dogs were not allowed in the community at the time. Often she called at Mr Everly's parents' small shop. "She'd bring Mother some little thing that probably she'd got down Twining Point or somewhere to sell, make a few cents; yes, and then she might give Mother something, a little keepsake."

Mrs Hines was not poor; her husband worked on the coastal schooners and as a mason in his spare time "for extra income for the old woman, because she came from a respectable family." She also came from a relatively large town (like Polly Mason), so perhaps she missed variety and tried to create it for herself by playing a role. If Mr Everly saw her as greedy rather than needy, he was also impressed by her entrepreneurial spirit. "She was outstanding, I don't say you'd get a woman like that in many communities, that choose their profession."

Some women, it seems, achieved witchhood while others had it thrust upon them. Anyone who wanted to be seen as a witch would likely be taken at her word – and *by* her words, whether she constantly issued predictions (like Polly Mason) or spoke ominously only in a moment of anger. Once a reputation was made, however, it could endure without confrontations or neighbourly feuds or indeed any contact at all. Jim Weller, who grew up in Port Antler in the 1950s, is not even sure if he ever actually saw Polly Mason or merely imagines an old woman tending fruit trees in her yard at the far end of town.[8] But "Aunt Polly was this mystical figure among my buddies," he said. "It was fascinating just looking at her house, because it was a witch's house." The older boys would scare the younger ones with stories about her black heart book, which Jim pictured as an evil Bible containing a list of enemies' names and how to put spells on them. One Bonfire Night in November, on a dare, he and some other boys stole a punt belonging to her and burnt it. "And I lived in fear for my life for months after. I mean, this woman definitely had magical powers that she could harm you remotely ... She could just *will* pain or hurt."

When Jim asked his older sister about Polly, yet another face emerged: one with bright red lipstick. The makeup and unusual clothing recalled by Jim's sister would have been considered "sinful" in Port Antler, Jim said, where a rigid fundamentalist Methodism prevailed until replaced by an even more fundamentalist Pentecostalism. Mr Riall had told me that Polly was ordinary-looking, but her later adoption of flamboyant style fits into a story of increasing alienation from the community. When she first arrived there, Mr Riall said, she worked as a midwife; but after a while "people wouldn't have her anymore" because she was "hard to get along with," and his mother took over the job. But then I have only Mr Riall's word for it that Polly was unpopular; competition over the job might even have been the source of the strained relations between the two households, with their brooms in the doorway and dead puppies. This intimate history of neighbourly rift eventually led to the remote witchly figure – almost a figment – of Jim Weller's boyhood imagination.

Social and economic relations were often inseparable in outport life, particularly in the pre-cash era. Discord between individuals, especially over money or goods – asking too much, giving too little – breached the larger tacit social contract of fair dealing and mutual aid.

 ## Seeing the Seers:
On Prophecy and Visiting Witches

Dire prediction is the cornerstone of witch lore. Witches may also predict good things, but they do so much less frequently, and often only after an offence has been rectified. The crux of the typical narrative, the point that events lead up to and play out from, is the fateful utterance that casts a pall on the offender's future. No sooner is it out of the witch's mouth than everyone – the offender, the hearer of the tale – knows what to expect.

They also know what to expect when a person does the right thing. In the following story from the Northern Peninsula, a family's fluctuating fortunes are traced from two remarks made by Mary Hand. An unprepossessing figure with her uncut hair and fingernails and dress made from brin (burlap) bags, Mary would go visiting during the Depression in search of food, clothes, and tobacco for her husband Jack (saying that he would pound her with a stick if she went home without it).

My uncle Eli French, who died in 1957, had a spell placed on him by Mary because he refused to give her a pan of flour. She didn't say anything angrily, but simply said, "That's okay, Eli my son, you'll be sorry before the fall." It was in the winter when she asked for the flour. That summer Uncle Eli caught only one quintal of fish to feed a family of five. He lost part of his cod trap with ice. He put out a trawl, but never saw it again. By October, things were so bad he borrowed flour and gave it to

Mary. She responded, "Bless you, my son, you'll have plenty after this." A week later Uncle Eli got a job in Dr Grenfell's mill at Roddickton for the whole winter, which enabled him to feed his family and still have enough money to pay the bills he had taken up during the bad period. (70/13)[1]

Notice that Eli's bad period was called a spell but his prosperity was not; although Mary's benediction was implicitly a reward, the fact that it has no name, no special "marked" category, suggests that it really only restored the status quo. The refusal was the exception, and the norm was to help Mary. "My father says he can remember my grand-father spending a whole day hunting for rabbits, because Mary had come to the house looking for rabbits, and he didn't happen to have any at the time," the student wrote.

As the narrative fulcrum, the prophecy is often fixed as a memorable phrase and may be the sole quotation of direct speech. "The boat might be loaded and ready to set sail, but you'll never reach St John's," said Emily Condor, another reputed witch of the Northern Peninsula, to a merchant who had refused to give her food and boots from his store where she already owed a large amount.[2] His vessel set out on a beautiful night, yet it struck something at sea and lost its cargo. The student who reported this in 1984 was hearing of long-ago events, yet the language of all the stories retains a sense of immediacy, as if the events happened yesterday. When Emily asked his great-grandfather for some fish heads for fertilizer, "my great-grandfather replied that the fishing was far from good, but told her that if they caught any fish at all, he would surely give her some for her garden." That day and for the whole season thereafter, his traps were full even when everyone else's were empty. The fullness of his courteous response replaces the curse as the decisive moment of the narrative.

Some people, like Mary or Emily, issued predictions mainly as a strategy in personal negotiations. Others prognosticated in a more gen-eral way and derived their reputation from their accuracy. "Everything she said came true," said Millicent Kelly of Jane Gricket. Mrs Kelly's family lived on the north shore of Conception Bay but fished during summers in the 1930s on the Northern Peninsula where Mrs Gricket was a permanent resident. Mrs Gricket was not called a witch, but she would say "I'll witch you" to anyone who displeased her. Far from frightening or repelling people, however, she was a "pleasant, attractive woman" with three daughters, and her immaculate house was a popular gathering place because she was amusing and "always had something to tell you." Men with water pups (sores) on their wrists would come for a poultice, which consisted only of flour and water but would not work if applied by anyone else. This was a kind of proprietary cure Mrs Kelly called "old women's rinkles" – her spelling, but nothing to do with wrinkles on the face, and nothing to do with witching. (Mrs Kelly's own mother made a poultice for burns from castor oil and lime – the chemical, not the fruit; people could bring their own ingredients, but they had to be mixed and applied by her mother because somehow she had a "special cure" in it.) As to spells, no one feared Mrs Gricket because she would only put a spell on you "if you did anything against her," so if you promised to do something, you'd better do it, and "that's all there was to it." Mrs Kelly never failed to send a package of chewing gum when she returned home at the end of the season.[3]

Although the association was not automatic, it was a small step from fortune-telling to witching. A student wrote of an otherwise ordinary woman, "her reputation as a witch stemmed from her ability to foretell the future by reading tea leaves and by telling people where to find lost items" (83/14). The techniques of tea leaf reading were available to all through local publications such as *Dr. Chase's Almanac*,[4] but specialists were in demand. One student wrote that if a certain woman attended a social function, "it was a common thing to see her surrounded by women waiting to have their cups read. Besides this, no one would dare do anything to displease her for she was able to cast a spell on people. We all feared her and thought of her as a witch" (68/15/FSC). The writer Helen Porter (now in her seventies) told me that her aunts often read one another's cups for fun, but that "Mary Ann the Duck" was a different story. Mary Ann would call about once a month at certain houses to have a lunch and tell fortunes by cards, not for money but in implicit return for the meal, Helen wrote in *Below the Bridge* (1979), her memoir of life on the South Side of St John's;[5] in an interview, she told me that while no one said so outright, there were "little whispers" to the effect that "you've got to let her in, and you've got to give her something to eat and a nice cup of tea, or they'd be a bit afraid she might put a curse on them." While Helen's aunts never predicted anything harsh, "Mary Ann didn't care, she would tell you everything," which is why "they really believed her." Parties of women sometimes ventured to her miniscule house on the outskirts of town to get their fortunes told.

Men also told fortunes and had their fortunes told. A Northern
Peninsula student described Ned Opper, a fisherman and woodcutter
who died in the 1950s and who was "locally known as a wizard"
(83/16). Ned not only told fortunes by "cutting the cards" but helped
people find lost cattle and advised on supernatural affairs; he told his
niece, for instance, not to worry that her house was haunted because
the ghost was only her grandfather. And he didn't need cards to foresee
something bad for someone who offended him – dispensing with the
props in a moment of anger being one way a fortune teller crosses the
line into "witch." When a boat operator refused Ned passage because
he was too busy guiding "sports" (visiting hunters), Ned said, "He'll
be lucky if he gets to Parson's Pond." The boat drifted for hours before
the engine would start and was then blown off course by a sudden
wind. "Only for the innocent people aboard, I'd put her to the bottom,"
Ned remarked. From this it seems that he wanted to remove any doubt
that he had *caused*, rather than merely predicted, the boat's difficulties.

Prophecy or curse? Either way, no one wanted such ambiguous
words directed at themselves. That didn't necessarily keep people away
from either fortune tellers or reputed witches; they simply exercised
due caution. "Everyone who went to see her always brought something so she wouldn't put a curse on them," wrote George Wareham
of Mrs Hynes of Placentia Bay (70/17/FSC). George's brother, the folklorist Wilf Wareham, recorded their mother's story about what happened when *her* mother (their grandmother) forgot the prophylactic
gift, circa 1870. He gives her exact words as follows:

> Old Mrs Hynes in Port Regal was a witch, or so they said. One
> time Mother and Aunt Lizanne went to visit her but they didn't
> bring her anything. She used to be mad if you didn't bring her
> anything when you came. They brought nothing and when they
> were going through the door she said, "You won't reach Mussell
> Harbour Arm this night." And as they were rowing home it filled
> in fog and they rowed out to the bay. Next morning they [people
> from their home] went looking for them and brought them back.
> They were rowing just about all night. I often heard Mother
> speak of it. (68/18/FSC)

George noted that Port Regal was a kind of way station between two
other communities; so it may have been that passers-through made
for more company than in a typical household (70/19/FSC). Since

custom demands (to this day) that visitors be fed or at least given tea, entertaining many of them could quickly strain household supplies; anyone who received many guests would naturally hope that they did not arrive empty-handed. Elsie Rossiter of Calvert on the Southern Shore told the folklorist Gerald Pocius that "the old people" had a saying: "Stay home, you'll get nothing. Go out, you'll get something," meaning that an offer of food or drink was assured.[6] Mutual visiting maintained a balance between giving and taking, but if a person did not go out much and was always a host but seldom a guest – perhaps like Mrs Hynes in her run-down house – she would not be repaid in turn; so if she had to remind her visitors of this with a little spell now and then, they could hardly object. The Warehams' aunt and grand-mother took the point, according to George: "They said that Mrs Hynes had jinked them and they never went to see her again without bringing something."

Not only was it safe to consort with reputed witches if the propri-eties were observed, there were even some witches whom it was dan-gerous *not* to visit. The niceties of exchange were elevated to ritual in the pre-season oracular consultation, first described (to my knowl-edge) in 1904 by Dr Edward Rutherford of Bonavista in his diary of a seal hunt:

> There is a certain fair septuagenarian, a modern witch of Endor, living in one of the outports, whose benediction is considered absolutely essential, to assure a successful catch of seals. Some of the captains even make it a point before sailing to lay at her feet votive offerings of sugar, tea, and other modern substitutes for the classic burnt offerings of rams and turtle doves. The men then went on to speak of a steamer lost within recent years and it seems that this malevolent beldame had put her "spell" upon this vessel. They both agreed that no navigator, however skillful, could have brought that ship safely into port. I was much relieved to hear that her ladyship was understood to be favorably disposed toward the *Virginia Lake*.[7]

A handful of archival accounts attest to these conferences in tantaliz-ingly scant detail. A north coast student wrote, "There was one old woman on Indigo Island supposed to have been a witch. Seamen used to go to her so that she would predict what kind of season they would have; Dad said if they treated her right she would tell them they would have a good season" (84/20). "Most settlements have some old lady who was looked upon to be a witch," wrote another. "Ours controlled the fisheries, rightly or wrongly." Skippers of Labrador schooners gave her a present when they left and brought her fish for the winter when they returned (71/21/FSC). A third student was given this written note: "In one northern community in Newfoundland there lived an old lady who was supposed to be a witch. Before some of the men went to the Labrador or Seal Fishery they would carry her a present to ensure them of a good trip, and the strangest part of it was it happened that way. But if she asked them for anything and they didn't give it to her, they would have some misfortune or bad luck before the year was out" (68/22).

Here is a mutually beneficial, almost symbiotic relationship: the witch receives gift-bearing visitors and probably prestige, while the visitors have a scapegoat ready in the event of misfortune – no need to retroactively figure out who offended whom. But how did these oracular figures come to be singled out for the role? The dearth of information may be due to the secrecy that surrounded some trans- actions. A student told me that in the 1970s, he and other children were afraid of a hermitlike old man in his town. Groups of fishermen could be seen visiting his decrepit house, but there was something furtive about it all, and only later did the student discover that they were going there to "get a charm" so that their fishing would be good.[8]

Information from other countries is equally scarce. Fishers and skippers of Fife in Scotland cultivated the goodwill of "certain old men" by buying them whisky before sailing.[9] In Yorkshire, the Prim- itive Methodist Nanny Jenk was so "highly esteemed by the fishermen" that they engaged her to pray for them in return for a percentage of proceeds from their catch.[10] Newfoundland's highly developed Meth- odist culture may have fostered counterparts for Nanny Jenk, espe- cially after the literary phenomenon of "How the Fish Came to Hant's Harbour Sixty Years Ago," written in 1894 by the Reverend Moses Harvey (a Presbyterian who said he got the story from the Methodist minister at Hant's Harbour).[11] The story tells how, when a poor fishing season threatened the town with starvation, a special prayer meeting was held at which saintly Aunt Lydia prayed so fervently that the fish soon arrived in shoals. Circulated widely in tracts and published repeatedly up to the present day, it sent the message out in a big way that wishing with intent and intensity worked; so perhaps less pious controllers of fish than Aunt Lydia (that is to say, witches) gained credence from her success. Another possible influence on the pre-season consultation was the Methodists' annual prayer meetings held before the seal hunt, intended to "fortify" the men's minds against temptation;[12] the sealers probably wanted a blessing for material success as well. Of course the influence of religious and folk culture is reciprocal, with the former often adapting the latter's more popular forms. Once religion becomes the "official" version of a tradition, the folk or secular manifestation may fall into its shadow – become a little shady, so to speak, and therefore kept quiet.

There is something grandly pagan but also paradoxical in according command over the very fishes of the sea to the most homely individuals. A northeast coast student wrote, "Everyone believed that Aunt Mary White was a witch. Any bad luck or good luck in the community was always attributed to her. Stuart Quince wouldn't take his schooner to Labrador without first going to see Aunt Mary and taking her a little gift ... [He] claims that he never got another load of fish after Aunt Mary died" (64/23). Yet the same account portrays Aunt Mary as a nuisance, subject to the malicious mischief of boys:

> She spent a lot of her time visiting her neighbors. One of her most common haunts was the home of George Cristopher [the informant]. George was then but a boy (now in his forties). He and his brother became fed up with Aunt Mary's always being in their house. They heard that one way to get rid of a witch was to drive a nail into her track. One day they watched Aunt Mary leaving the house and when she got out of sight, they drove a six-inch spike into her track. Aunt Mary became crippled on the way home with a bad foot and never walked another step until the day she died.

A student along the same coast knew a woman who was "definitely a witch," whom she describes as "a very kind old lady ... very fair and a lovely person ... a very capable woman, strong, healthy – very friendly" (82/24). She was also generous and apparently a good talker. "If she offered you something, well, you were just as well to take it whether you liked it or not. She had a lot of friends of course. She'd tell lots of little stories." Somehow these characteristics translated to such charisma that "when people went fishing they would always favor her or else she would turn the fish away."

It seems a safe guess that an "oracle" had in some way a strong personality, which can also be said of most of the witches in the preceding examples: some were attractive, some repellent. But maybe the answer to the enigma – how were oracles designated? – lies less in the witch than in the clientele. After all, no one can force others to come bearing gifts; there had to be something in it for them. Perhaps the visit itself was the important thing. Its association with the Labrador fishery and the seal hunt, rather than the inshore fishery, accords with the anthropological truism that people turn to magic and ritual in endeavours whose outcome is uncertain. All ocean fishing is danger-ous, of course, but the boats of the inshore fishery left and returned each day rather than disappearing over the horizon, not to be seen again for weeks or months, sometimes never.[13] Schooners were lost in gales, and hundreds of "ice hunters" perished amid the fogs of March, as they pursued seals on the shifting pack ice without so much as a lifejacket.[14] If ritual imparts a sense of control (as the "uncertainty" theory suggests), perhaps that is what the pre-season visit did. At the same time it acknowledged that not everything was in the mariners' hands. A caprice of wind or weather could send everything to the bottom, as everyone knew. For captains especially, in charge of many men and goods, the responsibility was huge; hence the relief of locat-ing at least some of it outside themselves. Too much rode on those voyages to leave anything undone that *could* be done, and the oracle's psychic insurance was cheap.

Because their predictions were so powerful, it might be expected that witches would be healers as well, but this was not often the case. Cursing and curing may be two sides of a proverbial coin, since it would stand to reason that anyone who could harm could also help; but plenty of people "charmed" various ailments (cured them magi-cally) without being called witches. Possibly this was because many of them were men, to whom the "witch" label less readily applies. Pos-sibly the requisite faith would not be placed in a too-threatening fig-ure. It is likely, too, that the connection is obscured by the secrecy which is a feature of the tradition of charming. In 2006 a student of mine did a series of interviews about a healer who had recently died in his nineties. Most accounts described his success in treating a vari-ety of ills through word, touch, and medicines he concocted from ingredients he got from the woods, but there was also mention that he "could make things happen when he said they would happen." Once he arrived too late at the dock for a boat he had planned to take out of the lumber camp where he was working. He muttered that the boat would never make it across, and "sure enough" it broke down halfway and had to be dragged back to the wharf. At the informant's request, this was removed from the student's paper before it was deposited in the archive – only the positive testimonials remained.[15] This is the opposite of what happens with the witch, whose curse is her defining legacy.

 Jinkers and Male Witchery

"If you went with a fisherman and he got a water haul, i.e., no fish," wrote a north coast student, "then you were considered a jinker or Doone dinker ... and it was highly unlikely that they would let you go with them again" (70/25/FSC). The jinker, like the oracle, served as a ready scapegoat when things went wrong, but he did not prophesy – rather, the people around him did, because he was a man, as George Patterson noted in 1897, who was "recognized as unlucky."[1] His reputation sometimes adhered in a nickname: "Foggy Bill" and "Squally Jim" seemed to attract bad weather;[2] "Jinker Joe" of Conception Bay was not wanted on voyages, I was told, because he always seemed to bring bad luck with him.[3]

H.F. Shortis described the jinker's undesirability in the early 1900s:

> It was in the days of the great sealing fleet that the jinker came forth in all his glory. In my opinion, many and many a first class jowler [sealer] lost his hard-earned lawrels [*sic*] through the unfortunate circumstance of having the jinker smuggled on board, either through the influence of the merchant, to whom he owed a large amount, which accumulated spring after spring, or otherwise that the skipper was imposed on by his tidy and healthy appearance, and was thereby induced to give him a berth to the ice-fields.[4]

Shortis almost seemed to have had someone in mind, and indeed he claimed to know a "fine-looking" fellow who "'jinked' every sealing master he went with" for twenty-five years.

Even a long-standing reputation, it seems, did not necessarily keep men off boats. John Sainsbury set off with the *Neptune* in 1929, according to Job Barbour, the ship's captain, but quit after the first leg of the journey when no one would speak to him; after his departure, the ship was blown off its coastal route and ended up in Scotland.[5]

Although Barbour discounts the crew's belief, its prominent place in his book, *Forty-Eight Days Adrift* (1932), nevertheless invited readers to entertain the possibility and added the authority of print to a normally oral tradition.

Somehow jinkers found their way to the bottom of a male pecking order. Perhaps it was kinder or simply evasive to say that they were "unlucky" rather than incompetent or unlikable, or whatever it was that made them the designated blame-bearers. The folklorist John Ashton thinks that they were in some way "outsiders or deviant," and he should know because as a native Englishman married to an outport schoolteacher, during the 1970s he was "singled out on numerous occasions as the underlying cause of failed fishing or hunting expeditions, not to mention broken-down cars or boats."[6] The same thing happened to the English anthropologist James Faris, in the same area, in the 1960s.[7]

Usually, the jinker's baneful influence was portrayed as involuntary, an unfortunate personal attribute rather than the product of malice; but it could shade into more typical witchery, and then some:

> Some people in Channing Cove could put spells on people in order to punish them. One man in Channing Cove had this power. The people called him "Jinker." He could put a spell on you, preventing you from doing something you could normally do well. Mr Carter [the informant] said his father made the old jinker angry one day and couldn't shoot any birds, even though he was an excellent shot. The old jinker stood on the stage [wharf] and grinned when he came back empty-handed. Some people in Channing Cove had "antidotes" for the jinker. One such man had heard that boiling one's shot [ammunition] in human urine would cancel the jinker's powers. This man would jeer at the jinker and then go out birding to see if his "antidote" worked, and it did, the man shot more birds than usual. Many people feared this jinker, especially after he said he had sold his soul to the devil. Seven years after he said this, the old jinker died for no apparent reason. People believed that the devil had collected what was his. (84/26)

A woman who did this, or made the same claims, would very likely be called a witch. Since the default of the word "witch" is a woman – that is, a witch is a woman unless otherwise specified – men may be underrepresented in this category even though they do the same things. As Richard Bovet wrote in 1684, "It is Observable that Witches are commonly of the female sex, and some there are that confine that Term wholly to them."[8] The term may be confined in Newfoundland, too, but not the power of witching; no one would say, "He can't do it because he's a man." And man-made spells are, on the whole, similar to those laid by women. A southeast coast man, for example, put a spell on a magistrate who convicted him of poaching moose: "Six months from today you'll be in a crump." The judge had a stroke and died shortly after that (69/27/FSC).

Men do tend to be associated with devilish or ritual aid, like Elias Joffrey, who used "a cat's heart stuck full of pins to do his dirty work." When another man shot a wild duck on the island where Elias lived by himself and considered everything to be his own, Elias correctly predicted that his fifteen cattle would die (66/28/C). Enoch Riall, who told me about Polly Mason, also told me about Uncle Dave, who owned a "warlock's book." The strange thing about Uncle Dave was that he never went away to work like the other men did, instead staying in Port Antler fixing up houses and doing other odd jobs which people gave him because they were afraid of him. Loners like Elias or Dave, left to their devilish devices, could be imagined to get up to anything. Laurence Noftall of Placentia Bay "always seemed a little different," according to Wilf Wareham, although no one called him a witch or wizard "or anything like that" (68/29/FSC). In 1961 he was fired after five years as skipper of the *Claire Alice* because he was too slow getting from port to port, so he "quietly told the owner that he had cursed the boat so she would never pay." People laughed at this, but a series of calamities dogged the schooner to the point where it was abandoned two years later, "a lost cause."

Personal characteristics aside, the big question about male witching is this: why was it almost never directed at women? One answer is that many men don't like to do things that have strong female associations, whether it's wearing a dress or witching. Another is that the societal prohibition against assaulting women extended to witching, for a spell is, after all, an attack. (*Counter*spells attack women gleefully enough, but never as a first strike, and only after the target has been dehumanized as a "witch.") A third possibility is that women had more to gain from witching than men did – it served more of their needs and desires than it did those of men. This is obvious in the case of poor women who had to forage for food; but there were many strictures in ordinary women's lives that witchcraft could mitigate or evade. A few examples follow.

 ## Witching as Equal Participation and Social Inclusion

When Job Barbour took John Sainsbury aboard the *Sea Bird* (some time before the *Neptune* made its accidental voyage to Scotland), the ship was so wracked by storm that Barbour held the wheel himself for eleven hours. "I was quite satisfied to make myself the 'goat' for poor John," he wrote, "seeing that I had taken him against the wishes of all, including my mother who I believe, was appealed to by the crew before we sailed."[1] Whether Mrs Barbour shared the crew's opinion or not (maybe she simply saw that his presence would sap confidence), their appeal to her is of interest for it raises the grossly neglected issue of women's influence in the ostensibly male precinct of fishing affairs. As matriarch in a prosperous mercantile clan, Mrs Barbour exercised more visible authority than less advantageously placed women; but all women had a deep interest in the fishery – the family depended on it, after all, and most of them worked in it at least as hard as the men. Their uncontested responsibility for the household was only part of their job in the days of the salt fishery, when women often made up the "shore crew" who processed the fish for export. This was backbreaking work that had to be done right, and right away. If the fish was salted too lightly it would spoil; left in the rain, it would rot; too long in the sun, it would burn – any of this would lower the price or make it unsellable. All day and often all night, women would be carting, cutting, gutting, curing, loading, turning the fish. They were at it through the mid-twentieth century, until processing plants finally supplanted the old methods.[2] At an all-male fishery conference in 1962, Newfoundland's first premier, Joseph R. Smallwood, professed surprise that women were still engaged in such "slavery." Welcome at the splitting table but not the conference table, "women, their issues, their work in the fishery were largely invisible," as the sociologist Barbara Neis put it.[3]

Of course women were not invisible slaves in their own communities; on the contrary, they could be autocrats of high degree. Leslie Harris, historian and former president of Memorial University, describes visiting his cousins' house in Little Harbour, Placentia Bay, where their grandmother reigned:

At the door, we would be met by our Aunt Bess with a whispered greeting (one did not speak loudly in the presence of that mother-in-law) and led forthwith to pay homage to the personage who ruled the domain with a rod of iron. She would be seated in her rocking chair with a clear view through the front kitchen window of the gardens as well as the flakes and waterfront premises, for she, literally and figuratively oversaw every aspect of the family's domestic economy. She alone ordered the comings and goings of all about her. When should her men sail for Oderin Bank or Cape St Mary's, or wherever the exigencies of their fishing might take them? When should the salt bulk [fish] be washed? How long should it stay in water horse [piles]? When should the fish be spread, or put into faggots or packed in piles? When should the grass be cut, or, the potatoes trenched?[4]

With age and luck, women could move beyond doing the work to supervising it; but they could be forceful enough while still on the stagehead. Women who cleaved metre-long cod at a stroke were hardly shrinking violets. Barred though they may have been by custom and law from political decision making and the actual fishing, they nevertheless found ways to participate – and one of those ways was witchcraft. This is one reason why witches are so often seen to "act" on behalf of husbands and sons (but not daughters). The folklorist Larry Small described how every spring in his hometown, inshore fishing crews vied for the best spots. Some communities used a lottery,[5] but in others, like his, berths went to whomever got there first.

Competing for trap berths was always a sort of "hell-time" for fishermen at home. This particular spring [c. 1955] one fisherman and his crew were able to get to a certain trap berth before anyone else. It was a good berth and was usually occupied each year by another crew. Anyway, the whole thing caused an uproar. The wife of the man who always occupied the berth became enraged. She bet with all her power that the crew who had taken her husband's berth would not get any fish whatsoever if she could do it. The berth was a failure all that summer. From that time on everyone feared her as a witch and didn't cross her in any way, especially the fishermen. (67/30/FSC)

Notice that it is the wife, not the husband, who is said to be furious. At the same time that witching offered women a voice in fishing affairs, it allowed men to remain diplomatically silent. A man could find it very handy to have a witch for a mother or wife. In this instance the issue was resolved without the husband's having to confront the usurpers, with whom he still had to fish year after year.

The men were also likely to have been lifelong acquaintances if not necessarily friends, for although men ranged widely in pursuit of work, they did not typically have to uproot permanently from their home communities as women did. Women were more mobile in this respect. Girls as young as ten went "into service," working as unpaid servants in return for room and board, sometimes far from their homes. Young women were expected to move upon marriage to their husband's residence where their livelihood would be based. As "strangers," these wives were the very ones who could be suspected of witchcraft in "Cat Harbour," the pseudonymous north coast community where the anthropologist Faris worked in the 1960s; in fact, according to Faris, natives of the place could not be considered witches at all.[6] I did not find that this applied as a rule everywhere (nor did I find that only men performed counterwitch rituals, as he noted in Cat Harbour), but since "new" women were an unknown quantity (from the native point of view), they might be first choice if a witch was desired. For their part, the women might not have minded having this potential, if it could help them negotiate some advantage within the virilocal system. That men preferred not to blame one of their own is perhaps why witches were cited more often than jinkers for fishery failure – the onus was cast farther away, out of the boat, to someone on the distant shore. By deflecting conflict from itself, the group could remain harmonious, united in the (imagined) face of opposition.

That face often belonged to a conveniently well established witch – someone like Mrs Bombey, for instance, who lived near the Barbours and who, like Mrs Barbour, enjoyed a strong influence on the men around her and their work. (Bombey and all names but Barbour are pseudonyms in the following accounts.) She was the bane of the merchant Rogers family, according to one student. "Whatever her son Paul asked for, the Rogers would always give him," he wrote. "If they had to turn around and buy the thing he wanted the very next day, they'd give it to him. They were afraid that his mother would 'witch' them if they did not give him what he wanted" (69/31). Paul seemed to have trouble finding and keeping work. "A fellow by the name of Arthur Howsell wouldn't give her son a berth on his fishing schooner which he had recently built. She uttered something to the effect that he would never use it himself. That very night the new schooner broke clear her moorings and was smashed to pieces on one of the islands nearby" (ibid.). A story from a different source tells how Paul was hired to repair a schooner, but "another fellow undermined him" and got the job instead (65/32/c). When the vessel was finished and ready to launch, it burst the cables and wouldn't come off the blocks. "The man in charge had to humble himself down, go to Grandmother Bombey and ask if she had the schooner hung up." She merely told him to go back and his schooner would go off, which it did.

Witching was not just about material things: getting respect was important too. Another of Mrs Bombey's sons, Harold, was once the only skipper (out of more than a hundred) who had not been invited to a birthday party. "No, Mother, I suppose I wasn't worthy to go to the big shindy," he said, to which his mother replied, "Never mind, my son, I don't suppose they'll enjoy theirself too good." The party was held in a room with a kerosene chandelier. "Before they sweetened their cup of tea, down comes this lamp and he [it] beat every bit to pieces and spoiled the whole issue and there wasn't one person had a bite to eat" (65/32/c). This tale hints at social stratification that would be less marked in smaller places, where it was typically assumed that all would attend a festive event. "Every one in the community was invited. No matter how poor you were," as Hilda Murray wrote of weddings in Elliston.[7]

Despite the lively detail and dialogue of the chandelier tale, the narrator was not in fact from the Bombeys' area but said that he heard the tale "every year" during the seal hunt. Men carried a stock of stories on their various voyages, which were effectively flotillas of motifs from bay to bay. In the next large community along the shore from the Bombeys', for instance, it was Granny Copper who brought the party to a crashing halt.

Once there was a wedding to which most people were invited except Granny Copper. Just as they were all sitting around the table and about to eat the wedding dinner, a large chandelier which was hanging from the ceiling fell right into the middle of the table. This upset the tea, broke a lot of dishes and spoiled some of the food. The next day someone told Granny what had happened and she replied, "Ha ha, Granny wouldn't waste her tea." From that time on Granny was always invited to all social functions. (68/33/FSC)

In both versions, the attempt at exclusion is dashed along with the dishes.

In 1964 ninety-year-old Enos Spires recalled both Mrs Copper and Mrs Bombey by reputation, and from what he said it is easy to see how the same stories affixed to both (64/34/C). Enos knew a woman who thought that at the age of thirty she was too old to marry, but she went to Mother Copper ("a pure witch") before a trip into St John's "to see what she had to say about things." Mother Copper told her that before she returned she would have a man, and that if she did, she would have to give her a present. The woman did marry and did give Mother Copper a gift, but it was not what she wanted: "She never did right, what she give her." The woman's new husband embarked on a voyage to the Labrador Straits along with Enos, and when they had no luck, the skipper guessed the problem: "If you promise Mother Copper anything and never give it to her you won't get a fish." He wanted to leave the husband in Nain, but Enos had a better idea: "'Tis cheaper to shoot her." He tied an empty shotbag to a pole, and shot it, hitting it three times in the neck. The fishing was fine for the rest of the season, and upon their return in the fall they found that Mother Copper had been in bed all summer with a pain in "the crook of her neck." ("That's where I shot the bag," Enos explained, meaning it literally and not as a pun or metonym.)

> Yeah, that's what the old stuff we'd be doing them times, see, I doubt if there was anything to it. Anyway, seemed like she was a witch, they put a wonderful dependence on her, they wouldn't do nothing against her, this old Mother Copper in Green Cove ... whatever she said would be the law. There's an old Mother Bombey in Nettle Cove, just the same with she down there ... Captain George Barbour, before they'd go to the ice, Captain Job Barbour, them fellas, when they used to be going to the seal fishery, they'd do everything for her [so they] wouldn't lose their luck, afraid she'd – Lord knows what they used to give her, give her a whole lot of stuff.

The more people obliged, the more demanding a witch could become; requests could move beyond necessities to "luxury" goods. Someone once gave Enos's father-in-law a canary, which he put in a cage on the verandah. Mrs Bombey "admired this bird and she want en [it] wonderful bad. Well now, he said, Grandma, he said, I can't give 'ee that one … I had en given to me. She said she'd like to have him all the same, you know, and the next day he was dead, she witched him, witched him dead." Some pigeons died, too, when Mrs Bombey asked for one; Enos's father-in-law didn't refuse but he didn't jump to comply, telling her, "If you can catch one you can have en."

I heard a bit about the Bombeys myself when I visited the area. Two sisters, Ellen Martin and Dorothy Wise (probably in their seventies), told me that Mrs Bombey had always been welcome at their house, but if she were seen approaching, they would rush to put away any fresh flowers because if she saw them she would want them, and if she didn't get them they would die anyway.[8] Dorothy's son told a story of Paul enjoying power in his own right. He said that Paul once wanted a ride on a sled but the sled owner said that there wasn't enough snow for the dogs to pull it. "That's all right, you hitch them up, they'll do it," said Paul. When this was done they sailed off smoothly with both men aboard, over the gravel and rocks.

There is simply no shutting them out: magically or literally, witches put themselves where they are not wanted.

One fall old Mrs Bombey wanted a trip to St John's on a schooner belonging to the Barbours (businessmen who sent boats to the Labrador fishery). For some reason or another, they said they couldn't take her. The next morning the Barbours were ready to go to St John's. However, they could not get the anchor off bottom. This happened morning after morning. By now the Barbours were firmly convinced that "old Mrs Bombey" really was a witch, had them "witched," and that they would never get to St John's unless they took her along with them. The next morning, with "old Mrs Bombey" on board, there was no trouble getting the anchor up and they went on to St John's. (69/34)

Where the witch insinuates herself, most of all, is in the victims' thoughts. The student who described Mrs Bombey's boat trip related another incident.

One day a group of men … told her that the next morning they were going out "birding." "You won't get nar one," she said, "you

won't get nar one." Apparently the men had said or done
something she didn't like. Anyway, the next morning the men
went birding. They said that birds were never so thick – there
were thousands of them, but fire all the guns they like and they
couldn't kill a bird. The men were firmly convinced that
Mrs Bombey had "witched" their gun.

The men weren't bad hunters – it was Mrs Bombey calling the shots.
   Maybe Mrs Bombey would have liked to go hunting herself. There
must have been many women who would have preferred sailing a ship
to baking bread or any of the other repetitive tasks that made up
"women's" work (just as there must have been men who lacked the
stomach for life at sea), but traditional gender roles were not easy to
get around. Dona Lee Davis notes the derisive term "shore skipper"
for a woman who is "bossy and interferes excessively in her husband's
affairs,"[9] but in the fishery, those affairs were her business too. Prophecy
could be a bid to be heard and taken account of.

 ## The Victim Strikes Back

When people who suspect that they are bewitched try to "counter"
the spell, they undertake the only unambiguously purposeful, unde-
niably "magical" acts of the whole scenario. These procedures are thus
the material heart of witch lore and could also be called its material
culture since the actors use objects, not just words. The artifacts would
constitute a very small museum display: some old bottles and pins;
boards or a door painted with hearts or human figures bearing bullet
holes; a handful of cut-up coins. But the forms and imagery of counterspells mirror the violent, corrosive feelings at the core of a curse:
the hidden stoppered bottle festering like a grudge or boiling like an
overheated imagination; the gun exploding into the facsimile witch;
the totemic heart cut through with a knife.
   Sometimes remedial action is the main event – a victim might not
know who put a spell on him or why but is only concerned that it be
broken. Two brothers on the south coast, for instance, had a bad start
to their fishing season, so they "collected all their fish hearts," stabbed
them full of holes, and threw them in the stove. The lids of the stove
flew off with a bang:

Shortly afterwards Mrs Newhouse, who was about ninety years old and lived on the other side of the harbour, took sick and was straightway taken to bed where she died some months after. [The brothers' mother] said that it was Mrs Newhouse who had cast a spell over her sons, because the beginning of her sickness coincided with their heart-stabbing and better luck ... The important thing for them was that their luck from that day changed, and during the rest of the summer they did as well or better than anyone else. (69/35)

The student explained the operation in terms of the curative properties of fish hearts, which can be kept as talismans against various ailments,[1] but it is also of a piece with visceral counterspells everywhere. Paul Pinter, a ship's mechanic on Chart Island, told me about two young men who after a successful season on the Labrador were having trouble getting home with their load of fish.[2] Prior to the voyage, they had been able to offer a berth to only one of two sons of a certain woman (an ordinary woman, not a reputed witch) and they decided that she must be taking revenge:

> So one fellow said to the other fellow, "Must be the old woman, I suppose, where we couldn't get her son to the Labrador." So they carved a heart in the piece of wood, one fellow did, and the other fellow cut his finger and let the blood flow in the heart. And they drawed her name in the center of the heart and fired at it. And apparently they come on home with no problem. And when they got home they found that the woman was after falling down and broke her leg that bad that she ended up dying with a limp in her leg, the rest of her days. That's true, I can remember that, seeing her getting around, you know, with a limp in her leg.

In Paul Pinter I met a lively storyteller with a deep interest in many traditional forms; he was an accomplished accordion player and had just been invited to tell ghost stories at the elementary school. He and his wife Susan were in their forties at the time of our interviews and had several young children who were also present. Susan was quieter but knew all the stories; in fact, most of Paul's witch tales came from her grandfather. They concerned the grandfather's next-door neighbour, Janet Black – "He could tell hundreds about her." Paul didn't identify Janet but Susan wrote her name on a piece of paper as we talked. One story in particular conveys the antagonistic relationship between the neighbours, for the grandfather accused Janet of magically preventing him from landing his fish.

> [He] used to be down in the run, bringing up loads of fish, and she'd be up there in the pond, there with a, like a boat in the pond [a facsimile boat representing his own], and she'd be making all kinds of motions, making all kinds of wind storms in the pond, right, and saying all kinds of old stuff, and he couldn't get up out of the run then … And he caught her … making all this wind. They had some row over there, over on the point.

The stories about Janet Black were good, but even more fascinating, as I sat listening, was that I happened to know that they formed the background to Paul's own experience of bewitchment. A witch-driven wind whipped through his very own tale, I would discover. But here I should backtrack and explain how I met the Pinters. I went to their house at the suggestion of an older neighbour whom I met through a contact in another town; at first the Pinters' neighbour told me that, concerning witches, no one under fifty would know what I was talking about – but then he remembered something about Paul and a bottle and a man named George. He swore me to secrecy about this, however. So I walked around in the road for a while to get up my nerve to knock on the Pinters' door, but I needn't have worried because when I did, I was welcomed enthusiastically before I even explained my errand. Paul had mistaken me for someone he met on the ferry who was interested in the accordion, and by the time we cleared up the confusion I was in the kitchen having tea. Later, after recording the stories about Janet, I asked Paul the same question I asked everyone I spoke with: Had he ever heard about "putting up a bottle" to break a spell? At this, the children burst into laughter; they knew what I was talking about. After a moment of surprise Paul embarked on the following story, growing more animated as he went on. Susan offered critical clarification at key points.

> PAUL: Oh! That happened to me. That happened to me, I gotta tell you. You heard that, did you? Yeah, well, I'll tell you this one now. It was a Monday morning, just after we got married, I suppose, and so anyway, I had to go up to the store for

something, and Susan was here washing clothes, I believe she had sheets and all that stuff washed. Anyway I went to get aboard the car, and when I went out I had a flat tire. So I thought to myself, well that's all right, got the pump and I started to pump him up, this tire, and when I started to pump him up I looked through under the car, and the other one went flat, before me eyes, eh?

So here was two flat tires, now, right off the bat, I didn't even have a chance to move. So at the same time, a big gale of wind, a squall of wind hit, and sheets went everywhere, wet sheets on the clothesline, all out over the garden, busted line. So Susan come in, in a big rage, I was out there changing tires, and she looked out through the window here, and she said, "Well, everything's happening," she said, "and now," she said, "they got my wedding ring split in two." Her wedding ring just split in two.

SUSAN: And our wedding picture split in two.

PAUL: And our wedding picture split in two. All this happened, now, a Monday morning, in about an hour, everything going to pieces. So I got in a rage. And I started to swear. I said, "Brother," I said, "you'll die." So I go and gets the bottle. And I pissed into it. I put the cover on good and tight and I turned the oven on and put it in the oven. I said, "You'll bust, you son of a B, you'll bust." And about two hours later I'd say, or three hours, the helicopter was landed on the other side to pick up this woman who was gone to the hospital piss-bound blocked solid! [Everyone laughs.]

SUSAN: Yeah, but I don't think she was the one.

PAUL: Well, no, you don't think it, but I don't know that; I don't know, see. But it happened.

BR: But when you were saying that, were you thinking of her?

PAUL: Not of her, no. "Whoever you might be," that's who I had in mind, eh? And I was raging [laughter]. And it was just bubbling then, in the bottle –

SUSAN: Someone trying to bust up our marriage.

PAUL: Yep. But everything happened in about an hour, eh? That was it. Pumping up a tire, and the other one going down before your eyes ...

They didn't say why someone wanted to break up the marriage, but the broken wedding ring and wedding picture make the objective clear (as do the tangled sheets and deflating tires to the symbolically minded). They also didn't mention a suspect, although Susan doubted that the woman was behind it.

BR: So maybe it got kind of misdirected, your energy?

PAUL: [laughs] Yeah, but anyway, got it straightened out again after that ...

SUSAN: But now I don't know if this person would be guilty or not, I don't know.

PAUL: I used to always figure out, every time I'd see her she'd be giving me a bad eye.

The emphasis on looks becomes notable when they started talking about other people. The exuberant performance gave way to lowered tones, their voices dropping at points so that it was hard to catch every word.

BR: Are there still people who have that reputation [of being a witch]?

SUSAN: Oh yes. Yeah, there is a person not too far away from us, I think he got power.

PAUL: Who's that, a fellow here? Oh yeah.

DAUGHTER: Are you talking about Roddy? The power of the seventh son?

SUSAN: [Too low to be heard clearly, but she identifies a different man, George]. I think he got power.

PAUL: Oh yeah. Guaranteed. Guaranteed.

SUSAN: You only just got to look at the way he's [strong?]. And I think whatever he wants, in his mind, I think, you know, it could happen, eh?

BR: So what is it, he's just an unpleasant person?

PAUL: Oh, very, very, *very* unpleasant.

SUSAN: And very sarcastic, and he would turn you away from his door, eh, from his door, right?

PAUL: Devilish [ways? voice?].

SUSAN: Very grudging. And the look that he got, you know, is something else. [Vicious?]

BR: He's like that with everybody, is he?

SUSAN: Most everybody -

PAUL: Most everybody.

SUSAN: He hasn't got a good word for anybody, you know, that type of person, eh?

Paul and Susan's testimony is remarkable on many fronts. Perhaps most striking is the wild physical energy swirling through the affair, snapping the clothesline, cracking metal and glass. Paul's rage whizzes missile-like across the island where it strikes the woman like a bolt of lightning. The very language – raging, boiling, bubbling, busting – is charged, and very different from archival descriptions in which counterspellers appear to go about their work in brisk workmanlike fashion. This comes, of course, from oral performance, a "live" versus a summarized event, full of emotional content and shifting moods. The stress on "looks" also contrasts with archival accounts, and it is easy to see why: it is hard to describe the fleeting and subjective impressions that make up "looks," whether in reference to how one person

looks at another (what exactly does a "dirty look" consist of?) or to
the general "look" of a person, like the saturnine George. It is much
easier to document words, and because of this, the threatening utterance might be given undue weight in the description of witch tradition – that is, behind the words may lie an entire silent history of
inimical "looks." (In modern France, Favret-Saada found that "even
more than speech or touch, the witch's look has devastating effects.")[3]
The same may be said of counterspells – that because they are easily
described, they distort the overall picture of witch lore, looming too
large over subtler signs: the "bad eye" Paul thought he was getting, or
the "grudging" and "sarcastic" attitude that Susan sensed in George.

These "currents of malice," to borrow Persis W. McMillen's memorable phrase,[4] are the alchemical fuel for the spells. George's magical
malevolence is an extension of a general social offensiveness; his indif-
ference, even antipathy, to his neighbours means that he is not bound
by the same rules they are. Since he is always angry, he is always powerful, whereas Paul was only powerful in the grip of his rage; and
despite the heat that launched his counterattack, he was only deflecting, not generating, magical damage. Even for that he used a traditional prescription, and one does not have to look far for its source.
A Chart Island student wrote:

> A friend of mine was starting a business on Chart Island in the
> fall of 1978. From the beginning he was plagued with difficulties,
> such as machinery breaking down without explanation. Almost
> every day something went wrong. My friend believed that a
> certain man had "witched" him. Being a believer in witches he
> decided to break this spell. He urinated in a pint glass bottle and
> heated it with a blowtorch. The urine had to be heated until it
> was boiling. If it was overheated and the jar or bottle broke the
> spell would not be broken. My friend claims that from that day
> on he never had one problem getting his business started. He
> said that while he was heating the urine he was thinking about
> the man who had witched him. (80/36/FSC)

The source for this story is unclear (which is unusual for archival
material); Paul was an informant for this student on another topic,
and this might have come from him as well. He certainly would have
heard it, and perhaps he appropriated or adapted it for his repertoire;
as I mentioned, Paul is a good storyteller and as such always on the

lookout for material. Does this mean that he made up his story of the bizarre Monday morning, or that he doesn't believe in witches? Not at all: I have no doubt that he and Susan both believe that certain people have magical power and that it had at some point been aimed at them; and I am sure that he actually put the bottle in the stove. Whether he really believed that it sent someone to hospital is another matter, for it is possible to perform such a ritual with no belief, with half-belief, or for comic relief. (I know because I have done it myself.) A striking coincidence, like the woman going to hospital, is icing on the storyteller's cake.

It does seem clear that Paul and Susan felt that at some early stage their marriage was in danger. Locating the threat outside themselves reaffirmed marital solidarity, closing ranks against an unseen foe. Someone, it follows from this, must have been jealous. Someone perhaps had wanted Paul or Susan for themselves, or someone envied their (supposed) happiness: both kinds of coveting are well documented motives for spells. The married state is also a common target for revenge. Flora Parsons of the Northern Peninsula, for instance, told me that when the witch Aggie Tackell overheard Flora's cousin making fun of her (the cousin was calling Flora "You Aggie Tackell"), she told the cousin that she would get married but have no luck. The cousin and her child died in childbirth.[5] It is not always so clear what is at stake, however, because private areas can be hedged about with layers of symbol, metaphor, and sublimation. Is the following tale about cabbage or sexual jealousy?

> My father's brother-in-law … told Dad that his mother during
> the first years of her marriage had fallen under the spell of an old
> maid of the community which contributed to her bad luck and
> that of her husband because she did not give the old woman a
> meal of fresh cabbage when she wanted some, but this was
> because it was just mid-summer and the cabbage was not fully
> grown. Anyway, another man of the community told Mr Marden
> to mark out or paint (not sure) the resemblance of the old
> woman, stick it up, then shoot at it. The idea then was that
> a good hit would overcome the spell. In this case Dad said it was
> a success, because the spell was soon broken. (69-7/174/FSC)

Some symbols are obvious enough, like the patent male associations of common counterspells that can hardly escape the most literal mind.

Both employ male tools, for one thing, and many metaphors equating guns and penises play on the parallels (both can be "rods," an infertile man is "shooting blanks," and so on). In counterspells, both are discharged at the witch effigy (or into her, when she is represented by a bottle, in which case she may even swell and burst as if pregnant). Given their phallic nature, does it stand to reason that they counteract a threat to male sexuality? I could hardly ask Paul or Susan. Symbolism may be subconscious in any case, its whole point being to deal with matters that are not addressed directly, or to express fears and impulses unacceptable to the individual psyche or society.

And who would come right out with it anyway, if he feared for his personal prowess? One man seemed to hint at it while talking to a student in 1974 (74/37/4 FSCS). The student was being regaled with witch tales by Abbie Gray, who named at least three other women in the community as witches (one of whom told another woman that "she would never enjoy married life"; the woman died a week after her wedding). Listening to it all was sixty-two-year-old Edward Parrish, who was less forthcoming.

Mr Parrish told me, when I asked him, that he had shot a quarter that he cut up at the heart on the store door [a painted heart common on outbuilding doors]. I asked why and he said he had been witched. He said he was having hard luck. I asked him this when we were all sitting around the living room. Aunt Abbie was there, too. Mr Parrish seemed very secretive. We went into the kitchen and I asked him what his hard luck had been and had the shooting worked. He said it had been a sickness (a personal thing) and other things. Then I asked him who the witch was. He gave me a look with the eyes and then he took a piece of paper and pen and wrote, "I blame it on that woman in there." "Aunt Abbie?" I asked. He nodded his head. Later on, after she had gone, I asked him whether the shooting worked. He said he didn't know whether she got hurt or not when he shot the heart because he didn't see her for a while but the sickness went and his luck wasn't bad anymore. He really believed this, was dead serious, but his wife thought it was foolishness. Mr Parrish said he tried the bottle cure first. He did his pee in a bottle, corked it and stuck a big stocking darning needle down into it and left it in the store. This was supposed to drive the witch in a frenzy and she would come pleading for mercy. But it didn't work and he went to the store to look at the bottle and the cork had blown off.

That firing the gun and urinating in the bottle are supposed to "work" in the same way make them what Alan Dundes, the late great Freudian interpreter of folklore, would call symbolic functional equivalents.[6] Mr Parrish's big darning needle is another, along with other piercing projectiles. Dundes would have loved the story of the man who retaliated against a witch by "ramming" a six-inch nail into her heelprint in the mud, giving her a permanent limp (67/38); as Dundes's students know, shoes are a common psychoanalytic symbol for female genitalia. This woman had "a reputation to have the power of causing death of an animal offspring – you know, a calf or lamb." She had killed the man's cow simply by looking at it, although she didn't mean to; she had even done it to her own livestock: "Her cow had a calf and it died after she looked at it." Dundes's model of phallic practices against the evil eye could hardly find a better illustration.[7]

There is no mistaking the evil eye in Newfoundland, although it seldom goes by that name. The destructive gaze or wish may be inadvertently cast, an almost autonomous force rather than a directed vengeful spell; it is dangerous to anything desirable, especially animals, plants, and children – anything, in other words, full of budding life that someone might envy. In the only actual use of the term I have found, a midwife spelled it out: infants should wear a religious medal against the evil eye, she said, which was "envy by other mothers." She added that they might say "What a lovely baby" but don't always mean it (79/39). Expressions of admiration are dangerous, in the evil eye world view, because the admirer is assumed to want the desirable object, and the hungry eye drains life with its covetous gaze. Paul Pinter told me that people would give Janet Black things "just to keep on the good side of her," but one man refused her some pork. She "shuffed her hand across the pig's back, brushed him down, like, and said, 'That's a lovely pig, isn't it?' And the next morning he was dead in the sty."

The lethal compliment figures in a story recorded by a Chart Island student from his grandmother about her first son. He was born in the 1920s and was two weeks old when Janet Black came to call; the young mother didn't want her husband to let Janet in because of her reputation, but "he said it was all foolishness" and did. "Oh, what a nice baby," Janet said. After that "it refused to suck the breast and continued to refuse it until it died three weeks later. My grandmother was convinced that the 'witch' had caused the death of the baby" (79/39). When other family members expressed scepticism, the student added, his grandmother cited further evidence, such as how a silver bullet and a bottle of urine hung in the chimney both worked against Janet (on separate occasions).

It can't be pleasant to think that a witch has killed one's baby, but it is probably preferable to blaming oneself, or having others blame one. A reputed witch makes a perfect substitute, especially someone already "known" by all to be wicked. Her very words can be turned against her, and perfectly ordinary behaviour seen as sinister. No conflict need precede a noxious encounter. Paul told a story of a close call during a visit from Janet.

> She went to another person's house, here, and they had a small baby ... She went to see the baby, and the baby was upstairs asleep ... This woman was sort of scared, she wouldn't bring her down. So anyway, she [Janet] waited, and waited, and waited, kept on wanting to see the baby. So anyway, she [the mother] goes up, and when she goes up, the baby was black in the face, just about gone. Brought her down, and the old lady caught hold to the baby, and [the baby] recovered pretty fast. And apparently that's true, too, I've heard several people talking about that one, you know. She was a bad egg.

The implication here is that Janet's thwarted desire was sucking the life out of it as it lay in the crib. Ironically, if the baby really was asphyxiated, then Janet's persistence saved it; perhaps she even suspected neglect, which would explain her insistence on seeing it in the first place. The child-killing witch could be the perfect projection for parents who unconsciously (or even consciously) would like to be rid of their offspring – the unacceptable impulse imputed to someone outside the household. (In early modern France, says Maria Tausiet, parents often killed or abused their children and blamed witches.)[8] Another form of projection could be by a mother suffering from postpartum depression or psychosis who, fearing she might harm her baby, transfers the obsession to a witch – *she* is the one who imperils the baby.

In order to answer the needs of an individual psyche, however, there has to be a degree of social consensus on at least the *possibility* of witching; it is one thing to tell the story oneself, another to get others to buy into it enough to pass it on – it has to be slipped into context among other examples of a witch's toxicity. The woman whose baby died had a deep personal stake in blaming Janet; Paul had none. Paul and Susan, however, stress that George is nasty to everyone, not just them. In closing the case of the Pinters, I should add that it is readily observable, sitting in their kitchen watching Susan field phone calls, looking at the pictures on the refrigerator and other accoutrements of family life, that they are full members of the community, in no way socially aberrant or odd. Embodying deviancy is the job of the witch.

Not every situation demands a prefabricated witch like Janet Black; sometimes, as noted at the beginning of this chapter, almost anyone will do. And they could be anywhere – distance did not weaken the link between victim and witch. A northeast coast student described envy without borders:

> When a family has a period of bad luck, they begin to think that
> someone has put a spell on the whole family. [They can break
> the spell] if they draw a crow on one side of a sheet of paper and
> a woman (or man, if they think a man has put the spell on
> them) on the other side. Then a member of the family takes his
> gun and shoots at the crow. If a man or woman takes ill or dies
> during the next couple of weeks, they believe that person was the
> witch and the spell is broken. Shooting at a crow was common
> among fishermen who went to the Labrador in the summer.
> If the fishermen were having a poor summer, they would say
> someone home was jealous they might have a good summer and
> make a large amount of money and so they put a spell on the
> fishermen. (80/40)

The two-sided drawing – crow on one side, witch on the other – graphically depicts the suspicion that neighbours might have two sides: one normal to all appearances, the other an ill-wishing witch (the crow being a common witch avatar). If "envy was the motor of witchcraft as seventeenth century people understood it," as Lyndal Roper asserts,[9] it equally propelled spells in twentieth-century Newfoundland.

How counterspells were supposed to work seldom seems to trouble practitioners, but as Gustav Henningsen said of Denmark's anti-witch arsenal, "one thing runs through almost all of them like a scarlet

thread: it is taken for granted that some part of the witch's supernatural person or being is literally attached to the bewitched thing or
creature."[10] Thus exploding fish hearts explode the spell; and the man
who each day found a single bright red fish in his trap knew that a
certain red-haired woman "had something against him, you know.
And he used to swear on that red-haired bugger." He burnt the fish,
the woman died, and the fish returned to normal in colour and
number (64/41/c). (The narrator, who worked with the perpetrator,
actually saw the fish – "Yes, a red codfish, bright red" – a phenomenon
that a marine biologist informs me is rare, but possible, through hem-
orrhagic disease.)[11] The occult physical bond between victim and
witch explains why the victim's urine – not the witch's, as might be
expected in standard image magic – works against the witch: the
victim expels someone who has "gotten under his skin," then attacks
the expelled product (which equals witch). Putting it in a bottle is in
effect returning the witch to herself (since the bottle represents the
witch) and trapping her inside her own body, so that she suffers and
swells until she "removes the spell" (withdraws her presence from the
victim's body and mind).

Did anyone really believe that he or she really injured or killed
another in this way? If so, would they really go around bragging about
it? One student wrote about a young man who, convinced that a
reputed witch had "hexed" his family, got his friends together to shoot
the woman in effigy three times. The young man was eager to take
credit for her death soon after that, according to the student. "I knew
the woman in question and had heard the same things about her, that
she practised witchcraft. I also know the young man who told the
story of what they had done at the 'back of the island.' I did not witness the target practice and to my knowledge it was the only time it
happened, if it did happen. This fellow often told it and he stuck to
the same story and details in relating the incident. I also know for a
fact that the woman in question was hale and hearty up to three days
of her death" (72/42). There is no information about how this tale was
received; probably those who hadn't liked the woman enjoyed the
vicarious deed, while others just rolled their eyes. However much a
would-be killer might like to think he has witch's blood on his hands,
or have others think it, all he really has is a story.

A handful of archival reports counsel direct physical violence. "If
you think anyone is a witch, chop her across the thumb and get her
blood; this would make her power useless" (68/43/FSC). Illustrative

narratives are few (there is one in Part Two), but that is only to be expected if they were true. One concerned a strange woman whose arrival in town coincided with a slump in the fishery; the fishermen began to suspect that it was her fault, especially as "she didn't mix with the women" and had the habit of coming to the wharf each day to enquire after the catch.

> And this particular morning she came down on the stage head and the men were splitting their fish – the few they had. She leaned across the splitting table and said, "Boys, no fish again today," and one of the men there at the splitting table came up and chopped her right across the arm, and if you got cut with a splittin' knife you know it's quite a cut. So she just drew back in horror and went on up to the house – blood goin' everywhere. That was the last morning she ever came down on the stage head. I don't know if she left the community, but she was never seen again in that community and just like that the fish came back again. (67/44)

Truth or fiction? Both the location and the woman are unnamed, but again this would be normal if it really happened. It would be surprising, in fact, if a physical assault were recorded at all, especially voluntarily and for an archive; yet one man described to a student, with considerable relish, his attack on Lizzie Moreland. He was the pilot of a local ferry, and she was a witch who "had the heart frightened out of everyone, young and old alike, from one end of the bay to the other." His mother and everyone else would give her anything she wanted when she went around "begging," this being before the days of social assistance, he explained, and since Lizzie was unmarried. One stormy night she was aboard his ship and she told him that if he didn't stop it from rocking she would put a curse on him. She was holding a picture of the Virgin Mary and one of the Sacred Heart, the spoils of her latest round, he said, and he didn't want to hear her "prating": "I finally grabbed the two pictures from her arms and hauled em frames and all down over her fat head. She never opened her mouth again til we pulled in to the wharf – course she couldn't if she tried, lookin so much like yoked oxen" (81/45).

The man's hatred is palpable and there can be no doubt that he would have *liked* to hit Lizzie over the head, but I don't think he did. Men simply did not go about bashing women, even witches, in public.

It is equally implausible that the fishermen slashed the strange
woman; more likely it was a modern legend of its day, an outlandish
story told as true (and believed by many).

I do not mean to discount the possibility of vigilante witch-bashing,
which has been documented in England into the 1800s.[12] But in
Newfoundland, it can't have happened often, if it happened at all.
Magical attacks were enacted precisely because real ones were out of
the question. For one thing, if a person believed in a witch's powers
that strongly, he or she would probably have been too afraid to try;
in fact, witch lore could have been a useful defence against aggression
for vulnerable persons, old, eccentric or alone. But most witches did
have family and friends, and most places had little in the way of public
violence. Even verbal expressions of hostility had to be muted where
everyone knew everyone else, many were related, and almost everyone
worked together in one capacity or another. People saw each other all
the time whether they wanted to or not. Open enmities would simply
be too disruptive in such a setting – the claustrophobic conditions
that foster witch incidents in the first place. So the pressure of a victim's covert grievance or anxiety builds until he seeks relief in counterspell. He blows off steam (even if he'd prefer to blow off the witch)
so it doesn't really matter whether he believes in it or not. It was
cathartic theatre as much as belief. Meanwhile, on the surface all
remained calm.

Domestic violence is another matter: everyone knows that it happens,
but assessing its extent is (as everywhere) beset by problems of secrecy
and denial, compounded when dealing with the past. It is possible
that a magical attack that was supposed to have injured a witch from
afar could be a cover story for violence closer to home – that is, a
husband or partner did the real injury. More likely, witch tales allowed
men symbolically to attack wives in the guise of demanding, overcon-
trolling "witches." One man, for instance, shot a nagging wife who
hadn't wanted him to go woodcutting.

In spite of this he left his home, got into his punt and rowed
away to the place where he had decided to cut the wood. When
he got to a place which we call Pointers Cove, a fox came out on
the bank and barked at him. He shouted at it but it did not go
away. The fox followed him along the shore until he got to a
place called Easter Cove. The fox was still barking at him so the
man grabbed his gun and fired at it. He crippled the fox but he

did not kill it. The fox then crippled away before the man could get another shot at it ... When he got home he found that his wife had been hurt in the leg and the wound looked like shot wounds, but the woman insisted that she had fallen down. (68/46/FSC)

Only a foolish man would hurt an indispensable working partner. Who would make the man's tea now? If we accept that the tales embody more than their literal meaning, we enter a speculative world where reality is flexible. While the tales take their structures from everyday life (such as the directionality of male to female violence), they mirror some but invert others in fugues of symbol and fantasy.

Still, if the violence of witch lore is on the whole abstract, some perpetrators sincerely intend their rituals to harm. They proceed without compunction because they see their acts as self-defence, magical tit-for-tat, a paradigm that leads back to the central problem of witchcraft: why do "victims" feel attacked by "witches" in the first place? Obviously they think (with or without justification) that the witch hates or envies them, or at least has something against them. But they also hate the witch, not only for the perceived attack (the spell) but for having frightened them or made them feel uncomfortable in the first place through some disagreement or unpleasantness (notably the refusal of a request). Here the psychological mechanism of projection comes into play: the "victim" disowns his or her hostility by projecting it onto the witch, crediting *that* person with destructive rage. John Demos explained:

> Victim accuses Witch – in effect saying, "I am not angry, *you are*; I do not wish to attack, *you do*." This is the essence of projection: the attribution to others of inner states which are unacceptable to, and in, oneself. And yet there is one more twist. In making an accusation Victim does in fact attack, with consequences that may be very damaging, even fatal, for Witch. In a sense, therefore, projection allows Victim to have it both ways: the intolerable affect and the inadmissible wish are disowned and indulged at the same time.[13]

An accusation could be fatal in the New England period of which Demos was writing because the witch could be arrested and charged. Newfoundland victims dealt with the problem themselves, which is only reasonable since they created it themselves.

Indian Witches

Projection is not always a retroactive process, occurring only after a confrontation has taken place; vengeful impulses may be endowed in advance, so to speak, upon anyone whose behaviour is known or merely *expected* to provoke anxiety. The worrisome parties, in other words, are made into witches before an encounter even takes place. Nowhere is this clearer than in the case of the Mi'kmaq, widely said to "cause bad luck if they are not treated properly" (64/47) and to "put a curse on whoever refused them" (71/48/FSC).[1] Well into the 1970s, this reputation preceded them wherever they went calling on their Euro-Newfoundland neighbours. In 1967 a student wrote:

> I can remember very well when the Indians came to Small Cove for the first time to sell baskets. They came home [to the student's community] for the first time about ten years ago. When the people knew they were in Hermit Cove, which is ten miles away from the community, they began to gather together in bundles, talking about them. The main topic was whether they would be witched or not. These people believed that those Indians can really witch. Whether they can or not, I would not be able to say.
>
> One thing the people home made sure of and that was to buy a basket from them. The women not only bought a basket, but gave them clothes as well. They were so scared when they wanted lunch, they hardly knew what to say. They wouldn't dare say no, though.
>
> These Indians were not wanted in the community because the people there, and mainly women, were so scared of being witched. However, the trips were always rewarding, and still are, because they received piles of goods each time ... However, there was one woman in our community who did not respond to them so generously. She was the bold type. Every time these people went to her door, she would drive them away without buying anything from them. One time when a particular old Indian, Mrs Jones, was driven away, she became very angry. Before leaving this home, the old woman (Mrs Jones) cursed this woman. She told her that before next year on that particular day, she would not be feeling so well in health. Sure enough, before two months were up, she became sick. She came in here [to

St John's] to a specialist, but they were unable to find her
trouble. This woman had gone from 190 to 130 pounds and she is
still sick, but no one can find the trouble. This woman believes
that she was actually witched. The old Indian has never turned
up since in the community. This incident changed this woman's
views and those of others like her. (68/49/FSC)

These callers were not the resident Mi'kmaq of Newfoundland, who
live mostly on the south and west coasts, but visitors from Nova Scotia
who used the passenger ferry service to visit relatives and to sell baskets, medicines, and other small goods. The Mi'kmaq had been crossing the Cabot Strait since at least 1600, but the late-twentieth-century
crossings carry the greatest archival freight of witch lore.[2] The tales of
these calls epitomize the direct request as threat, the cash "sale" as
extortion; they are an extraordinary testimony to the power of such
encounters to create resentment and dread, and therefore to create
witches. The peddlers' visits confounded traditional rules of hospitality
and put people in the position of refusal or reluctant compliance – in
other words, the classic witchcraft scenario.

It seems, too, that there was tradition already in place upon which
to build. "People buy these baskets [from the Nova Scotians] because
they believe the Indians can cast spells," wrote a student. "This seems
to go back to the earliest days of the community. In those days Micmac
Indians came from Bay D'Espoir [in Newfoundland] to the area and
a number of stories are told about spells being cast on the early inhabitants." He relates the tale of a child who threw a visiting Indian's cap
on the stove, whereupon she pronounced, "None of you will live to
wear out a cap." The mother, who was sewing, stuck a needle in her,
and by drawing blood was safe; the father was not present and so also
escaped the spell. "The children, however, all died and are buried in
Ruby Cove. The old people at French Harbour still maintain that they
died because of the spell cast on them by the Indians" (68/50/FSC).

Lacking data from before the late 1960s, it is impossible to know
whether witch beliefs influenced early settler-Mi'kmaq relations.
Unlike the indigenous Beothuk, who made only fleeting contact with
the Europeans and who were extinct by 1829 through disease, loss of
habitat, and murder,[3] the Mi'kmaq formed good relations with settlers. "On one of my distant outport missions they had unbounded
faith in an Indian doctress," reported a Methodist minister in 1903,[4]
while the Reverend Power, a Catholic, observed in 1910 that "the

Micmac is often the subject of grateful anecdotes amongst the white settlers he has befriended."[5] They were in great demand as guides by foreign big game hunters like the naturalist J.G. Millais, who wrote, "These Newfoundland Micmacs do not like to be thought the savages many of the fisherfolk consider them to be." He added that the Mi'kmaq regarded the settlers with equal disdain.[6] Nevertheless, intermarriage was so frequent that in 1908 the English governor declared, "As an ethnic unit the Micmac can therefore hardly be said to exist here." Yet he articulated the double bind that held for the rest of the century: "At the same time the Micmac community, such as it is, will not, at least for several generations, be absorbed into the European population of Newfoundland."[7] Assimilation was taken for granted; it was not until 1973 that Conne River was officially recognized as a native community, and it was 1985 before the inhabitants gained governmental status as native Canadians. Meanwhile, colonial administrators and "educators" did considerable damage to native culture. "Let us endeavour to preserve the race and language, and likewise the strange yet beautiful traditions of the children of the forest," the Reverend Power urged, but most of his successors preferred to do the opposite.

Doug Jackson's history of the Newfoundland Mi'kmaq traces the deterioration of relations with the non-native population over the century along with the decline of their fortunes.[8] A railway put across the base of the Great Northern Peninsula in 1875 allowed hundreds of great white hunters to line the tracks and ambush migrating caribou, then pile the carcasses on the train; when the herds were decimated by overhunting and logging, some accused the Mi'kmaq of wholesale slaughter, which in fact was the speciality of visiting trophy hunters. (The "elite" foreign sportsmen came to the Mi'kmaqs' defence, pointing out that they were the most economical and respectful of hunters.)[9] In the 1920s fur markets declined so steeply that Conne River was impoverished by the thirties, and lumber mills, once a seasonal adjunct to income, became the only option. Substantial houses built when the mills were new and fur prices high gave way to shacks without water or heat. Hopes rose in the 1950s when workers were needed for the hydroelectric project on the Salmon River, and in the 1960s for the road being built down the middle of the island, but the economic boost was short-lived. Worse, the dam flooded caribou calving grounds and hunters' campsites, while the road gave instant access to prime hunting and fishing (and traditionally Mi'kmaq) territory.

Only in the 1970s, when the Mi'kmaq began to organize politically, did conditions improve.[10] Looking back over the course of events, it is hardly surprising that Mi'kmaq-settler relations were, as Jackson puts it, "somewhat ambivalent."[11]

Witch tales encompass that ambivalence and function ambivalently as well. On the one hand they fostered distrust, but on the other, they encouraged civil behaviour, even amity. "They can do some terrible things, but they can also do some good things," a man assured his son. He often took Mi'kmaq in his punt while working in the lumber woods, and one day on the way to autumn payday, he turned the boat back to pick someone up, although other men didn't want him to. The office was crowded when they arrived but the paymaster called them first. "My father still says this was because they had helped the Micmac" (68/51/FSC). He does tell of a destructive spell but suggests that it was justified:

> My father would tell me about the merchants ... where he used to deal. [One was William Gaynes] who was very mean. There were Micmacs living in Conne River and they would row out to Gallows to sell their furs. Of course "they didn't sell them but gave them away." One Micmac came out to sell a beaver skin. William Gaynes wouldn't buy the skin from him. The man was very poor and didn't have anything to eat. On leaving, the Micmac said to him, "By next spring you won't see the colour of a beaver." This became true within a few months, when he lost his eyesight gradually.

All the versions of this tale imply that the merchant deserved it. One makes the play on racism even more explicit: William Gaynes rejects the furs on the grounds that the colour is bad, and the Mi'kmaq tells him that soon he won't know if a colour is good or bad. He becomes colourblind, unable to tell "if a man's face was white or black" (69/52/FSC). A third account names a different Gaynes merchant who is colourblinded after paying too low a price: "We'll be back with more furs next year but you won't be able to tell the color of them," the sellers said (68/53/FSC).

This story may have achieved special currency through its poetic justice, with the offender pronouncing his own fate and its almost punlike fulfilment. Moreover, the Gayneses appear to have been widely despised. "All the people seem to agree that the Gaynes were crocs [sic] and did all they could to hurt the residents rather than help them. According to the reports by these old people you had to be on your toes in order to keep them from cheating on your account," one student heard (68/54).The Indian as agent of retribution may have satisfied the settlers' own desire to punish the merchant, just as "supernatural" forces in another text expressed contempt:

> Harry Lea was staying with William Gaynes when he died.
> After they had William settled away they thought it called for a
> celebration and a big one at that, so Harry went down in the
> basement and got the rum and alcohol William had down there.
> They drank until everyone was loaded. The day they buried old
> William, Harry said he and five more men carried him up the
> hill to the cemetery. He swore to his God, he said, that the devil
> must have been in the coffin with him because he was so heavy
> they could hardly carry him. After the funeral was over and they
> had him buried and nearly everyone was gone except Harry
> and a few of the others, a crow came and shit on the grave and
> flew away. (68/55/FSC)

The Gaynes story is one of only a few witch tales reliably documented from the Mi'kmaq themselves (by Jackson);[12] in it the merchant's clerk is blinded after offering a poor price, saying "he wouldn't look at them for anything more." Jackson gives two more that differ from European stories only in that the spells are relatively mild. An RCMP officer's boat breaks down after he confiscates out-of-season moose meat from a Mi'kmaq family (in a settler version the boat runs aground: 69/56/ FSC). An old woman, annoyed that some visiting hunters set off on their own without hiring her husband as a guide, renders the caribou off limits – the hunters see them but cannot advance until they return for her husband. If in real life the Mi'kmaq had to deal with shrinking resources and growing restrictions, in folklore they remained masters and mistresses of the game.

Predictably, many witching incidents between Newfoundlanders (settlers and Mi'kmaq) centre on competition for resources. The informant for this tale said that he heard it from the Mi'kmaq.

> Most springs in Bay D'Espoir the geese wait in the bay for the ice
> on the ponds to melt. The birds come close to the beaches to
> feed. Years ago, men built "gazes" near beaches which geese

passed while feeding. A "gaze" was a simple structure made of boughs and sticks to conceal the hunters who fired through holes in the gaze at the geese. One day in the spring of 1905 a Micmac and a white man were in a gaze waiting for geese to come within shooting range. When the birds were close enough, the men fired at the same time, which was always the custom although each man would fire at a different group. On this occasion the white man was lucky enough to get three geese but the Micmac got none. The Indian became angry and told the white man that he would never shoot another goose, that his sheep would be no good for mutton, and that he would die behind bars. Everything happened to the white man as the Micmac stated. He never did shoot another goose; his sheep drowned and therefore the meat was thought to be unfit for human consumption; and the man died of mental illness less than a year later in St John's.

Some of the people in Bay D'Espoir thought that the Micmacs had such powers, especially the daughter of the deceased. Others in the family just looked at it as a coincidence and gave the Micmac a lunch every time he visited them. The Micmac used to bring the mail. (69/57/FSC)

The curse seems unfair, since the white man did nothing wrong and had not shot his geese at the expense of the Mi'kmaq's; it sounds more as if the Mi'kmaq man's pride was wounded over being the unluckier or less-skilled shot, and he lashed out jealously with the spell to reassert supremacy in the natural world. If he did anything at all, that is – maybe the whole thing was just another case of "blame the Indian." And maybe the Mi'kmaq were willing to take credit, for that and other incidents, in the hope of using it to advantage.

One point of agreement between Europeans and Mi'kmaq was that Indians could witch Europeans but not vice versa. In a review of the literature for Nova Scotia, McGee goes so far as to say that for the Mi'kmaq, "most of the folk history concerned with Micmac/white relations relates to mistreatment of the Indians by the whites with the consequence that the whites are punished by supernatural intervention."[13] In New Brunswick, the Miramichi fire of 1812 was said to have been caused by a white man's refusing a drink of water to a Mi'kmaq; the Campbellton fire of 1910 spared only the house of a Scots merchant who had been kind to the Mi'kmaq.[14] Although the Mi'kmaq appear to be united against Europeans (magically speaking), Philip Bock noted in 1961 that the New Brunswick Mi'kmaq held a stereotype of their Nova Scotian counterparts as "hostile, unpleasant, and (according to some informants) potent witches."[15] I have no information about internecine witching among the Newfoundland Mi'kmaq other than what archaeologist Gerald Penney told me: that among the Mi'kmaq at Conne River, only certain people were supposed to be able to witch.[16]

Powerful as it is portrayed in each story, witching proved a weak weapon in the larger battle for rights and respect, and one that was easily turned against the Mi'kmaq, for clearly the tales made ready fuel for prejudice. "Nobody liked the Injuns," declared one man. "That's the name the people gave to the Micmacs from Bay D'Espoir that used to come out here selling baskets. They had witched people before." His example was of a Mi'kmaq couple, lost in a boat in the fog, who lodged at a certain house. They had a dog with them, which a boy in the house liked so much that the woman gave it to him. A few days later during a storm a thunderbolt came through the roof and killed the dog as it lay next to the stove. "[The householder] always said the old Injun witched the dog because she didn't want to part from it" (68/58). An ordinary enough witch incident, had it happened between Europeans; here it is used to justify dislike of an entire group. "Some of them wasn't fit to have around, you wouldn't know what they would do if you crossed them," said another man (but at least he said "some"). His rationale was the tale of an angry Mi'kmaq who told a man that "his son won't do him any good and his pig wouldn't give him any meat for Christmas." The pig and boy both died (69/59/FSC).

A particularly nasty charge involved "a Micmac superstition to get the power to witch" by putting a live cat in an oven. "If you can stand the screams, you supposedly sold your soul to the devil." You then cut the front paws off the dead cat and put them in a river; one would go upstream, and that one you could use to witch people (71/60/FSC). While there may be a superficial plausibility in ascribing this rite to native tradition, in which bones can have magical properties,[17] it bears a closer resemblance to the English "toadman" who had special powers over animals. A description written in 1953 tells how to get these powers by catching a toad and skinning it alive or killing it in some hideous way, then drying the bones and throwing them in a stream at midnight. There they "let out such screams that only a brave man can stand for it. One bone, still screaming, points or even moves upstream. This bone must be taken out of the water, and carried about by the toadman who is now in league with the Devil."[18] Archives in Cleveland, Ohio, hold a boiled-cat-and-floating-bone prescription similar to the alleged Mi'kmaq rite,[19] and black-cat magic was supposed to have been performed by Jews in London in 1680.[20] Clearly it is just another floating bit of stereotype, although to be fair, one account does say that anyone can do it (68/61/FSC). A Mi'kmaq man turned the tables by saying that burning a black cat was "the only way a white man will know if he can be a witch" – if the bones go upstream, he can (69/62/FSC).

Still, in most stories (which are almost uniformly from the settler point of view) it is the Mi'kmaq who are said to perform destructive rites. "Sometimes when a Micmac witches a person he will fire a load of shot into a decaying tree stump. As the stump decays the person witched will become sicker and sicker until he dies. When my informant told me that I had to laugh, and he agreed that it sounded silly but some people in Moor Point still believe it" (69/63/FSC).

As always, it is hard to know how seriously people took these ideas, or how much they influenced behaviour. One student traced the evolution of his own belief:

If a Micmac comes into your house and you get into an argument with him causing him to become angry, you will wonder if he will witch you for doing so. The way to tell his intentions is by noticing the way he leaves through the door. If he leaves by walking backwards, you then know that he has put a "spill" on you. To render the spill useless is by sticking a pin into the person to draw blood. When blood is drawn, the spill will not take place. Micmacs will tell you that themselves. A few of the old people in Bay D'Espoir believe it but most don't, or say they don't. When I was a boy I believed everything about witchcraft but I can laugh at it now. George Janes, a Micmac, once told me that the flyhook I had caught my salmon on was no more good [*sic*]. I asked him why and he said, "Because I have witched it." I replied, "You and your witchcraft." This caused him to laugh. As a coincidence I broke the hook later. I was telling George about it the same day and he, trying to keep a serious face, said, "What did I tell you?" Then he laughed. I answered, "I know there is no such thing as witching, so stop your bloody foolishness." The last incident really

happened while fishing on Conne River in the summer of 1967.
(69/64/FSC)

Familiarity bred contempt for the idea of witchcraft, at least in this
student. It might be harder to laugh off an unpleasant exchange with
a stranger, if one had grown up believing in witchcraft or even just
hearing the tales. Peggy Martin found that witches were strangers in
all but two of thirty-six archival accounts she surveyed (also that the
majority were male). She suggests that the settlers may have transferred
to Indians a long-standing fear of English Gypsies from whom it was
obligatory to buy in order to avoid being cursed.[21] This is supported
by the fact that some people even applied the term to the Mi'kmaq.[22]
"I remember when we used to get them Gypsies coming around all
the time selling flowers and baskets," said one man. "Boy, if you didn't
buy something a curse was placed on you. They would say a magic
spell, then that was it. Once Ann Moore didn't buy anything so the
Gypsie cursed her. When Ann had her next child he was retarded. And
Jack Sanders up in Jack Cove wouldn't buy anything either and he died
two weeks later in his sleep and he wasn't even sick" (79/65).

Like all witches, the Mi'kmaq made excellent scapegoats, especially
those who were just passing through and would not be around to get
embroiled in a drawn-out feud, as a neighbour-witch might be. Nor
could they be seen to suffer the result of counterspells, as Sara Jane
did. A Mi'kmaq married to a settler, "she had a dark complexion and
looked very much like a witch, in fact almost everyone believed her
to be one, since everything she said would happen did happen" (68/
66). Almost a hundred years ago, the story goes, a man got lost while
hunting partridge and spent the night at her house. She issued no
prediction for him because he sneaked away without seeing her,
taking his birds with him. "On leaving early next morning, before
Aunt Sarah was up, he decided he just couldn't afford to leave one of
these fine partridges behind (*as no doubt Aunt Sarah expected he
would*)." The emphasis is mine because the assumption of reciprocity
is the core of the tale, and everything follows predictably when it is
breached. The blundering hunter falls through the ice and almost
drowns before getting home nearly frozen, "with a determination to
get revenge on Aunt Sarah whom he was sure had 'witched' him." He
drew her figure on a board and shot it and later claimed to have heard
that Aunt Sarah was "crippled in the legs and blaming him for it."
Sarah's ethnicity is incidental to the tale, her colour only a support

for a reputation based, like that of many another Newfoundland witch, on prophecy. Like any resident witch, too, she was subject to the machinations of her abominable guest.

Not so the travelling Mi'kmaq. Itinerancy also allowed them be indifferent to long-term relations in favour of immediate gain. Harmful as witch lore was in fomenting ethnic tensions, it involved a certain collusion that could have short-term mutual benefit: goods or good treatment for the Mi'kmaq, explanation or excuses for misfortune for the bewitched.

Did the travelling basket sellers deliberately use fear to coerce "customers"? Several south coast people assured me that they did, but their information was second-hand, so this could just be more negative (if unintended) stereotyping. Yet the Mi'kmaq were aware of the belief that they could witch, and it might be hard for anyone in their situation to resist using a tool that was practically forced upon them.[23] It is not exactly a threat to observe that a homeowner might not have a house the following year – unless the observer was someone who has just been refused admittance. Outside the language of witching, this could be taken as a philosophical comment, not a curse causing the refuser's house to burn down (as I was told happened).[24] In any case the tales, and therefore the sales, of the basket sellers got a boost from a spate of ship mishaps in the 1960s. The real names of the vessels are given in the following because the story is well known.

About five years ago [c. 1963] Mrs Gold was coming to Newfoundland on the *William Carson*. They struck a severe storm and a number of her baskets were damaged. She demanded payment from the CNR [Canadian National Railroad, which ran the ferry service] but they refused. Mrs Gold retorted, "You pay more than the worth of the baskets in a short time." A short time after, the *Cabot Strait* ran aground in the Cape Ray area. Most people around French Harbour claimed the reason for this was a spell cast on them by Mrs Gold. (68/67/FSC)

The media helped spread the story, according to another student, who wrote that when several of the company's coastal boats ran aground the summer after the curse, "the press and radio made quite an issue out of the incident and people in Goat Cove and surrounding communities were 'on the watch' for her." Everyone bought a basket when Mrs Gold came to town (68/68/FSC). In Bonavista Bay, where many

CN crew members lived, the *Northern Ranger* ran aground on a rock. "When a person refused to buy a basket, all he had to do was look out his door or window to see this boat on the rock to see just what would happen" (69/69). In Notre Dame Bay, I was told that the grounding of the *Nonia* inspired people there to make precautionary purchases.[25] Eventually (in 1977) the *William Carson*, the ship that started it all, sank in mysterious circumstances.[26] Recently I learned that the story is still known on a reserve in Nova Scotia; my informant (a man of Mi'kmaq ancestry) heard it from the daughter-in-law of the woman who allegedly laid the curse ("You *will* pay"). She was supposed to have been a "goodin" (my informant's phonetic spelling), a reputation now held by her daughter.[27]

The tales I have been quoting paint the Mi'kmaq as very much "other," alien, remote. But the divide between settlers and Mi'kmaq, especially within Newfoundland, was really not so huge. Both struggled to wrest an uncertain living from water and land, and both had to deal with merchants and outside authority figures. Their separate cultures and sometimes competing claims to resources could create problems, but they were too pragmatic to stay apart when it was to their advantage to be together (as the many mixed marriages attest). Ethnicity allowed Europeans to cast all Mi'kmaq as possible witches, but it is not the whole story; for this didn't happen with the Innu or the Inuit of Labrador (or for that matter, with the French, or with the travelling Jewish and Lebanese sellers of small goods). Perhaps the interactions with these groups lacked the tension between closeness and distinction that characterized the Mi'kmaq/settler relationship or the specific incidents (housecalls that blurred the line between commercial transaction and traditional hospitality) that were so rich in witching potential. To what extent the Mi'kmaq were willing partners in realizing this potential is unknown. In closing, I must emphasize that settlers are the source of almost all the available material; how it might, or might not, dovetail with Mi'kmaq tradition awaits analysis from within the Mi'kmaq culture. Welcome too would been Mi'kmaq perspectives on how it feels to have been pictured as witches.

 ## Magical Jerseymen

A completely different "class" of witches marked by ethnicity were men from the island of Jersey (and, to a lesser extent, Guernsey) in the English Channel. Prosperous, even rich, the merchants were proprietors and agents of large mercantile firms in Newfoundland and along the Gulf of St Lawrence; their workers came from Jersey as well, often on seasonal contracts. Newfoundland operations began in Trinity and Conception Bays in the late 1600s, moving to the south and west coasts and to Labrador as entrepreneurs sought sparsely settled areas in which to set up shop. The fewer the people, the better they were able to control an area's resources, which they did very well until the late 1880s when the last of the firms closed down. Real place names are used in the following accounts, since by now they have become impersonal. They are tenacious, though. Commerce in Forteau, Labrador, ended in 1873, but a hundred years later it was still said that "the early settlers at Forteau, the Jersey Men, were very strange people. Every weekend when the week's fishing was finished they were believed to have gone home on their cabble, or some kind of stick. They even told some people such things as, we were home last night on our cabble. Some people believed them to be witches of some sort" (74/70/FSC). The cabble was possibly modelled on real ships so swift as to have aroused jealous comment. Edward Chappell remarked of the Guernsey merchants at Forteau in 1818 that "by being the most industrious, they are generally the most calumniated. The vessels of these thriving islanders are slightly built, and calculated to make speedy voyages: so that by hurrying out to Newfoundland as early in the year as possible, they quickly procure cargoes of cod; and speedily recrossing the Atlantic, they by this means succeed in getting the first of the Spanish and Portuguese markets."[1] While visiting Forteau in 1848, Bishop Feild observed that the Jerseyans' main occupation on Sunday evening was washing clothes,[2] but a company manager on the south coast had his laundry sent out to Jersey on Saturdays and got it back Monday (65/71/C).

Whether of people or goods, magical transport is the hallmark of the Jersey tradition. A south coast student heard this from his father:

There was an old fellow here one time who had two youngsters [first- or second-year apprentices] and every Saturday night he would lose them but on Monday mornings they were back again. The old fellow tried to find out where they went but he was unsuccessful. One Monday morning he got up quite early and went out fishing. He took hold of his "rodes" [anchor rope] and started to "haul off." When he did so, he looked up to the

westard and there was a sail coming down towards him. When it
got near to him he recognized it was a coal grate and his two
youngsters were on it. This was what they were using to go back
and forth to Jersey. (68/72/FSC)

The travellers transformed not just objects but themselves. Two Jersey
youngsters would disappear from Francois every week; on Monday
morning two seals would swim into in the harbour, and "it was suspected that they turned themselves into seals and went to England for
the weekend" (68/73).

Just as the "cabble" mirrored real-life speedy vessels, these apparently most fantastic of tales actually reflect a basic reality about the
Jersey merchants, namely, their deep lack of commitment to Newfoundland. Firms were not only owned but staffed by Jerseyans; all
skilled workers were imported, often as indentured servants for part
of the year, and fishing crews signed on by season as well. "A far-flung
form of maritime transhumance" is how Rosemary Ommer describes
the system and its purposeful Eurocentricism:

> The nerve centre of the Jersey merchant system resided in Jersey
> itself. This was the organization and ownership base for the
> trade. Here were written the political petitions which sought to
> create and maintain a favourable politico-economic framework
> within which the trade could operate at maximum efficiency.
> Here also some of the supplies for the fishery were manufactured
> or assembled, the exchange goods bought with the produce of
> the fishery returned, labour recruited in the form of clerks,
> agents, captains, shorecrews and fishermen. Here the vessels
> returned when all was done. This was home, the metropole,
> master-minding its outpost across the Atlantic, deploying the
> capital that created the trade, and most importantly receiving the
> profits that flowed out of it.[3]

On lush green Jersey, stone mansions or "cod houses" still stand as
monuments to fortunes made; on the south coast of Newfoundland,
Jersey Harbour is an empty cove where among the rocks one can pick
up worn imported bricks, remains of the once substantial premises
there.

Jersey firms were not alone, of course, in siphoning profits away
from the island. Newfoundland was long without a business or

corporate tax, or an individual income tax; instead, through the 1940s, government was supported by taxes on imported goods that everyone needed, such as flour and shoes, while the wealthy invested their profits abroad. (One law firm on Water Street was "world" headquarters to thirty international firms, registered here to take advantage of this peculiarity.)[4] But even within this context, the Jersey firms stood out as rootless, and maybe ruthless too, their close protection of property marked in memory as surely as in stone. The "Jersey Rooms" near Harbour Grace in Conception Bay[5] may not feature on present-day maps, but a student from the area wrote in 1984:

> My grandfather told me one curse legend about two people from Jersey who lived in Upper Island Cove. These people were believed to have powers, but my grandfather didn't refer to them as witches. The story is that these two Jersey people would go home to Jersey every Saturday night. How they did this was to place a bowl of water in the middle of the table, and then they would go into a trance. At this time they were supposed to go across the water to their homeland of Jersey. On one Saturday night while they were doing this, a man went into their garden with a knife and a bag intending to steal their cabbage. The Jersey people saw this man, and as he bent over about to cut the cabbage, they put a spell on him. All that night and the next day the man was in this position and couldn't move. As people passed the house on their way to church they looked at the man, and knew what had happened. When they finally took the spell off the man he left the garden as fast as he could. Sure enough, he never tried to steal their cabbage again.[6]

This public display of control is of a piece with other tales of superiority to the locals, such as the south coast Jerseyman who defeated three men in a fight, so that "people thought he was a witch" (72/74).

Elizabeth Beaton Planetta recorded similar traditions at Chéticamp in Cape Breton, Nova Scotia, where the Jersey-Huguenot *sorciers* flew to the Channel Islands on pigs, or on horses driven by *les lutins* (leading some people to conclude that *les lutins,* or little people, themselves came from Jersey); carriers for local flights included a pile of firewood and a barrel.[7] The *sorciers* could change not only themselves but others into animals. Anselme Chiasson, who also noted the tales, suggested that the Chéticamp merchants used them to "abuse the credulity" of the fishermen, whom they already held in thrall through the credit system;[8] some of Planetta's informants also suggested that the *Jersais* tried to frighten the Acadians in order to strengthen their economic hold.

Martin Lovelace put the question of exploitation to Pius Power (1912–1993) in an interview about Mr Power's grandfather's dealings with Jersey firms in Placentia Bay.[9] On the contrary, Mr Power said, the merchants were "good fellows" who purchased raw materials, like his grandfather's furs, and brought in necessary goods. The importing was done in good time, too: when his grandfather needed a suit, it was ready the next morning – fetched overnight from Jersey. Rum could be had from a hole bored into a tree, from which it flowed from the "puncheons in Jersey" – but only if it were paid for first. If the merchants were close accountants, it was only because they had to answer to their masters overseas; as one explained when he required Mr Power's grandfather to pledge his gun as collateral for a stove, he'd be "hung in Jersey" if he didn't get the funds. When the grandfather asked one Jerseyman how he got his powers, he was told that it was through special training that required that they never get "vexed" with anyone – they could have "no temper at all" or they would lose their magic. They could never mention God's or the devil's name. Mr Power told of a merchant who owned a birch broom that "he could make [into] a yacht or a square rigger or whatever kind of boat he wanted." Once he took on a passenger who marvelled at its speed: "By God, can't this one go!" In an instant it vanished and the riders found themselves in the water.

Mr Power did not consider the Jerseymen to be witches, or at least they didn't abuse their power as witches did ("fellas jinking shot," turning into loons, and the like – "that was true too"). People who did think they were witches would never call them that, just as they wouldn't call the fairies anything but "good people." He said he couldn't swear to the truth of any of this, as it was not personal experience; yet he didn't think his grandfather would lie. "Perhaps he went through the air on that birch broom," he said of the merchant, but then again perhaps it was all illusion like his uncle saw at a magic show in the Nickel Theatre in St John's, where one audience member witnessed a person beheaded on the stage, while his companion saw only a cook slicing a cabbage.

Lovelace points out that the neutrality in religion and comportment that were claimed as ritual requirements made good business sense in minimizing friction with clients. L.E.F. English spoke of their reserve and their magic in the same breath. "Among the qualities of character and physical appearance which tradition ascribed to some of the old Channel Island merchants," he wrote in 1950, "were a saturnine reticence and the ability to transport their bodies through air by a process of thought." They were also supposed to have "remarkable faculty of curing disease," not by magic but with material remedies such as bottled brown jellyfish for rheumatism. "These shrewd old traders were astute business men ... unrelenting in driving a bargain, and austere in their mode of living," he said, but they were not without feeling:

> A story is told of an old "Jawseyman" named Greeley who had a thriving business at Little Bell Island in Conception Bay. So passionately fond was he of his ancestral home in the Channel that he used his magic power to revisit Jersey each week end. It happened that a fisherman went down to the shore this Saturday to shoot for a Sunday dinner a sea duck or whatever wild fowl that chanced to wing its way in range of his long musket. Just at nightfall a giant bird was seen to pass eastward, and the hunter raised his trusty weapon and fired. The strange bird fell beyond a point of rock, and the fisherman on rushing to the spot found the bewildered and bewhiskered Jersey planter [landowner] picking buckshot from his legs.[10]

The ultimate commuter fantasy, these tales offered business-class flights of fantasy for merchants. For workers, they were perhaps wishful escape clauses from contracts that contained harsh penalties for failure to put in the full term.[11] Many of them had farms and families in Jersey to which their thoughts (if not their brooms) surely flew; homesickness figures even in a parenthetical remark (in a book on Jersey sailing ships) about a Jerseyman at Harbour Grace who "could be seen jumping over a puncheon of water, believing that in this way he could spend the weekend with his family back in Jersey."[12]

Not surprisingly, analogues thrived in other isolated workplaces. Acadian lumbercamp workers availed of the *chasse galerie*, the aerial canoe that departed of a Saturday night for the passengers' hometowns or wild dances abroad. Piloted by the devil himself, it would crash if anyone mentioned God's name.[13] Seasonal fishers on the Labrador sometimes decamped, voluntarily or otherwise, aboard strange devices. One man was "taken away by the fairies" on a piece of birch rind that "went fast over the water" (76/75).[14] Martin Walsh, "the fairyman of Chapel's Cove" who lived in the 1800s, was still remembered in the 1990s for his trips between Labrador and Conception Bay aboard a chip of wood, a birch rind, or the back of a pig; he would tell the summer fishers on the Labrador everything that was happening at home. (In Chapel's Cove, "Martin Walsh's gang" – the fairies – helped him with chores and other tasks.)[15]

Martin may have been the unnamed man in an earlier account who cried "Hi ho!" along with the name of his hometown, jumped on a chip of wood, and was not to be seen back in Labrador until Sunday night (67/76). The boarding cry is a direct link to old-world fairy and witch lore. "Que-hou-hou!" called the gens du Vendredi of Guernsey, witches who flew to Friday-night revels. (Born sorcerers could transport themselves at will, while ordinary people had to make a pact with the devil.)[16] "Ho for Par Beach!" launched a Cornish man along with the pixies.[17] The accused Scottish witch Isobel Gowdie said that she and her companions called "Horse and hattock ... ho, ho!" as they mounted corn straws and beanstalks to ride to their revels along with the fairies.[18] Isobel was executed in 1622; a Somerset woman who "confessed" to riding a broomstick was sentenced to death (but killed herself first):[19] today's playful Halloween motif was once dead serious.

The grisly business of witch prosecution explains why, in Newfoundland, Jerseymen but not regular witches rode brooms and other enchanted objects. Broom-riding was a relatively late development in England compared to continental Europe,[20] because England did not allow the use of torture to extract descriptions of whatever diabolical doings prosecutors wanted to hear.[21] The Channel Islands had proportionately more witch trials than England, replete with torture and killing (and, notably, confiscation of property.)[22] In Newfoundland, aerial transport aligned better with fairy tradition, since the fairies were well known for carrying people away.

The Jersey and Guernsey witch trial records display the full complement of more pedestrian witch lore, with the typical offence/revenge pattern. Not apparent from the limited evidence is a special connection between magic and merchants. Yet it appeared early in North America in the case of Philip English, originally Philippe L'Anglois from Jersey, one of the richest men in New England and one of the few men accused in the Salem witch trials. Underlying his accusation and possibly the whole Salem episode, Mary Beth Norton sees the English colonists' fear of the French and Indians; but she adds that as an aggravation, Philip English had violated custom by going to court in a bid to claim land that had been left by oral agreement to someone else. "Under normal circumstances, his claims to his wife's uncle's land would have aroused resentment, even anger – but not witchcraft accusations," Norton says.[23] But maybe there was more to it than that; maybe the greedy salt-fish trader already belonged, folklorically speaking, to a guild of magical merchants. His ships, plying the banks of Newfoundland on the triangular route between the northeastern seaboard to Jersey and Spain and the Caribbean, would have trafficked as busily in folklore as in material goods.

Here it is worth remembering that the flow of tales is not all one way. Tracing antecedents is fun and important for tempering culture-specific interpretations, but Newfoundland gave as well as it got, according to an account written in Jersey in 1786:

> There are many curious anecdotes about Newfoundland which are the subject of conversation in Jersey at the knitting soirées (*à la veille*) during the winter months, when some twelve or fifteen men, women and children worked by the dim light of a crasset, filled with Newfoundland oil of the coarsest quality. The young men who had spent some time "*daeux éstais et un Hivé*", [two summers and a winter] on the "*Banc de terr-neuve*," made it a point to go in and to tell them cock and bull stories, which made the humble rural party shudder and cry bitterly. Those who had been to Newfoundland were looked upon as great navigators and as having made "*le tour du monde.*" They had issued a table of commandments made by one Moise Le Ruez which were engraved on the hearts of the poor fellows who toiled often night and day, Sundays not excepted, on mountains of ice and snow, as the fishermen called them. We give here the first commandment: – "Siex jours tu travaillas et le septquième à la chivière tu porteras!" [Six days you work and on the seventh you carry the handbarrow, i.e., you keep working.] We hasten to add that this commandment was altered some fifty years ago – working on Sundays was, after a struggle, declared impious and unlucky. Men took to go[ing] to church and reading the Bible.[24]

But according to legend, some preferred to visit Jersey on Sundays.

Little known today, the magical Jerseymen tales are a ghostlike tradition, tenuous afterimages of a vanished past, materializing from time to time in startling full-blown form. (Even in 1950, English noted that they were "fast fading.")[25] They never entered popular culture like the flying canoe of Quebec, which has featured on postage stamps, pub signs, a beer label ("Maudite" brand), and in an animated film. The Newfoundland images are more like pictographs, inscrutable without the story behind them. Rum pours from a tree – one has to *know* it is from an invisible pipeline to puncheons in Jersey. A man sits in a coal grate at sea – one has to *know* he is on a ferry to Jersey and back.

 ## The Black Heart Book

The black heart – or art – book allowed its owners to conjure up objects and illusions, and to cast spells or foretell the future. A sinister aura surrounded the book, and often its owners as well. One less than solid citizen, for instance, deported himself with the aid of the book:

> As well as [the informant] could remember there was only one
> such book on Bell Island, but he was unable to recall what it
> looked like or how it got there. It was used mostly for evil
> purposes, and infants born deformed or with bizarre physical
> characteristics (having, for example, two heads or the head of a
> pig) were often cited as the work of people who practised the
> Black Hart. There used to be a man over there, he said, who was
> somehow connected with it. He was sitting idly on the wharf one
> day, whittling a stick and wishing that he could cross over to
> England. Throwing the chips in the water he expressed his wish,
> which immediately materialized in the form of a huge vessel
> there before his eyes. He arrived in England and spent some time
> there, but when he wanted to come back again, the Black Hart
> failed him, and he was never seen on this side after. (70/77)

The student who recorded this noted "hart" as the pronunciation of "art," but when people speak of the book, it is seldom clear which word they mean since in many areas an "h" is pronounced in front of some words beginning with a vowel ("hice" for ice) and removed from others ("art attack" for heart attack). But many student collectors write "heart," so for them at least that is the meaning. It makes sense as an exchange for the soul, as by a man who "sold his heart to the devil" to get "a devil's book, known as the Black-heart book" (69/78/c). It also evokes the close, secretive nature of some book owners. Virginia Dillon recorded the case of a man who had traded his soul for the "black heart book" and who inspired such fear that her informant (a fellow student) didn't want her name in the archive lest he "come after her" – despite the fact that she had never met him but had only heard about him from her father, who had worked with him in a central Newfoundland woods camp around 1947. The men in the camp had seen the book, but only the covers, for they were afraid to touch any of the owner's belongings.

> One night as they were playing cards the man with the book got the queen of hearts. Before the eyes of everyone he turned the queen into a real woman who walked across the floor. She was dressed like the figure on the cards, mostly in red. She wore high heels. One fellow who was about twenty-two fainted. The men never wanted to let this magician in on their games for he knew all the hands around the table and would win all the money. They were afraid to refuse him after they saw the woman, for they thought he had the power to change them into anything he wished ... He looked just like anyone else except that he let his hair and beard grow long ... He was never cold like the other men and would go out to chop wood with his shirt open and with no mitts on.
>
> If he insulted anyone they let it pass because they were afraid of him. In his hometown, a man once did something to him and he told him that he would never have any luck as a result ... soon after [several of his children died, and all were sick].
>
> One night in the lumber camp the magician put up a thousand dollar bet that no man in the camp would meet him between the two camps at eleven o'clock at night. All the men were afraid ... when the men talked about it after they said they were afraid he might have appeared in some other form, for example, a snake.
>
> [Once he offered everyone cigarettes.] Each man took one in his hand but as he raised it to his lips it disappeared. When they all began to look for their cigarettes they saw that the magician had them all back in the package.
>
> None of the men would talk very much behind this man's back ... The thing that most fascinated the men was the book. There was no way to destroy it. No one ever saw him burn the book

but there was a belief that if he burned it, it would still be in his pocket. The men were afraid of the book and they believed that if they once saw what was in it they would become just as bad as the man who owned it. (64/79)

Strange as he was, this man had counterparts throughout the northeastern United States and Canada, where would-be magicians bought or bartered for the book in lumber camps.[1] In Newfoundland it could also be imported from abroad – India (83/80), the West Indies (87/81), France,[2] the mainland (73/82/FSC) – all increasing its exotic appeal; or it could be acquired by ritual: "A person has to make himself over to the devil and then go to the same place every night for twelve nights in a row. He must go to this spot at midnight. On the twelfth night the book will be there waiting for him" (68/83/FSC). Once gotten, it was hard to get rid of; one man kept trying to burn his "but it always turns up some unexpected place in the house" (68/84). (The thought gives slight menace to an early Newfoundland alphabet-book rhyme: "My book and my heart will never part.")[3]

The indestructibility of the book is of course a standard international motif, just as some of the narratives are widespread legend types. "Inexperienced use of the black book," for instance (the theme of the sorcerer's apprentice), is catalogued as Migratory Legend 3020 in Christiansen's Norwegian index; analogues date from classical Egypt and Greece.[4] It appears on the south coast in the tale of "Old Kelly," who usually locked his black book in a chest when he left the house. But one day he forgot:

> The girl he had working for him wanted to find out what was in the book so she took it and began to read it and the house filled full of little black imps. Kelly felt there was something wrong so he hurried up and scrabbled home. When he got back the imps nearly had the girl killed but he read something else and they went away. The girl never told nobody what she read in that book from that day to this. (68/85)

Another curious woman took a book from a man's hand and read until little black pups appeared and the man snatched it back (65/86/C).

Men, it would appear, make better masters of such infernal conjurations. A man in need of a crew swore, "I'll have somebody next year spose tis the devil and 'is himps." They showed up and went to work:

"One of the himps would cut the fish open and cut around the head, one would clean the guts out and take the head off, one would draw up the water and clean the fish, and another would carry it into the stage, lay them in the 'pin [pen], and another would salt them." In the fall they vanished in a ball of fire – without even getting paid (68/87/FSC). Another man lived and fished alone; the other men never saw or heard him go out in the mornings, although they knew the sound of everyone's boat. When everyone began having a poor catch but this man, they followed him out to see how he did it. There he was asleep in his boat while a strange young man leaned over the gunnel, tapping it with a stick while fish leapt out of the water into the boat as he chanted, "Tappity, tap em in, tap em in" (67/88/C).[5]

Surely the busy himps and prodigious fisher inhabit the fabulous end of the belief spectrum. The characteristic latitude of legendry is especially wide in the case of the devil; for all the talk of him, was he really sure to appear? If so, why did the Faustian bargainers make such measly deals? One student heard: "Anyone who makes a pact with the devil will get the black sticks. You go off to a secret spot and make a pact with the devil at night, you sell your soul in return for the black stick. The Black Stick is a burnt stick which you use to make magic with, especially against someone who has crossed you. However you can use it to make many kinds of magic. Each year you have to go back and renew the pact. William Burke ... was supposed to have them." So what did Burke do with his fiendish device? Stalled a bulldozer on a construction site until the foreman gave him a job (69/89/FSC).[6] Another man settled for small beer when he and a buddy found themselves short of drinking money. He "went into his house and looked into this Black Heart's Book, and by doing so changed the change (quarters and dimes) into several dollars, enough for several beers each." Despite this boon, the book kept changing hands: "no one would keep it very long because it was cursed and brought bad luck" (71/90/FSC). A few book owners did fare better, like the man who had "no need of working any more as the devil supplied him with all the money he needed" (73/91/FSC). Dave Gaze was once ferrying a corpse when a sudden storm threatened to swamp his boat; he "began to rhyme off the curses," and the waves calmed around them – though they raged everywhere else – until they reached port. "I've heard ... that Dave always gets away from having to pay fines, e.g., for killing a moose without a license," wrote the student. "It is only thought that Dave has a Black Art Book, no one

has ever seen it. It's just that he seems to get everything he wants"
(68/92/FSC).

Women book owners never seemed to get set up like this; nor did
they use the book to amuse or amaze, as men did. But then women
seldom performed the card and sleight-of-hand tricks more typical of
male gatherings (not to mention spectacular tricks like chewing glass
without being cut: 73/93/FSC), tricks that really could be found in
how-to volumes on juggling and illusion-making, and that really did
include "black art" in their titles.[7] These books circulated for centuries, and it is easy to imagine that they would have been prized diver-
sion, especially aboard ships or in camps or other isolated work
settings. It is unlikely that they reached Newfoundland in any great
numbers – no books did. But it wouldn't take many in a print-starved
culture to make an impression; in fact the paucity of print could only
further exoticize the books, so often heard of but seldom seen.

Ordinary books, too, could have fed into the legend-making process.
While the oral tradition of West Country England is the motherlode
of Newfoundland witch lore, there are bound to have been literary
influences as well. In the English chapbook "The History and Wicked
Life of Dr. John Faustus Shewing how he sold himself to the devil
…[etc.]," Faust was not a tragic intellectual but a trickster "resolving
to make himself and the town's people merry by his conjuring Art."[8]
Dr. Faustus was among the chapbooks translated from the German
that were imported into late-seventeenth-century New England,
where it was outsold only by the Bible, books of Psalms, and a few
school texts.[9] Newfoundland's extensive trade with New England at
the time would certainly have carried some of these to the island, as
personal possessions if not commercial commodities.

Later, North American publishers continued with "ancient" secrets,
like *Herrman's Book of Magic: Black Art Fully Exposed* (1903), a copy
of which resides in the Northeast Folklore Archives at the University
of Maine.[10] Also on offer were compendiums of material, medical and
magical advice such as Dr William Earle's *Illustrated Silent Friend:
Being a Complete Guide to Health, Marriage, and Happiness*, published
in New York in 1848, containing information on disease, hypnotism,
monstrous births, beauty tips, and a UFO sighting in Ohio.[11] *The Long-
Hidden Friend*, assembled from European "occult" sources by the
German immigrant John George Hohman, enjoyed huge North
American circulation in various editions and is still advertised on
the Internet.[12] One of this family of "friends" was the *Silent Friend*,

Marriage Guide and Medical Adviser sent by a Swift Current man to the Department of Justice in 1942, urging them to send "2 strong willed men, who understood sorcery combined with some of the things written in this book" to act against witches whom he accuses of killing his horse, his father and grandfather, and numerous others; he fills an entire page with the names of witches in the town. A ranger from the local enforcement unit actually went to investigate this case of tradition run amok.[13]

In most homes, the Bible was the closest thing to a repository of arcane secrets, such as the "Black Psalm" that a west coast woman threatened to "read on" anyone who offended her (68/94)[14] and charms. Aunt Betsy Dean, for instance, was "a kind of witch-doctor" who cured warts by drawing three crosses on the stove, then writing a certain verse from the Bible on a piece of paper to be worn around the patient's neck until the warts disappeared. No one knows what the verse was, and she died before revealing it to her son, as she had intended (81/95). The early missionaries' determination to bestow the Bible on everyone, whether they could read it or not, could only have furthered its fetishistic quality, as well as that of its devilish counterpart. That the black heart book is the Bible's evil twin is made clear in one student's text:

I was told this item by a friend whose father was formerly a resident of Spanish Bay [c.1920–25]. It concerns a little item which they called the "Black Heart." It was, in fact, the Devil's Bible which was carried by his disciples. These disciples were people who had sold their souls to the Devil, and whom he had placed here on earth to recruit more. The legend goes on that the "disciples" would wait for an opportunity in which a person would be in a position to bargain with them. When they thought they had a prospect here, they would present him with "the Black Art." The person would be safe until he agreed to accept the Black Art, thus signifying that he had sold his soul to the devil for some favour in return. (70/96/FSC)

Never mind that it is probably sacrilegious for a Christian to suggest that the devil can put people on earth – the point is simply inversion of a religious icon to indicate wickedness, just as the Lord's Prayer can be said backwards to put a spell or "the hag" (a kind of waking nightmare) on someone (82/97).

Even the shadiest black heart practitioners, however, were hardly as bad as one might expect satanic covenanters to be. If they were masters of any art beyond legerdemain, it seems to have been that of suggestion. Their words, according to some descriptions, had an instant transforming effect.

> There's a fellow down in Shore Cove by the name of Vince Carver. He has a reputation for doing tricks. The tricks he does are really supernatural. For example, making snow fall in the house. One time his father-in-law went into his house. That was when he had very little done to it inside. His father-in-law said to him, "I suppose you'll be getting some furniture soon." "Furniture," Vince replied, "I've got plenty of furniture. Come in the front room and I'll show you." When he went in, the room was furnished with the most expensive furniture. The floor was covered with a beautiful rug. Only moments before there was nothing there. When they went back to the kitchen, one of Vince's children was there dressed in the ordinary overalls etc. of an outport child. His father said, "You might as well get some new clothes for him while you're at it." "Why, he hasn't any need for new clothes," says Vince, "he has the best." Looking at the child, the father-in-law saw that he really did have the best, when only moments before he had only overalls. (68/98/FSC)

Vince was not called a witch, added the student, but it was said that he had gotten the black heart book from the devil. Another student added a dancing stove to Vince's phantom furniture, as well as the ability to cut up socks and then retrieve them whole from the wood-box (70/99/FSC). Simple tricks like the sock repair could set the stage for less explicable feats by building conviction in the audience, whether as witnesses or simply hearers of the tale.

The "wizard" Bill McCall didn't even have a black book, but he seems to have been a hypnotist extraordinaire. Otherwise normal, he was "supposed to be able to do whatever he wants to" (67/100/C). He could levitate cups from tables, and "just by making certain movements with his hand made other people strip off their clothes entirely." No wonder he could order people around: "if he told one of 'em to do something, well, just snap the finger and they went and did it." He could put away three bottles of rum without effect, "just drink it down like water" (possibly explaining why he looked much older than his thirty-odd years). He was a seventh son but not a healer; he prepared the dead for burial and was supposed to have found treasure, perhaps in the course of his career as the local grave robber. ("Sounds to be a versatile character," remarked the folklorist John Widdowson, while recording this.) His greatest talent seems to have been the induction of trance. On a hunting trip with another man, he conjured up the image of "a very dim past" with volcanoes and high smoking rocks, tall leaves of grass and a big lake. "And this lasted about five minutes and they'd build to something else and [then] they were back sitting by the campfire again." A low-lit setting, a persuasive talker, and a receptive audience were probably the basic elements of a black heart experience.

Expectation and atmosphere combined to hypnotic effect in a story recorded by Mark Ferguson in coastal Labrador in 1990.[15] The informant, Norm, was a Metis man in his mid-thirties; he heard it from a trapper who was a young man in the 1920s when the event took place. The story goes that a group of seal hunters were having no luck one spring, nor was there any other meat to be had. So they went to visit a kinless old woman (not named in the story) who lived alone and who owned the "Book of Black Hearts." She took out the book and began to tell them a story about seals and hunting, and within minutes they heard the baying of seals under the floor, and water splashed up through the floorboards (although the house was not near the sea). They were too frightened to run but left when the story ended; within days they found seals, which remained plentiful all season.

The faith that led the hunters to this woman and primed them to expect something extraordinary could only have been based on other stories about her, like that of a trapper who went to her because he was catching nothing and his family was destitute. She opened the book and told him that he would have a great round on his next trip to his trapline, and it happened that he had his best haul ever. The importance of animals was embedded in the book itself: Norm knew a man who had actually looked into its pages and seen their pictures there. He was visiting the woman (the man told Norm) and saw the book, normally kept in a black leather box, lying on the table. A black heart was on the black leather cover, and while the woman was busy elsewhere, he opened it and began flipping through. On each page was a single black heart, and inside each heart were little coloured animals: foxes, marten, mink, and lynx, as well as domestic animals like horses and goats, all increasing in number with each page until they crowded the hearts by the middle of the book. At the bottom of each page were scratches like writing, but not English. Even stranger than the book, however, was the man's observation that although the kettle was boiling and the room was warm, he couldn't hear the fire; he touched the stove to find it "stone cold."

As Ferguson points out, "distinctively indigenous Labradorian motifs" imbue this essentially European import. (The book was even said to have come from Scotland, where one clan had stolen it from another.) Animals, hunting, scarcity, and perhaps most tellingly, the book's use for common good rather than individual gain: all bespeak aboriginal themes. The seal-conjuring woman recalls the supernatural animal-controllers of circumpolar lore, as well as the shaman inter- mediary between the human and spirit worlds; she might even have been a shaman. She is also reminiscent of the Inuit "Old Woman" deity herself, who lives at the bottom of the sea and withholds sea mammals if offended by humans. When that happens, the shaman has to travel to her abode (like the visiting hunters?) passing many dangers on the way (including in one case a boiling kettle).[16]

Another woman with a mystical tie to the hunt was noted by Millais in central Newfoundland in 1907. Anyone who dreamed of a certain Mrs Bury, his (white) guides told him, would be sure to get a stag: "There's some connection 'tween the deer and dat lady."[17] No infor- mation was offered about her except that she was married to a shop- keeper; yet there must have been something special that made her the dream-companion of the deer.

Or was there? The grand power over the natural world accorded to even the garden variety witch, who keeps fish from the nets or kills plants with a glance, goes oddly unquestioned. The ancient equation of women with nature, embodied in the Artemisian Mrs Bury, seems to hold for witches whose power is innate rather than acquired. A man who felt himself persecuted by a neighbour made a clear distinc- tion: "She can put a spell on you cause I believe she got a black heart book. She's not a witch, but she's possessed by the devil" (66/101/C). On the whole, it was men who needed a manual, and even then their feats were relatively paltry parlour games. (Jerseymen's magic was more spectacular, but that too was gotten by rite rather than right.) The black heart book was like a counterspell in being a device through which owner-operators could manipulate reality – unlike the "real" witch's unmediated deployment of natural force.

Religion

Reams have been written about religion and witchcraft, inextricably and horridly linked in the hunting and persecution of "witches" past. I will not have much to say about it here; devilish book contracts notwithstanding, I do not find that it figures hugely in people's thinking – and talking – about witches. The stories seldom convey a sense that any "higher" *or* "lower" power is involved; rather, witching is something that happens between people, independent of divine or diabolical aid. Prayer is rarely mentioned as a remedy for spells. People may cite the Bible to justify belief ("I often wondered, too, about it because the Bible says, 'Suffer not a witch to live,' it's really there cause I saw it": 79/103), but it is typically as an afterthought or aside to the main discourse, which is about who did what to whom and why. Narrative and experience, not theology, supply the best evidence for most people. This is why I see witching as essentially an areligious phenomenon, an energy akin to electricity or radio waves, operating mysteriously but not necessarily "supernaturally" in the world. Some people (witches) generate it naturally, through inborn ability or strong emotion, while others (the bewitched) might rechannel it through the mechanical motions of counterspells.

This is not to say that religion was irrelevant in shaping people's world view so as to encompass (or reject) witch lore. The churches have had a huge impact on almost every area of Newfoundland life: they ran the public schools until 1998, for instance, and clerics had the right to fire teachers for "moral" offences, such as dating someone of another religion. But they did not always enjoy such a stranglehold. "Religion is scarce to be found in this country," wrote the Methodist missionary John Stretton in 1770.[1] By the 1800s missionaries were fanning out across the island, setting out by boat and overland for remote places where they were sometimes the first and last agent of religion to be seen. Even when religion was a fixture of cultural life, many small places received only occasional pastoral visits, and even in larger centres with churches, people might be away for months at a time in Labrador or inland winter quarters. William Wilson, upon the decampment of his flock from Burin in the winter of 1828, followed them to Freshwater Pond, where they obligingly built a tilt for him and his wife, and he rechristened the place "Wesley Vale" (after John Wesley).[2] But it was he who went after them, as they pursued their customary itinerary and folkways.

The practices (and possibly preaching) of the various religions nevertheless had much to offer to the non-denominational tradition of witching. Bible-reading Protestants, for instance, were apt to find scriptural endorsement while Catholics looked to their priests for the last word. Sometimes clerics competed with lay people for authority in extramundane affairs. In 1833 Wilson was accused of using "the black art" after he reassured a terrified woman that a fortune teller's prediction that she would die in her twelfth childbirth had no validity. (He read the Bible to her and urged her to look to God, he said, and "my exhorting her thus, was construed into an Astrological Prediction!!!")[3] P.K. Devine wrote in 1915 of fortune tellers in St John's known as "widows," although they had husbands who helped gather information for their practice, which apparently catered to out-of-town fishermen. He tells how one Father Fitzgerald disguised himself as a fisherman and went to have his cards read. When the fortune teller was done, he announced that she was in trouble and withdrew a whip from his coat, "and there were 'ructions' in that domicile for the next five or ten minutes."[4]

Like Father Fitzgerald, many Catholic priests wielded power far beyond church doors. They banished fairies and ghosts, cured people, *and* meted out magic punishment. A man who insulted a priest by slapping his (own) buttocks, for instance, was forced to perform the gesture constantly for the rest of his life (73/104). A student wrote that in Dark Harbour on the south coast in the 1960s (population about eight hundred), the priest "was still held in awe because people believed that if you crossed the priest, he would put some kind of a spell on you or your household (much the same as a witch's spell) that would definitely bring bad luck or misfortune" (80/105). He recounts how the priest was enraged by the rumour that he (the priest) was "having a relationship with a woman" and demanded that the accusers take their charge to court, "but fear was greater than boldness and no one accepted the challenge." In a sermon the priest announced that he was leaving and that "family problems, economic problems, sadness, misfortune and grief would strike the community in payment for their evil deeds." Among the misfortune following the priest's departure, the student lists illegitimate births, marriage breakdowns, adultery, alcoholism, and unemployment, and sixteen accidental deaths within ten years: all evinced (by some) as proof of the curse. (Dark Harbour was not the first town to be cursed by a cleric.)[5]

Earle Mackay told me that in his Conception Bay community, "older people had a great fear, years ago, that the priest, that if you rubbed them the wrong way, they'd put a curse on you." One Sunday morning Father O'Boyle came out of the church, pulling off his vestments and saying, "I'll curse the man who cut a tree out of the graveyard." The culprit was Michael Hurder, a charmer who would "tie a worm knot" for infected children. (This was done by knotting a string – always the same one – over their bellies; this knotted the worms themselves, which were expelled several weeks later.) Although the priest had been speaking "half in jest," Michael, who was old and "a bit senile ... took it seriously, took it to heart. And eventually he died over in Waterford Hospital, because he figured, you know, the curse was on him." Father O'Boyle had apologized to him, but it didn't shake his conviction; perhaps as a "magic" practitioner himself, Michael had a special respect for invisible vectors of health and disease.

Margaret Flight, who grew up in the 1950s in a tiny Irish Catholic community on the west coast, described to me the absolute power held by the priest there.[6] As a child, she was haunted by the image of an emaciated baby, almost as long as the crib it lay in. She had never actually seen this baby, only heard how when the baby was born (in the 1940s), the mother wanted to give her an unusual name and the priest refused to christen her because it wasn't a saint's name. The mother, a "hard ticket" (a rebellious sort), said that she would take her to the next community to be baptized by the Protestant minister. "You'll regret it," said the priest. The baby withered, and people said that the fairies had taken her and put one of their own in her place. Lights would dance around the crib and she would catch at them, but eventually she died. Margaret said that it was not that the priest called up the fairies but rather that the woman had left her family open to danger; people said she had "brought the wrath of God on her head." It is hard to express the enormity of the woman's transgression, Margaret said, in the sectarian climate of the time.

Morbid divisive hostility is the theme of some Catholic tales. A priest who found a rat crucified on the church door said, "Whoever was the instigator of this will, before he gets out of this, get more rats than he wants." The Protestant perpetrator, suddenly plagued by rats, sickened and died; at his wake, rats overran the coffin (73/106). Barred from the bedside of a dying Catholic woman by her Protestant husband and his brother, a priest "took off his hat and passed it to one of them and said, 'Here, now you hold that.' Then he cut [made] the sign of the cross at the other fellow. Both of them froze where they stood as if they were statues." They were released when the priest emerged from hearing the woman's confession (73/107).[7]

The extra-church activities of Catholic priests could also explain the remark of the Reverend Charles Jeffrey in a letter written in 1878 from Bay St George on the west coast. A woman there thought that her daughter-in-law was a witch and was causing poltergeistlike disturbances in her house. "As her own clergyman could do nothing to break the spell," wrote the Anglican Jeffrey, "she applied for the assistance of the R.C. priest and he though I suppose accustomed to such things, was able to effect just as little." Jeffrey tried to convince her that her neighbours were right and her own daughter was behind the mischief, but "she would not receive it."[8]

The tight priestly grip on instruments of power (from whips to sacraments) may be one reason why there seems to be less witching among Catholics than Protestants. There was an exception, however, for widows – real widows, that is. "A widow's curse will always fall," agreed the late Queen Maloney and Alice Hayes of the Southern Shore, both of Irish Catholic background and otherwise unacquainted with witch lore. Frances Kavanagh, a specialist in ghost stories (and also of Catholic background), told me that certain widows could put a "wish"; she gave the hypothetical example of a widow who had a son who was hanging around with a questionable crowd: she might put a spell on the crowd, not the son.[9] Several published stories (from Catholic sources) contain dramatic cursing scenes and utterances ("My curse be upon you, you robber of the widow's mite," and, "Let the sea take him and those who would help him, and never may their bodies rest in earth"),[10] echoing perhaps the histrionic performances of "the widow's curse" in Ireland.[11]

Certainly widows of the past (of any denomination) could use all the help they could get, given the lack of social insurance and the practice of patrilineal inheritance laws. Sean Cadigan's review of court cases in Conception Bay from the late eighteenth and early nineteenth centuries shows that women were generally left without property, their husband's house, land, and fishing gear going straight to his sons. This could happen even against his will: when John Lecoux died in Western Bay in 1789 leaving the fishing rooms (premises) to his wife Jane, a son from Jersey whom Jane never knew existed showed up to claim the property; the surrogate awarded it to him, allowing Jane only a third of any proceeds from its lease.[12] Wills typically contained a provision that sons must care for their mother or mother-in-law, an arrangement making her dependent on the goodwill of male relatives, which, as Cadigan notes, "could be disastrous for a widow."[13]

In Protestant tradition, it seems as if widows were subsumed in the general run of witches, even though the Bible stipulates that they are not to be offended. In 1656 Thomas Ady admonished his English parishioners who met with trouble after refusing charity that they should not ask "what old man or woman was last at my door, that I may hand him or her for a Witche; yea we should rather say, Because I did not relieve such a poor body that was lately at my door, but gave him harsh and bitter words, therefore God hath laid this Affliction upon me, for God saith, Exod. 22.23.24. If thou any way afflict widows, and the fatherless, and they at all cry unto me, I will surely hear their cry, and my wrath shall wax hot against thee."[14]

Except for urging the Bible on everyone, the Church of England was no more eager than the Catholic church to share spiritual agency with women. The Anglican missionary Wix, travelling the south coast in 1865, was disgusted to see women taking the same liberties as men – drinking, smoking, swearing – but was especially incensed to find in Burgeo the presence of "a young woman who had, a few years before, practised with her father upon the ignorance and credulity of her neighbours and strangers at Gaultois, by affecting to receive divine communications, and to prophesy."[15]

Only Methodism offered women a leadership role, allowing them to be lay readers (though men were preferred).[16] A big force in Newfoundland history, Methodism arrived in Harbour Grace in 1765 in the person of Lawrence Coughlan, who had the five thousand souls in Conception Bay to himself, there being no other ministers there.[17] Coughlan was a contemporary of John Wesley, an avid believer in witches who famously declared that "the giving up witchcraft is in effect giving up the Bible."[18] Wesley put much stock in oral tradition, saying of witchcraft that he had "stronger proofs of this, from eye and ear witnesses, than I have of murder."[19] Since Newfoundland, alone among North American congregations, adhered to Methodism "as taught and practiced by Wesley,"[20] there is reason to wonder whether that religion made an especially generous contribution to witch lore. For one thing, a distinct regional correlation holds between high-witch areas and the Methodist missionary circuits, although there were usually Anglicans and Catholics in these places as well. For another, Wesleyanism has long been held responsible for the tenacity of witch lore in southwestern England.[21] Owen Davies has recently disputed that claim, pointing out that Anglicans had their own clergy schooled (or said to be schooled) in popular belief, such as the spirit-laying, black-book-owning Parson Joe of Devon; Old Cleeve of Somerset, who conjured a thief into a willow tree; and sundry clergy who might pray over bewitched persons or bewitch people themselves.[22] Davies does note the suspicion that witchcraft went on at Wesleyan meetings and "love feasts"; and as Deborah M. Valenze notes, this could be an alluring prospect. She quotes the husband of the (English) Primitive Methodist preacher Elizabeth Smith: "It got circulated that we used the black art, and black books, and that Miss Smith was a fortune-teller. This brought many out, and led to their awakening and conversion."[23] Davies also acknowledges that Wesley's journals were full of references to witchcraft, and that his *Arminium Magazine* was rife with diabolical tales.[24] These were all on Newfoundland shelves "among our people where books were found," Wilson noted in 1865; Mrs Stretton's library, for instance, contained the whole of Wesley's works in sixteen volumes, his Christian library in fifty volumes, and all the magazines.[25] Even the pious must have scanned for the juicy bits.

Methodist ideology might also have supported witch lore indirectly. Methodists were supposed to respect if not actually love one another; complaints aired at a meeting in 1876, for instance, included one against a woman "for not showing a friendly spirit toward an old acquaintance," and another against a man "for speaking too harshly to Dr J. MacDonald."[26] Even acting correctly was not enough; one's inner life mattered too. In the so-called "heart religion,"[27] thought and emotion were as important as action – exactly as it is in witching. It may be that the furtive riddled-heart countercharms and black heart books may have been a kind of objective correlative to the festering subjective state of witch suspicions.

In 1991 I visited Wesleyville in Bonavista Bay (a real name, conferred in 1891 in a typical nineteenth-century conversion, like that of Devil's Cove to Job's Cove, Bread and Cheese to Bishop's Cove, or Bird Island Cove to Elliston in honour of the first Methodist missionary to visit the place).[28] There I queried the late Reverend Naboth Winsor, historian of Methodism in Newfoundland, about witches.[29] I received no doctrinal or philosophical opinion, only a tale like anyone else's. (The fact that he told it at all is interesting; when I spoke about witching with the late Reverend Fred Kirby, an Anglican, and Stella Kirby of Greenspond, they claimed never to have heard of it, although there are many stories from that community and certainly from Mrs Kirby's birthplace near Barrenville.)[30] Reverend Winsor had his story from the son of a man who, as a young fellow, was put in charge of a schooner when the regular skipper fell ill. The assignment angered another crew member's wife, who thought that her husband should have had the job, and she vowed that he would never have command of the vessel. When the young man was spreading lime in the hold in preparation for the voyage, the new brin bag (burlap sack) broke open and the lime flew into his eyes, putting him in pain for days; people said he was witched by the angry woman.

Here was a typical tale, with no religion at all, just business among people. These included not only the witch and bewitched but also community members who marked the woman's (note: not her husband's) anger and its result. Belatedly I realized that I did not learn whether the man eventually led the voyage or not. But maybe the seeming lacuna is revealing: it suggests that the prophecy, although the dramatic focus, is not necessarily its true centre. The crux of the tale is really the selection of one crew member over another. We will never know how the people involved felt (was the passed-over man insulted, or was his wife overly ambitious on his behalf? Did the young man feel badly about being picked, or nervous at the prospect of heading the ship?) but it was all important enough to be preserved in the medium of witch lore. The burst bag was no accident but the attendant of ruptured expectations. Religion is about the relationship between people and their god(s); witching is about their relationship with one another.

And "wishing" is, after all, not so different from praying, especially when intensity is related to outcome. All the religions taught the efficacy of prayer, and that is perhaps their greatest collective contribution to witch lore. For if a person can pray hard enough to "get an answer" – that is, a result – then maybe he or she could will other things to happen as well; at least it must have occurred to some people to try a secular version of moving whatever invisible powers that might be.

Lawrence Gough recently wrote of Wesleyville, "Everyone was a novel, everyone was a painting. Older men were called 'Uncle,' no matter what the blood relationship, and older women were all called 'Aunt.' It didn't matter how bloodlines flowed: the world flowed everyone into the same ocean, where they were all related. Every person in a town was seen as being responsible for every other person."[31] A romantic expression of the ideal outport perhaps, but it does convey the pervasive sense of connection that allows witching to "work"; for if everyone is responsible for everyone else, then no one can act badly with impunity. The Christian imperative to "do unto others" as one would be done by could only heighten this awareness and also facilitate the processes of projection: if the offenders put themselves in the position of the offended parties, they might well imagine that had it been them, they would want revenge. So they are punished through the witching ethic that one bad turn deserves another.

Although the witches and other magical personae (Jerseymen, priests, black heartists) discussed in Part One are all different, they have in common that they were empowered by the people around them, who used templates of proven utility to produce stories that were malleable according to need, belief, and desire. Almost always the animus was a breach of social accord: that is the heart that keeps the narrative corpus alive.

In the following chapters I attempt open-heart surgery, if that is not too visceral an image for a lot of talk about something that happens mostly in the mind. But words, thought, and emotion are the substance of witching, whether one believes that the phenomenon is real or not. And so on to Barrenville, to see what people there had to say about witches.

PART TWO

Hagridden Barrenville

Though bearing one name on the map, the town of Barrenville encompasses a number of distinct neighbourhoods with strong individual identities. A major fishing centre since the late 1600s, its inhabitants prosecuted the inshore, Labrador, and seal fisheries, bringing prosperity for some; several large fortunes were made there, and many families lived in relative comfort. But there was also profound poverty (and the profound irony that this should occur in the richest fishery in the world, where the catch was preserved). The museum curator, Marion Linton, likened Barrenville of the 1930s to a Third World country; people actually starved to death, she told me, as we sat leafing through lists of deaths from tuberculosis, childbirth, illness, and accident of every description.[1] There was nothing in the museum about witchcraft, although the curator knew all about it. Witch lore reached a pitch in Barrrenville, where witch-bottles enjoyed baroque variation, and the hallucinatory "old hag" was a recurrent collective nightmare.

The vigour of Barrenville's tradition explodes any notion that small, isolated places naturally harbour the most witch lore. On the contrary, its size gave impetus to a rich repertoire. There was a bank, for instance, where people went to get new pins needed for witch-bottles; and doctors who were supposed to have treated the bladder-bound witches and to have been believers themselves. The physical distance between neighbourhoods, with their miles of crisscrossing lanes, fostered a certain impersonality that would not be possible in a single clutch of houses. Across the open rambling spaces, people could observe one another's comings and goings (as to the doctor's) without meeting face to face; one could watch

witchy Birdie Howell on any number of occasions, for instance, as
she meandered along in her battered brown coat, eating snow from
the sides of the road, and never exchange a word with her. This,
I think, made it easier to entertain (and be entertained by) wild
ideas about witches; for Barrenville had not only more but more
lurid tales than the usual outport. As elsewhere, most witch
episodes occurred between people who knew each other well, but
Barrenville's were played out against a highly coloured backdrop of
stories about semistrangers in the semidistance.

Distance was not just a matter of geography but social and
economic disparity as well. Did the gulf between rich and poor,
wider than in small places, make the poor more resentful or
envious? Did the number of poor create crises of conscience among
those who were appealed to for help? Were issues of inclusion and
respect heightened by consciousness of class? Another possibly
divisive factor was that Barrenville had several churches, rather than
a single institution that might have united people at least on
occasion. (The population was mostly of English background, with
a few of Irish descent.) Furthermore, Barrenvillians were people on
the move: when the inshore fishery was in full swing, many families
spent the summer at makeshift quarters on the headlands, where
the fish were processed; in winter, many decamped to winter houses
in the woods to be out of the wind and near fuel. All this was in
addition to forays to the Labrador and the seal hunt and, for some
men, to ports around the world. This quasi-nomadism assured the
spread of tales beyond their immediate neighbourhood, and the
fruitful exchange of rumour and debate.

Seeking answers today is complicated by the distance of time, for
despite an occasional manifestation, the tradition does recede apace
and I heard of no living reputed witches, though I heard of a few
recent witch incidents. "They're thinned out today, there's nobody
knows them today ... but they're here," William Heywood told me,
suggesting another function of size, perhaps, since they can blend
in. I think the town's size also supported a kind of conceptual
formulary in that recurring ideas, motifs, and expressions abound
in my interviews and in the archival material: the doctors'
pronouncements, for instance, or the business of throwing the
bottle into the ocean to kill the witch. These echoes would
reverberate too insistently in the confines of a smaller space and
wear themselves out. Indeed they may weary the reader after a

while, but it is important to see the repetition in action, how the material is constantly reconfigured and recontextualized, since that is how it is transmitted and maintained.

Finally, a note before proceeding to direct testimony. Extensive quoted direct speech, besides being the best guarantee of authenticity (that the interviewer has not gotten the wrong end of the stick, so to speak), is critical in conveying the various ways that people relay occurrences and opinions of witching. Readers unaccustomed to verbatim transcripts sometimes complain that dialogue can convey an unfavourable impression of speakers when printed "as is," with no "correction" of grammar to formal style. Many people in Barrenville do not speak standard English; most older people had little chance for a formal education. But if such readers look beyond vernacular grammar to the narrative and commentary as a whole, they will see that it is typically constructed with flavour and flair. This is more than a matter of colourful expressions and dialect: it is a lively engagement and a willingness to hold the floor that comes from being part of a storytelling culture. Many Newfoundlanders, especially younger ones, switch between "standard" and Newfoundland English according to occasion, and no one familiar with the liveliness and warmth of the latter's idioms would want to give them up. To me, modern mainland conversation can seem truncated and flat in comparison.

 ## Charity Begins at Home: Sarah Haley

I knew no one when I first went to Barrenville, only that I had to go because of the richness of the archival data, but I was in luck from the moment I arrived at my lodgings with Ann and Ed Williams. Ann had never heard of witchcraft until she moved from Trinity Bay to Barrenville in 1950, but Ed is a native who grew up next door to Sarah Haley in the 1920s.[2] Soon we were peering at a photograph of a tiny woman with a bun of white hair, wearing the long dark dress and white apron in the old outport style. Ed doesn't know how Sarah came to be singled out as a witch, only that she could put a spell on you if you didn't give her what she wanted. This helped her through the Depression, when she went door to door for food, but even before that she would come to Ed's house most days at dinnertime in hope of leftovers. Ed's brother Gill Williams (who became my guide to

Barrenville) said that the boys would tease her while she waited, taking her hair down, pulling on her skirt, and even calling her an old witch. But she "never did anything to them" (that is, in the way of a curse) because "Mother used to give her things … she never bothered us." Their mother died when Gill was six, so these are vivid childhood memories for him; an older brother, Harold, also said that Sarah could have "done something with them" if she wanted. It hardly had an inhibiting effect on him and his friends, though, who as teenagers would hang about her tiny house of an evening. He recalls passing through a doorway so low he could heave it up with his shoulders; inside, one boy would distract Sarah's attention so that the others could peek into the mysterious stone-floored rooms. They played tricks on her, putting sods in the chimney, or turning back the hands of the clock when she snuffed out the candles to tell them to go. Sarah had no children, so the boys' company must have been welcome despite their antics.

Sarah's entire situation sounds remarkably like that of Agnes Chatwin as described to me by Fred Earle of the northeast coast.[3] Like Sarah, Agnes would make the rounds of the houses, especially during the Depression, looking for bread and butter and food; her husband had been "in bed for years" and the government assistance they received was not enough to live on. They had no children, and the young unmarried men of the community would go to her place in the evening to engage in horseplay and mild license. At fifteen, Fred was too young to go himself, and he recalls listening enviously to the tales about "what happened at Agnes's last night." They would "torment" her with little tricks such as pinging stones at the kettle until she "swore on them." It is easy to believe (as reported) that she would threaten to "stop their water for a week" by boiling urine. Despite the teasing, Sarah and Agnes at least had someone to keep the fire going in the evenings, and company besides their husbands. Sharing marginal status – the young men in the brief liminal phase between boyhood and responsible married life, Agnes and Sarah as poor witches – they nevertheless found a community niche.

No one remembered much about Sarah's husband Austin, who died about fifteen years before she did, except that he sometimes fished as a shareman – someone who fished in return for a share of the catch, rather than as part of a permanent familial crew – with little success. Ed's impression was that there was nothing exactly wrong with him, but that he was exceptionally naive, and rumour had it that he sometimes got cheated because he didn't understand money. Frank Tibbert told me that once, when a skipper underpaid him with a pile of one-dollar bills, he exclaimed, "This can't all be mine!"[4] But then the skipper was a notorious miser, and Austin and Sarah seem to have been the butt of stock "numbskull" tales, such as the one Gill told about Sarah's being given an ice cream cone, which she took home and put in the oven.

Sarah did not appreciate being made a figure of fun. Ann Williams recalls hearing that she once took a bit of dried fish she'd been given to the shop to trade. "Who've you been fishing with, Aunt Sarah?" the shopkeeper jokingly enquired. The next day all his cows were dead. "Well, I'll tell you one about Aunt Sarah Haley," Charlie Harper said to me.[5] "People used to mark her, the way she would talk: 'That'll be all right, that'll be all right.'" One day his father teased her by saying that he wouldn't bring her any fish that year (as presumably he normally did). His brother was dismayed: "Just as well to haul up the boat. We're finished," he said. But it was the best summer they ever had – they filled the flakes, under the stages, the puncheon tubs, leading Charlie's father to conclude, "She's no more a witch than I'm a wizard."

Philomena Abbinott told me that some people laughed at Sarah behind her back, at her poverty and her wretched clothes hanging on the line, but if you didn't "talk to her right" to her face, she could "crump" you – make you sick and unable to move.[6] "She would stop some people, and some would stop her" (that is, some "stopped" her with a bottle). Philomena recalled that as young women, she and her sister were out walking one day and encountered Sarah's black cat. "Get out of the way, puss," they said. Sarah heard them and told them sharply not to talk to her cat like that. She came out into the road and put her arms around them. "You two will never get married," she said, "and you won't get any of those men that come [here] either." This was just before the war and the arrival of Canadian and American servicemen in the area, whom many local women did marry – but not Philomena or her sister. They always remained single, though whether Sarah had issued a prediction or a curse Philomena could not say.

Frank Tibbert gave me another example of Sarah's predictions. He said that one day he and Stewart Adey (as young men) were on their way to jig for squid (that is, catch them with a line and hook) when Sarah wanted them to chop some wood for her; Stewart said they didn't have time, but Frank stopped to do it. Sarah told him that he would get plenty of squid and Stewart none, and that was how it happened, even though they were in the same boat.

If Sarah made such pronouncements in the hope of creating more examples like Frank's, she was supported by the ideal that young people should respect and help their elders. Outport children were expected to obey not just parents but more or less all the older people who were in charge of things while younger adults were busy with the fishery. These "aunts" and "uncles" could inspire affection, but there is bound to have been friction as well, especially as the children matured and began to chafe at authority. It may even be that typical developmental resentment toward parents was subconsciously redirected toward substitute figures, especially anyone whom it was already acceptable to look down upon as a witch. The historian Deborah Willis believes that "witches were women because women are mothers"; subconscious animosity toward mothers, she suggests, was deflected onto someone who resembled them in some ways but not others – a needy, demanding older woman, for example (someone, in other words, like Sarah Haley). Struck by how often quarrels between older and younger women led to witchcraft accusations in early modern England, Willis goes so far as to propose that witch-hunting at the village level was "largely a form of women's work."[7] Such is clearly not the case in Newfoundland, but the intergenerational female dyad does appear regularly enough to show it as a point of tension, and it has no comparable model among men: older men do not witch younger ones (only one another). Possibly Sarah's childlessness made her a good mother-scapegoat, and therefore a witch.

Having no descendants has definitely contributed to her posthumous reputation, in that people feel free to talk about her without fear of offending living relations. I am sure I heard more about her than about some other women for this reason. Ed Williams, for one, might have been more reticent. He was appalled when I returned from one of my visits and reported that Susan Adder had been mentioned as a witch. On the contrary, he said, she was highly respectable – it was her mother who was the witch. The subject could still be a touchy one. A school principal told me that recently a parent became enraged when another parent called her a witch – she took it not just as an insult but as a literal charge to be refuted.[8] But even if Ed hadn't told me about Sarah, I would have heard about her sooner or later. In fact it was sooner, from the second couple I met, William and Maise Heywood.

True Believers

If the Williamses tended to scepticism, a conversation about witching with William and Maise Heywood is punctuated with assertions of its reality. "Oh, they can do it, you know"; "they could do most anything"; "they was all real, maid." William, a successful fisherman, has in his energetic seventies become a kind of cultural consultant; anyone researching any aspect of traditional life or history usually ends up in the Heywood kitchen. William is also called upon by the community for help that others might be reluctant to undertake. On one of my visits, for instance, he had just transported a coffin from a nearby town. He is part of a band that plays in local festivals and seniors' homes. He and Maise raised several children who now work in international technical positions. In short, they are extroverted, well-regarded citizens.

William's story about Sarah Haley is among the most astonishing things I heard in the course of my research:

> Her brother went in her house one time, and her clothes was on the daybed, and he sat down and waited. He said, "She's gone somewhere." And he said, "I'll wait now," he said. After awhile her clothes just straightened out. She sat up [in the clothes]. "Oh my," she said, "you're here."
>
> "Yes," he said, "I'm here." And he told her off, he called her everything. "You was off now," he said, "torturing some poor people," he said, "wasn't you?" And she started to cry, you know.

The brother was accusing her of travelling invisibly, "like a spirit," to oppress people in their sleep, "what they call ag-rog you" (a local variant of "hag-rode" or hag-ridden). A devout Christian, Sarah's brother heaped abuse on her: "You're nothing but a dirty old witch, I'm not coming around here no more." ("You dirt!" he said, in a version William gave to Mark Ferguson.)[9]

Perhaps by spreading this tale (and several other people recall his doing so)[10] the brother was trying to disassociate himself from hereditary taint. "See, it more or less runs in the family," said William. "If

your mother was one, you could learn that from her, how to do it."[11]
Alternately, maybe the brother meant to imply that he too might have
powers, even as he professed to detest them. His tale shows a certain
power of invention, for the materialization of Aunt Sarah in her
clothes is an unusual motif.

Being hag-ridden is common enough, however, and not just in
Barrenville. People all over the world have awakened to find themselves unable to move, with a sense of oppression on the chest and
often of an evil presence. Some have no name for the petrifying experience, and different cultures interpret its meaning differently, but the
hallmark of an episode is the conviction that it is not a dream. While
science identifies temporary sleep paralysis and hypnagogic halluci-
nations as the cause,[12] throughout European history it has been associated with witchcraft.[13] In Barrenville the two are practically
synonymous. "Witches cast this spell on people and it's called 'the
Hag,'" wrote a Barrenville student of "a dream that something is going
to kill you, and you can't move" (70/1/FSC). According to William, "it
happens when someone is jealous, when you have something they
want." He adduced the time his mother got a new coat. "Now you can
give the old one to I," said her friend; but his mother said that she
still needed it for garden work and chores. That night while she was
in bed, she saw the friend enter her room, climb onto her feet and
ascend to her neck:[14]

> She come right up on her, she come up on her, and she had her
> down, she couldn't move an arm, she couldn't move a leg.
> She couldn't even speak, only she was there, you know, trying to
> get her breath. She was there for about four or five minutes, on
> top of her, thought she'd – think she was going to die, she was
> that bad. After awhile it left her again … She saw a shadow,
> like, going through the door. She knew, you know. So people
> was tortured to death with people. They ask, those witches,
> you know – if they want anything from you and you didn't
> give it …

Just so did Mary Trembles and Susanna Edwards of Bideford in Devon
(a major early port to Newfoundland) go invisibly to torment Grace
Barnes in her bed, after she refused them bread and tobacco in the
year 1680.[15] Hags were rife in colonial America, where "spectral
evidence" helped convict people in the Salem trials of 1692.[16]

Work patterns in Newfoundland were ideally suited to intensify this legacy. As Robert C. Ness and his informants pointed out, the hard labour and chronic sleep deprivation of the fishing season made people vulnerable – when they finally did get to sleep, it could be hard to wake up. (Using the Cornell Medical Index for sixty-nine informants, Ness determined that there was no difference in psychological or physical illness between those who had experienced the hag and those who had not.)[17] Physical conditions combined with cultural traits to predispose people to episodes. Melvin Firestone, an anthropologist who worked with fishing crews on the Northern Peninsula in the 1960s, suggests that it was part of the "Newfoundland social character" to repress hostility, which then surfaced when people let their conscious guard down, paralyzing the "aggressive" self, or projecting it onto a "hag" or other attacker. Particularly interesting with regard to witching are Firestone's observations on crews' decision making: "People attempted to maintain a *modus vivendi* through a kind of indirection which headed off the possibility of overt conflict ... When a man wanted to borrow something from a man outside of his fishing crew he never asked to borrow it but stated his need. The man being solicited understood what was wanted, but as he had not openly been asked, no one had been overtly rejected if the item was not offered."[18] In William Heywood's view, the male aversion to asking for things explains why there are so few known male witches – that along with the fact that men had better methods of revenge:

BR: What about men witches?

WH: Oh, yeah, there's witches and wizards. Oh, men can do it just as much as a woman could.

BR: But I never seem to hear of any men who have the reputation.

WH: No, well, men, see, is not like the woman. They never hardly ask you for anything, you know what I mean; but a woman, years ago, they used to ask for money and clothes and everything like that, you know. Then if you didn't give it to them, well, this is the only way they could retaliate with you, they couldn't up and hit you or take anything from you, but they'd put a spell on you.

The last remark recalls Keith Thomas's point that the sixteenth-century witch could be presumed to be in a lower social position than the victim, "for, had she been the stronger party, more direct methods of revenge would have been at her disposal."[19] It also echoes Christina Larner's comment about Scottish witchcraft, that "where men might use knives, women used words."[20]

Hagging, however, *was* considered a physical assault. Philomena Abbinott (she who never married as per Sarah's prediction) said that as a young woman, she went through a period of time when she would awake every night unable to breathe, move, or call out. Her father dismissed it as "bad blood," but she knew otherwise and told her mother, "There's a witch or something trying to pin me down." She didn't know who it was until one night she saw her: a friend of her sister's, looking just as she did every day, a heavyset woman in a low-cut black dress. "You blood of a bitch, you won't get me this time!" Philomena shouted, and the hag disappeared, never to return. Philomena said that she hardly knew the woman, and that the only possible thing she could have had against her was that there had been some talk of her brother and Philomena making a match, but it never happened. Philomena's mother was amazed by her audacity, but her sister was equally bold. When she (the sister) was witched by an older woman, Sally Addell, so that her cow got sick, she went to Sally and said that if she didn't take the spell off she would run her through with a knife. It did sometimes happen in England that people assaulted night "hags" in waking life; at least six cases were heard in Somerset and Dorset courts between 1852 and 1875 alone.[21] In Barrenville, the only case I heard of involved one sufferer who stuck a fork in Beatrice Daley's buttocks – her apparition's buttocks, that is, but Beatrice was supposed to have shown someone the marks of the prongs.[22]

Hannah Tibbert, Frank Tibbert's wife and a neighbour of William's of about the same age as Philomena, told me that she was once troubled by a bout of hagging. Like Philomena, she didn't know "who was doing it," until one night she saw a friend of hers – someone with whom she had no quarrel – enter the room, wearing a white blouse and black skirt. A Bible under the pillow solved the problem, as well as not sleeping on her back ("They can't get you when you're on your side, they're easier on you"). Hannah, like Philomena, also had a sister who was witched; she had refused to give money for a garden party to a woman she didn't know very well, and "she got sick over it." These sisterly afflictions suggest that family values help to make witching a viable explanation of certain events.

Philomena's and Hannah's accounts also suggest that hag victims are less likely than victims of "ordinary" spells to be aware of a motive for the attack. William Heywood, however, didn't buy the idea of any spell or hag attack without cause. When I told him about the apparently baseless harassment of Hannah, he pointed out that jealousy isn't always out in the open; a person might keep it secret, but it would come out in this way. The idea of hidden emotion chimes with various modern theories of dreaming, especially the idea that the subconscious can register social cues that are missed or ignored (not necessarily suppressed) by the conscious mind but that later come to the fore as "intuition" or in dreams. "Contrary to its popular name," the sleep specialist Charles McPhee writes, "the unconscious mechanism is acutely aware" of such things as a fleeting expression on a face, a tone of voice, or a turn of phrase.[23] It would not take an overt quarrel or refusal but something as subtle as a glance to set a cycle of hags in motion, so to speak. Suppose that x, for whatever reason (or for none at all) is hagged by y; she therefore looks at y differently the next time she sees her (even if she tries to hide it), causing y to be hagged by x and subsequently look at her strangely, and so on.

Then there is classic psychoanalytic theory that repressed impulses emerge during dreams, and it doesn't take a Freudian to see a sexual element in these nocturnal struggles (although they are never, by definition, pleasurable). One man's rejected suitor weighed so heavily on his mind by day that she weighed on his body at night.

> Maggie Wall was in love with Mr Crenshaw; she desperately wanted him but he did not want her. After he began courting another girl he used to be tormented at night by Miss Wall. Things got so bad that he used to stay awake as long as he could, sometimes sleep in the kitchen and even went to see the minister about it. Apparently the minister wasn't much of a help, he just told him to forget it. Someone told him to use the nails and board … Anyway that's what he did and that night before going to sleep he laid the board with the nails sticking up in it on his breast. He was later awakened that night by Maggie's yells, which he could not understand at that time. He couldn't go to sleep any more that night. The next day Mr Crenshaw heard that Maggie

was in her house with her hands and arms cut up. However she never bothered him after. (69/2/FSC)

Romantic rejection, like any refusal, was a risky business. Maise Heywood's uncle spent two years in hospital after Mary Barton "put beriberi on him" because she wanted him but he married someone else. (She took the spell off just before she died.) David Hufford recorded the tale of a man who was refused a kiss by a woman. He knelt naked by his bed, recited the Lord's Prayer backwards, then dove beneath the blankets where he drove a knife into a board, crying, "Hag, good hag!" His co-workers saw him do all this, but it is not clear how they found out that at that same moment the woman saw him standing over her with a knife.[24] Reports of men hagging women are rare, but this may be due to reticence about sexual matters. A student learned how carefully guarded such information can be when her grandmother told her that she had "the old hag" shortly after she was married; she was in bed when she saw her father-in-law coming toward her, and "he didn't have a tat of clothes on." He grabbed her by the throat and choked her, and she awoke screaming. According to the student, "This is the first time she has ever told my grandfather this and they will be married fifty years in March" (70/3/FSC).

Being based in physiology, the hag experience will endure, although the explanatory features will change. In my Newfoundland Folklore class in the winter of 2006, eight of the fifty-six students conducted interview projects on the old hag. Besides the general sense of presence or oppression, manifestations included hideous old women but also "spirits like misty horses" rushing into the room; a black cloud or fog; a "little midget dude" with a "giant buddy" at the door; a young blond woman mistaken for the sufferer's sister; and men well known to the sleeper, including her boyfriend with a suffocating kiss. Sounds (accompanying the apparitions or on their own) included hissing, heavy breathing, swishing as of cloth, and guttural voices. One young man was visited by an old woman hag so often that he named her Phyllis, but he saw others as well, including a Chinese man in a minivan asking directions to the porch. Only two of the essays mentioned a connection with spells. One was an informant who said that a broom in the bedroom would prevent the experience because a hag couldn't step over the broom. The second was the student, a sufferer himself, who heard from one informant "that her grandfather's father had done wrong to a woman who was well known in the community as a witch." When he refused to apologize, the woman said that "no one would sleep right again," with the result that "all have experiences with the hag on a regular basis." From this the student concluded that something similar happened to his own family. His father and other family members dismissed the idea, but the student wrote, "I firmly believe that my family does have a curse placed on them somewhere in the past as to the plain and simple fact as to how one can explain the same four family members all having the same experience?"[25]

The protean nature of the hag enables it to accommodate both individual psychology and traditional concepts. Ten years ago a student wrote about "the hag or hagrot as it is known in Barrenville" based on the accounts of two friends of his own age.[26] Both described an anonymous and unmotivated but still female entity. One was a two-foot-tall warty witch in black who sat on the sufferer's chest; the other was a circus clown for the friend, and for her mother, the devil. "Why do people see different things?" the student asked. One friend told him that "it is dependent on your fears. She has a deep inner fear of clowns, and has told me that since she was very young she always hated clowns … Her mother was a religious woman, and had a fear of the devil and hell." Despite this psychological insight, the informants maintain that the entity is real and that it is female. One never slept on her back after the attack, because "she cannot come if you are on your side or stomach," and both said that "no one knows why she picks certain people."

Older Barrenvillians usually looked for a cause. Marion Linton, like William, saw conflict as the source:

> Those people used to what the old people called ag-rog them …
> When they'd go to sleep at night, those people would come in
> the room and take them by the throat, almost like a nightmare
> … they'd feel as if they were dying … they claim this was done
> by people who could put spells on you. I don't think it had to be
> a person who was designated as a witch; it seemed as if this
> could be done by other people who had powers but who didn't
> actually function as a witch … This would be between people
> who had disagreements.

Also like William, Marion said that men could "witch" just as well as women but simply didn't become "known for it" because they didn't engage in the habitual public behaviour that led to the label. This was in response to my question whether an ordinary person, as distinct from a reputed witch, could cast spells:

> Yes, that sometimes happened. Wishes on people. We've all heard of those occasions ... Because with those community witches, I think it was a constant thing, you know, it was more a way of life. But with those others, it was only if you'd cross them. And so that would be a different situation, and they didn't get the reputation of it. And this could happen whether it was male or female, this wasn't something that was distinctly female ... it could be a disagreement between men who are fishing together or working together in the lumber woods or something similar to that.

Marion's family lived on the main street and so had a steady stream of importunate callers; there were simply too many to help them all, she said, so then you had to worry about a spell when you didn't. Her parents were well off enough to be saving to send Marion to school in St John's, an expensive proposition involving transport, board, and books; a dollar given at the door subtracted directly from her fund. The family's unease about solicitors thus exemplified Thomas's characterization of witchcraft as a struggle "between the fairly poor and the very poor."[27] Macfarlane found that while Essex witches were not the very poorest people, almost every accusation followed the request-refusal-revenge paradigm; he suggests that this was because the truly indigent could avail of parish aid, whereas the middling poor depended on neighbours and friends.[28] Conflicts over charity were exacerbated, in Thomas's view, by the sixteenth-century shift from the old system of neighbourly aid toward one of public assistance, with new "poor laws" that made it easier for householders to consider the poor to be someone else's problem.[29] A similar tendency to pass the buck may have operated in Barrenville, where the poor could be strangers, and rarely seen at that. In a smaller place of a few dozen houses, a needy person would have to freeze or starve more or less in front of everyone, prompting provision for care. In Barrenville, it was possible to ignore the poor until they appeared at your door; then, as Marion said, you turned them away at your own risk.

Not all cases of witching, as we have seen, follow the triple-R pattern, and some scholars think that too much weight has been given to what Marion Gibson calls the "denial narrative." Gibson points out that this summary form "does not represent all the interactions that make up witchcraft" and suggests that we ask, "Where does fact end and the stereotyping dynamic of narration take over?"[30] An interesting, but in my opinion rhetorical, question.

A set of stories from Lizzie and Don Wade, a couple in their eighties when I interviewed them, demonstrates the impossibility of isolating "facts," as well as the futility of interpreting narratives without relating one story to another. The Wades' experiences concerned their neighbour, Mrs Graves, whom Lizzie met when she moved to Barrenville as a young woman. Mrs Graves was about twenty years older than Lizzie (suggesting a quasi-maternal role?), married with seven children, and not poor. "She was a nice person, she shared whatever she had, and I shared with her," said Lizzie, and they were "not bad friends." Nevertheless Lizzie blamed her for killing a special plant someone had given her.

> [It was] a shepherd's prayer, it started to grow, and this woman come here, I don't want to mention her name, eh, and I said to her, I said, "Mrs Graves, my shepherd's prayer is growing; I was so long," I said, "before I got a flower like that. And I got en now, and I hopes he grows."
>
> "Yes," she said, "he's growing."
>
> [Points with index finger.] Right there with her finger. "He's growing nice."
>
> So she went on. That was Sunday morning. And she went on, and on Tuesday she come here again. And I took the flower – I got dirty, see – I took the flower and I brought it in and I showed it to her and I said, "Look," I said, "there's the flower," I said, "you looked at Sunday, it was growing beautiful," I said. "And you put your finger up," I said, "and Tuesday it was gone," I said. So he was gone then.

It is a fact that the plant died after Mrs Graves's visit, but why does Lizzie see a causal relationship? There was no request and no refusal. There was, however, implicit envy. Lizzie mentioned that Mrs Graves kept a small garden, as many women did, planted with potatoes, carrots, and turnips; perhaps the flower represented luxury, and Mrs Graves might be presumed to have wanted it. Witching was not always about dire necessity – one could hunger for a bit of colour too. But the import of Mrs Graves's visit becomes clearer in the light of other tales. A north coast student wrote, "It was told to me by an old lady that another lady who came to visit her witched her flowers. After the witch had admired the flowers they faded within a week. *She knew this to be true because it happened to someone else [too]*" (64/4/FSC; my emphasis). As Gibson acknowledges, each repetition of a pattern carries "more conviction because of the increasing recognition of typicality."[31] A person who had never heard of witching would never think to connect a friend's inspection of a plant to its death; the answers to many riddles of witching lie precisely in the stereotyping nature of tales. But Gibson's point is well taken, that behind every crystallized narrative lies a compounding history of incident.

Take, for instance, the time Lizzie and Mrs Graves were out walking and passed a group of girls who were laughing at some men digging a well. Mrs Graves thought they were laughing at her. "If I had known they was making fun at me, I would have done something with them," she said. She was not a "cheerful person," according to Lizzie. "She was strange, you could see it on her face when she was talking like this, eh?" Still, Lizzie hesitated to call her a witch – at one point she said she never heard of her "at that," but later she said, "people put that name on her," and, "I suppose she was one."

An early inkling may have come from Don, who had a run-in with Mrs Graves before he and Lizzie were married. Mrs Graves asked him for a bird he had just shot and he refused (although he said that if he had known she was a witch he would have complied). "That's all right, if you don't give him to me, all right," she said. Whenever Don shot a bird, he would look under its wing to see if it was fat, and this bird had been fine; but later, after the encounter with Mrs Graves, he began to pluck it and found it was black under the wing and therefore inedible. ("That was true," added Lizzie.) So, what is the "fact" here? Don's bird spoiled. But, attuned as any Barrenvillian would be to the nuance of exchange (of goods and of words), he knew very well that there was more to it than that. So "refuser-guilt syndrome" kicked in, as Robin Briggs calls the victim's response when "there were no clear boundaries to what might be demanded or should be given."[32]

Guilt, however, may not be exactly the right word for what many refusers feel; they do not necessarily suffer remorse for having done wrong but for having chosen a poor course of action. The refuser's knowledge of the likely consequences drives the denial narrative, which, it might be noted in passing, is not confined to European tradition. To take an example almost at random, Passin noted in 1911 among the Tarahumara of New Mexico an "almost compulsive fear on the part of those who do not share," because when "a man wants something from another, and when the latter does not comply with the request, he is bewitched."[33] It is only logical, after all, that in any culture containing the idea of witchcraft, witches would turn their power against those who displease them in any way.

Of course the refuser is sometimes seen as guilty, by others if not by himself; witches are not always thought to be in the wrong, and spells may be justified, or at least not totally uncalled for. When William Heywood told how a woman got sick after refusing to give Sarah Haley some boots, he was careful to explain that the boots had been the woman's only pair. The woman's mother put up a bottle ("naming it" for Sarah) and when Sarah duly appeared at the house and showed her swollen abdomen, she told her, "That wasn't fair of you, putting that spell on her" – a rebuke implying that in some circumstances it might have been "fair." Sarah promised not to do it again, so they uncorked the bottle, and she urinated on the spot.

Refuser-guilt is glaring enough, however, in the following account. A student wrote:

> Old Sarah Haley was a witch. She used to visit Dad's
> grandmother and often she overstayed her welcome. One night
> she stayed very late and asked Mom to bring in the "slop-pail"
> for her. Mom told her that it was time for her to go home; there,
> she could use her own. Next morning, as Mom was bringing the
> slop-pail out over the steps (it was customary to dump it every
> morning) she lost her balance and the pail swung over her head,
> getting her in a fine mess. Mom said this was the old witch's
> doing because Mom didn't let her use the pail. (89/5/FSC)

"Mom" was well aware of her offence, or she would not have connected the slip on the steps with the withheld pail.

For all her unwelcomeness at times, Sarah still moved within the everyday social world of visiting, borrowing, and talk – the episodes would not have happened otherwise. But sometimes there is no apparent relationship or interaction at all; bewitchment can be a self-contained affair. I heard about several men who nursed phobias about women whom they avoided assiduously, for reasons no one knew. John Kane told me that he used to go berry-picking with Harold Cuthbert, a "lovely person but a bit of a character," who would not leave his house if he saw Nettie Morgan or her daughter looking out their window.[34] It was Nettie he feared most, but he thought that if she was a witch, her daughter must be one too. If he saw either of them, he'd turn, make a step with a little kick to the heel, and go back to his house. He did the same step in the woods; if he knocked over a bucket, for instance, he'd say, "That's Nettie!" and do his skip. He was best of friends with Nettie's husband, who was unaware of his fixation (or obsessive-compulsive disorder, as a psychiatrist might diagnose). I also heard about Harold's hopping from George Bradwell, a lifetime resident of Barrenville in his seventies.[35] George said the step was a "constant protective action" because Harold "felt himself under a cloud"; a drinker, he always had some kind of ailment and died around 1980. George also said that Henry Thomas, who died at the age of ninety-four just a few days before my visit, believed that a certain Mrs Dunn "had powers," although he was the only person ever to mention her as a witch as far as George knew. Henry, who lived near her, went to great lengths to avoid her; he thought, for instance, that if she saw him set off to go trouting, he wouldn't have any luck. "That blood of a bitch is watching me again," he'd say. "I won't get anything this time!" Dan Button, too, according to George, "lived in mortal fear" of witches. He warned George of Susan Appleton, "She'll tie you up in knots, don't mess with her." Her mother had been a witch, and her brother Maxwell (now dead) was supposed to have powers: "You watch him, George, he'll put 'en on 'ee," Dan said.

I was unable to find out anything about Maxwell or any other male witch; it was surprising how stoutly people maintained the reality of "wizards" considering the paucity of stories about them. The most I heard was the vague recollection of a man who bragged that he could stop a boat out on the water just by looking at it; "If he only said it for a mouth-speech or if he meant it, I don't know," said Charlie Harper. Yet as we saw in Part One, the male witch is part of the conceptual repertoire and his shadowy presence must be counted as part of the thinking about witches, even if his potential is seldom realized.

In the same way, the connection between religion and witch lore appears to be more a matter of theory or hearsay than experience or belief. "Well, I did hear a story," William Heywood said. "I heard that if you want to be a witch you just go to a river and walk down through the river backwards and say the Lord's Prayer backwards while walking through the river, you could become a witch. I don't know. I don't know how true that is." He and Maise are typical Protestant churchgoers, not evangelical (although his parents were stout Methodists); they cite the Bible in a perfunctory way but segue almost at once back to narrative – yes, a classic denial narrative – that they know to be true.

BR: Did anyone ever say where they [witches] got this power?

WH: Well, see, the Bible speaks of it.

MH: Sold to the Devil, they says they are.

BR: So it's a devilish kind of thing?

WH: Yeah, it's a Satan – you know. The Bible says that, the Bible tells you to beware of witches and wizards; the Bible says, you shouldn't let them live, you should destroy them, you know, because they are wicked, you know. I got a friend of mine, they were going fishing...

The friend was Reg Foster, and the story was about how Reg and his brother Tom used to give money to Maud Foster (a relation of theirs) because they knew she was a witch, until one day they got fed up and refused. The next day, while returning from an unsuccessful fishing trip, their boat stopped dead in the water although the motor was still running. A crow flew at them, then turned into a white gull. Reg shot at it and broke its wing; as it fell, the boat shot forward in the water. Arriving back at the stage, they were met by Maud's sister with the news that Maud had fallen and broken her arm.

Coincidentally, shortly after William told this story, Reg himself arrived and confirmed it, except that it was a stove, he said, not money, that Maud had wanted, and the demand was just too much. Thus the spell was not the result of a random refusal but of the disruption of an arrangement the witch had come to count on. It resembles what happened just a few years ago, according to William, when Louise Smith became upset when Norma Jones didn't give her a ride to work as she usually did. Louise stuck a pin in the nose of a photograph of Norma, who then suffered terrible nasal pain until she resumed picking up Louise. The sudden turnaround in an established pattern may be perceived as an insult, implying that the witch has been resented all along – and so it is not just routine that is broken but the assumption that the arrangement had been an amicable one.[36]

Whether a request is occasional or habitual, implicit or overt, its denial is dead central to William and Maise's conception of spells. For all their conviction, neither of them has had any personal experience of witching; they have often wondered whether it could be the reason for Maise's sporadic bouts of weakness, but they always end up ruling it out because she never offended anyone.

WH: But nobody didn't put a spell on me, I don't know why.

MH: Well, I don't know if anyone put one on me ... maybe I had one on and I was too stunned [stupid] to know it.

WH: There was times I thought there was one on you, the way you was all your life, you know.

MH: Well, I still think sometimes, but – I used to be standing up there doing my dishes, I'd be perfect, my dear, and all of a sudden something would just go right through my body down to my feet. And I'd be so miserable I'd just have to let the dishes go, I didn't have the strength to stand up. And I've seen a crow come right down there by the window where I was doing the dishes ... yet I couldn't put my finger on. I didn't say anything to anybody, and I couldn't figure anyone that would do it to me. So what could you do? You know? I've never done anything to anybody; no one's ever asked me to give them anything or do anything that I wouldn't give them, or do for them.

BR: So if you don't have anyone you suspect, then you can't fill the bottle?

MH: That's what I said, what could you do?

WH: You've got to have somebody that you refused or anything, you know, cause you just can't fill the bottle unless you names the one who's doing it.

MH: Many's the time I swore that there was somebody had a spell on me.

We discussed some reputed witches of the past, and I remarked that there didn't seem to be any around nowadays:

WH: Oh, there was a lot of them, maid, there was a lot of witches on the go. Dr Hill … when he went away, he told a friend of mine, "There's more young witches in Barrenville today than what there is old ones." He knew who it was, he knew, you know. People used to have the bottle on them, they had to go to him for to get tapped, get the water tapped out of them. And he knew who they were. He wouldn't tell on them, you know, he was a doctor and that, but he knew them.

BR: So they weren't always old women.

WH: Oh, no, and they're in Barrenville today.

BR: Yeah?

WH: Oh, I'm sure of it.

MH: You can count on it.

WH: Sure of it. Yes, my dear, you can count on it.

 ## Egg Cove: Bodies as Battlefield

A few kilometres away in tiny Egg Cove, Myra Poynter, a widow in her eighties, and her daughter-in-law Dorothy (also a widow) echoed the Heywoods' view of the infestation of Barrenville by witches. We were speaking of witches in general, whom Myra took by default to be women:

MYRA: You was frightened to death – say I knew there was a woman like that, [who] could witch – I'd be frightened to death, be afraid I'd do anything contrary to what she wanted done; you'd try to please her, because [if you didn't] you'd be finished, she'd put a spell on you, see?

DOROTHY: That's what you're made to believe.

MYRA: That's what you're made to believe. But I don't think there's that much of it in these days now, I think that's done away with.

DOROTHY: I don't know; because Dr Hill – that was years ago, he was in here to Barrenville, a good many years ago now – that he said, that in the Barrenville area only, that he borned more witches and goblins than ever anyone could witness –

MYRA: Now. And that's not too many years ago.

DOROTHY: – when they were born, when the children were born, whether they were going to be a witch or just an ordinary person. And he said that he borned more witches and goblins in the Barrenville area than ever was borned in the world. And they're up in Barrenville, there are witches up there now.

MYRA: Oh yes, they is, they say Barrenville's a bad place, maid, they say there's lots of them up there, maid.

But Egg Cove had its share, and the incidents related by Myra and Dorothy, and others recorded by students, limn a struggle for control of psychic and bodily boundaries. Myra's principal story – the one she told first, with the most emotion and detail – concerned her Uncle Sam; she heard it from her aunt (Sam's sister), who raised her after her own parents died. As a child in the 1920s, Sam and some other boys were chasing a pig that belonged to Mrs Burge, who was "claimed to be a witch": she was a nice person, and "happy-go-lucky from day to day, but once you trip her up, that was it." The boys threw stones at the pig and crippled it, and Mrs Burge "pitched on" Sam as the culprit:

And she put a spell on him. So he got crippled in the two legs, couldn't make a step, my grandmother had to take him in her arms down around the fish, wherever she went she had to take him. Took him into St John's to several doctors, and the last doctor she took him to, he said it looked to him like the child was spellbound. And he asked her if she knew anyone in the community that could do those things, that was bad enough to do those things, and she confessed yes, she did. Because she heard of this woman doing those things before. So she brought him home, and she said to her husband, which was my grandfather, "Now," she said, "if Sam is witched, I'm going to do my part to try out to see what's going to happen." Now the cure, they said in those olden days, was you got a stopper, and got a bottle, and you let the little fellow or whoever it was pee in the bottle, make his urine in the bottle. And you get nine pins from the bank that never was used, common pins, and stick those nine pins in that cork and stopper. And hang it in the flue, it used to be in those days, open fireplace had what they call a flue. And she said, "If this is so," she said, "whoever got it done to my child," she said, "they'll have to come before the day is out, because," she said, "she'll be bursting." To pass her urine, she'll have to come.

The bottle in place, Myra's grandmother went outdoors to work in the yard. Mrs Burge soon came up the road and paced outside the fence, but the grandmother ignored her:

And she [Mrs Burge] was going up and down, nearly gone, you know, going up and down, going up and down … And by and by she sang out to her, "Susan" – Susan was her name – and she said, "How is your little boy?" And she said, "Oh, he's no better, my dear. No better." She says, "Can I come in and see him?" She knew, see, she knew that the trick was played on her. "I don't mind," she said, "you can come in." They used to wear the great big flowing skirts then, with the pocket in them, you know? She came in and she went in the room where Uncle Sam was, and he was on the bed, and she asked him how he was, and he said no better. "Ah, my dear," she said, "you'll be all right, you'll be all right in a little while." Put her hand in her pocket, and she takes out a whistle-pipe. And she gave him the whistle-pipe. And she said, "You'll be all right; you'll be all right." So she left. And Grandmother said, "Now I'm going to watch her now, I'm going to take down the stopper." She took down the bottle and she pulled the stopper out. And that woman wasn't clear of the gate before she had to stoop and pass her urine.

Only in the context of witching did relieving oneself outdoors, or visits and small gifts to children, acquire significance. ("Their diligent enquiry after the sicke party, or comming to visit him or her, unsent for" was a prime sign of guilt listed in early-seventeenth-century reference manuals for English and American witch trial judges.)[37] The reading of kindly concern as an admission of malice is yet another of

witchcraft's little ironies, a twist that makes it impossible for the witch
to win.

An Egg Cove case from the same era contains striking parallels to
Sam's case: adult tensions played out through a young person's affliction, diagnosis made by an outsider, and recovery following upon
reassurance by the witch (68/6). It also features medical consultation,
although for once Dr Farber fails to discern witchcraft at work. It was
told to a student in 1968 by his wife, Irma; she was sixteen in 1931
when it happened, and the witch in her early fifties. These are Irma's
words as transcribed by her husband:

Mother and I were shopping one afternoon in Toller's store.
Mrs Goudge came in and she began to talk to Mother. I am not
sure now what they were discussing, but it developed into a row.
Mrs Goudge said that Mother insulted her. She really blew her
top; she called Mother just about everything under the sun.
When I could take it no longer I told Mrs Goudge to shut up
and go home. She looked at me and said, "You'll be sorry for that
before the end of the month." We didn't think too much about it,
but a couple of weeks later I really got sick. I went to Dr Farber
in Barrenville several times, and although he knew I was very sick
he never did figure out what was wrong with me. I lost my
appetite and I really lost a lot of weight. You remember I used to
be a little bit on the plump side. I even stopped menstruating for
thirteen months; Mother thought I had TB [tuberculosis]. The
first week that I was sick, I was going upstairs one afternoon and
I was sure I saw a big black cat cross the living room floor in
front of me. It seemed as big as a calf. I yelled to Mother and ran
back in the kitchen. I couldn't be persuaded that there wasn't a
big cat in there. All the people figured I was going to die, but a
woman came in one day and told Mother that Mrs Goudge had
witched me and there was only one cure. Mother had to cut the
Lord's Prayer from the Bible and put it around my neck. I was
wearing it for a couple of weeks and still going to the doctor. I
didn't tell him what we knew. One day shortly after that Mother
was passing by Mrs Goudge's place; you remember Mrs Goudge
used to spend a lot of time in her garden and would always talk
to all the people that passed along. Well, this day, she called out
to Mother and said, "How is she?" Mother said, "She's still sick."
Mrs Goudge said, "She'll be better in a day or so." Mother did

scarcely stop to talk to her. Anyway, a few days after that I began to eat again, but it took more than a year for me to recover fully. All the women said that she had me witched. She really told one woman herself. A few months after that, Mrs Goudge was taken to the Mental [the psychiatric hospital], you remember that. She was in there twice. When Maggie was born – that was about five or six years later – I was passing by with her in the pram one day. Mrs Goudge had just come back from the Mental the second time; she came out and said to me, "I never did anything to you, did I?" Then she began to wander and talk in circles. Ask anybody home now around my Mother's age and even younger, and they'll tell you all about that. They all say she was a witch. Anyway, I began to get better after Mother put the Lord's Prayer around my neck. I don't believe in witches, but something like that really makes you think.

The only information given about Mrs Goudge is that her husband and father were both active in the Methodist church (a strong presence in Egg Cove). No reason is given for her hospitalizations; but whatever problems she had cannot have been helped by the rumours that must have reached her, to judge by her question, "I never did anything to you, did I?"

Irma, on the other hand, never doubts her own normalcy, giant cat notwithstanding. She claims that the idea of a spell didn't occur to her or her mother until another woman brought it up; instantly they seize upon it, while remaining defensive and withholding from Dr Farber "what we knew." The way Irma refers to her mother and herself as a unit suggests an almost unhealthy overidentification at an age when self-differentiation would be the norm. She seemed to perceive the attack on her mother as an attack on herself, and in the guise of defending her – although she was surely capable of defending herself – lashed out against an older woman (and possible mother substitute). In any case, whatever psychological factors might lie behind it, such a public quarrel would have generated major gossip, explaining how "all the women" came to their verdict of bewitchment.

The implications of her outburst must have frightened Irma severely, which could explain her anorexia and consequent amenorrhea. The giant cat (maybe a real one inflated by delirium or shaped from a shadow) suggests an overwrought mental state primed to produce conversion symptoms (somatic expressions of psychological distress). Having everyone predicting her death wouldn't help, either. Her recovery after Mrs Goudge's reassurance further suggests an impressionable mind keyed to cues from those around her (she was, after all, only sixteen). As Pierre Bayle observed in 1703, "An imagination that is alarmed by the fear of a witch's spell can overthrow the animal constitution, and produce those extravagant symptoms that exasperate the most expert medical doctors. This same imagination, forearmed with the confidence that the spell has been lifted ... arrests the course of the disease."[38] In fact, it is possible to see witches as faith healers, whose words or actions had a beneficial effect on whatever ailed their victim, whether or not they had influenced their health to begin with. Of course Irma's malady may have been merely coincidental with the quarrel with Mrs Goudge; but her careful accounting of it all, thirty-seven years later, shows that the events were firmly linked in her mind (if not in her body). The strangest part of her story from a cultural point of view is that only one woman suggested a cure, and that it was the "only" cure; Myra's story of Sam (among the myriad others from the area) shows that the witch-bottle was standard technique at the time. But perhaps resorting to that would have voided Irma's shaky claim to scepticism altogether.

It would not be easy to be a doubter in Egg Cove, given the strength of the area's tradition; and to appreciate Irma's fear it must be remembered that spells were sometimes said to be fatal. Egg Cove was too small to support local itinerant witches, but Myra Poynter said it was a "worry" when outsiders came around selling things. Her aunt always bought for fear of being witched; Myra told her she was crazy, especially if they were selling Bibles, but Myra herself always bought baskets from a Mi'kmaq couple from Prince Edward Island. They were nice people, she said, but one day when the man was turned away from a house, he told the woman, "I have no luck today, and you'll have no luck tomorrow." She pricked her thumb on a thorn and died from infection. "And no doctor can cure you, you know, when they put those spells on you," said Myra. A doctor's inability to fix a problem is another way in which modern medicine can further, rather than weaken, the idea of witching.

Witches themselves could face physical danger, according to Myra's story about a woman who spied on courting couples outdoors at night.

So after a while they got offended at her doing that, you know.
So this man was down in the stage this day, and they say that if

you cuts the witch and brings her blood, that ends her: she won't
witch anymore. So this young man was down putting away his
fish and she came down for a fish for her dinner. And she was
carrying on and joking, and he made a stab at her, and stabbed
her in the finger, and brought the blood out. And she never
could witch after. No, never could witch after, that was the end of
her witchcraft.

I asked whether people in town weren't shocked, but Myra said that
on the contrary, it was their idea in the first place: "The older people
said, 'Well, if you think she's out after yas at nighttime, and witching
yas, and you're against it, bring the blood out of her!'" The woman's
reaction was also explained in terms of witchcraft. "In a rage she was,"
Myra said. "That's because she knew she couldn't do anything else,
she was finished." No spell preceded the incident, nor did Myra know
other stories about the woman; but then she did not vouch for the
truth of it in the way she could for Sam's story: "a true one, the first
one I told you, because it happened in my own family, I know about
that." In a later family occurrence, her husband was hagged by a man
who was jealous over a job he had gotten; "the hag" appeared as a
woman choking him. (The landlady of the boarding house where he
was staying advised him to put a Bible under the pillow.)

I couldn't get any idea of how the spying woman came to be singled
out, other than by her snooping. In the archive I had read an Egg
Cove man's recollection that witches "were always peculiar in some
way, their dress or habit, and they were always old women" (89/7/
FSC).[39] But three witches described by Myra and Doris were unexcep-
tional except for their reputations. Mrs Burge, the pig's owner, was
poor; a second was of average means; and a third was well off and did
it "just for devilment." None were attractive: "It's a funny thing about
them, I think when they sells their souls to the Old Boy, they changes
in countenance," said Myra. Or perhaps they were just aging: in Myra's
view, "you grew into it" if you were a witch. Dorothy said that witches
were born (as per Dr Hill) but they "got more experience, learned
how to do this" as they went along. Both had heard that witches say
the Lord's Prayer backwards, and none of the witches went to church
(except to get married). "They say a witch has her soul sold to the
devil," said Myra. "She must be a bad person to do things like that."
Dorothy amplified: "They usually believes in nothing, see, and they
just dwells on devil's works, this witchcraft, and goes by the black art

book, and this is it, this is how they does it. They don't believe there's a God, there's a heaven, there's anything … They're working for the devil, something like the cult, or whatever, you heard talk of."

Contemporary events and modern folklore of the "occult" probably influenced these comments; the case of the Dravidian cult in Waco, Texas, was in the news at the time, as was the (true) case of some Newfoundland high school students who dug up a grave and removed body parts, apparently for magical purposes. Dorothy likened the black heart book to ouija boards, which are "the unluckiest things you can have in the house"; when someone sent one to her children in the 1970s, she threw it away. She said that "so many bad things have happened" with the boards that they are no longer sold in stores, but I saw one in the Avalon Mall at Christmas in 1992; that is St John's, though, where Myra thinks people probably get black heart books today. (She pronounced it as one word but spelled it h-e-a-r-t).

Mrs Colfax, whom Myra said looked "just like a Halloween witch," supposedly had a book. Sometime in the 1950s, her neighbours disappointed her expectations of them.

There was a family used to fish in on the [other] side, and apparently, this family hadn't been giving Mrs Colfax a fish, like for to cook or anything, and she kind of got offended and she said they wouldn't get no more fish. So she put the witchcraft, put the spell on them. And he'd go out and haul his traps, two and three traps, no fish, no fish. And after a while they figured well, this – they heard this woman could do it, but they wasn't sure. Because she had a book, see? Some of them has a book, and they goes by the book. A witchcraft book. What they call a black-art book. But you may not have heard it … but that's what they used to use in olden days. And after awhile they got wise to it. What they call a black-art book. And if you ever got hold of that, if anybody was bad enough to want to do some ill feeling against you, they could do it. So they figured out, well, that woman must have a spell put on us all right. So this morning when they come in they had just a few [fish], you know, twelve or so. So when he comes up, he brings up a fish and hands her, over the fence. And the next morning they went out they had the biggest kind of haul of fish in two of the traps. So they knew she had it done. So that's how they did witchcraft, my dear. Yeah, that's just how they did it.

In later years Dorothy sold Avon cosmetics and would always take some trinket to Mrs Colfax. She had a "dark, sly look," said Dorothy, and "you just didn't know how to take her. She'd think the world of you, but it was always that fear. Afraid that she'd witch you."

Another witch, who at the time of my interview with Myra and Dorothy lived in a nursing home in St John's, used to live in Spike Cove midway between Egg Cove and Barrenville. "She could do it, people was frightened to death of her … afraid they'd go across her, or do anything, 'cause she'd put the spell on you and that would be it." It was almost an involuntary thing, Dorothy suggested:

DOROTHY: And like you'd look at her, and you'd get the feeling like, "Oh my, she's not responsible for what she's going to do. You'd better treat her good."

MYRA: If you'd pass her in the car, you'd like to pick her up, 'cause perhaps if you'd pass her she's likely to put a spell on you.

DOROTHY: 'Cause we were going to Barrenville a good many times, my husband and me. And he wouldn't dare pass her. And neither would I. No way. 'Cause if I would, she could just put a spell on you, there, then you'd get the flats, and that's where you'd stay, perhaps go bottom up.

Except for the Mi'kmaq basket seller, the witches described by Myra and Dorothy were all women – until they remembered this woman's son.

BR: Did you ever hear of a man that was a witch?

MYRA: No, never. Never heard of a man being a wizard. Wizards, men are called, aren't they? Men are called wizards, and women are called witches. Never heard tell of a man … No, never, all women.

DOROTHY: Remember that woman we were talking about in Spike Cove, the witch? And remember, her son Phil was fishing with Earl? And so –

MYRA: Yes, that's a man, yes, that's a man, she's telling about a man, now.

According to Myra, "she gave her treatment off to him" and assisted in witching Earl, a friend of Dorothy's late husband Clark. Earl and Phil usually fished together in Earl's boat, but when Phil became undependable because of his drinking, Earl told him he didn't want to fish with him anymore.

DOROTHY: [Phil] said, "That's okay, Earl," he said, "you can go to work," he said, "you can put out your nets and that," he said, "but you won't get a so-and-so" – well, with the bad words on it. And so, all in all, he said, "You'll have more trouble than that, too." So Earl went fishing, but beforehand his truck gave out. He went and he got a new truck. He had all kinds of trouble with that, and that was brand new. He had the spell put on him. And he went out fishing, and that year he never done ... anything with it. His wife got sick, she had to be going back and forth to the doctor; Earl takes a heart attack. Then, when he got talking to Phil, then, they got buddy-buddies again, and he suspicioned that this was what Phil and his mother had done with him. They had him spellbound ...

BR: And then what ended the spell?

DOROTHY: Well, they got together again, and Earl suspicioned that this was the trouble, he knew what they were like, he'd heard rumours. And when it fell on him, well, he went down and he gave them fish, and whatever he could do for them, and he took buddy back again fishing with him.

MYRA: Took him fall fishing.

DOROTHY: Took him out in the fall, and everything went lovey-dovey.

BR: Made it up with him.

MYRA: Oh yeah, the spell was lifted, then he lifted the spell then, see?

DOROTHY: And that's really, really true.

MYRA: That's a true story.

DOROTHY: And that's only about three years ago.

MYRA: That's all, that's all. Clark was living then.

DOROTHY: Clark was living then, yes. That's my husband, and he's dead. "You know what the trouble is, Dorothy," he said. "They got a spell put on poor old Earl." 'Cause Earl and Clark were real close, see.

BR: Yeah, I see.

MYRA: So I'm glad you can understand now, and piece that together to suit yourself.

 ## Insiders and Outsiders: Two Student Chronicles

Two essays from the 1970s provide intimate contextual details of witch lore from radically different perspectives. Both writers were teachers, one a newcomer to the area, the other a native who set her material within the underexplored world of women's sociability and storytelling.

Max Bannock was assigned to Egg Cove for his first job in the early 1960s (74/8). He had never heard of witches while growing up in Conception Bay, but even so, he was less surprised by the tales than by the tellers. "The belief seemed to be the strongest among the more educated people, those people whom you would think would scoff at the ideas about witches," he wrote. "Over the span of the next few months I began to hear more and more about witches and the cures for getting rid of a witch." One tale concerned an old woman who lived by herself. "One of the neighbours found out that the doctor was taking water from her kidneys through a tube in her side as the poor woman apparently had kidney trouble. This was enough. Immediately the people said that someone had 'put up a bottle.'" Here it should be noted that doctors really did remove fluid from the abdomen in this way, and it was called "tapping" in medical (not just folk) terminology.[40] Causes for the edema (now treated with dialysis or medication) include heart or kidney or liver problems, malnutrition, or a combination of conditions, but the man who relayed the tale to Bannock credited none of these. "She finally burst," he said, "That's what she gets for putting curses on people."

Bannock's encounter with witch lore soon took a more personal turn, as he watched an interfering parent evolve into a witch, with himself nominated as victim.

> [She] was a troublemaker and caused no end of trouble for the teachers. She had several children, all from different fathers, and no matter what they told her when she asked them what happened each day in school, they were believed. If one of them said that a teacher did something to them, that was enough for a trip to the school and a yelling and cursing match in the principal's office. The more trouble she caused, the more she was shunned by the people of the community. Finally some of them began to suggest that she, too, was a witch.
>
> During the first year I was there, I did not have any of her children in my class, and therefore, had no dealings with her. The second year I had one of her sons and he was a continual pest. Several times his mother came along to school to explain how we should and should not teach. A few days after her last visit, I was sick in bed with the flu. One of the teachers told me that she had put a curse on me and that was why I was sick. I laughed and didn't say anything but I did have a series of colds all that winter. Each one was more proof that she had "witched" me. Several times I had been told that I should "put up a bottle" and see if she really was a witch.

One colleague asked, whenever he returned from a holiday, whether he had been sick while he was away. "Each time I told her no and she said, 'Well, you crossed water and her power was gone.'"

Bannock was regaled with further tales at a teachers' banquet, including one of a woman who was injured when a man shot at a quarter affixed to a fence stake. "After that incident no more of his cattle died and the local people said that 'he had put the fear of God in her.'" Bannock said he was not inclined to argue, because people "can give more 'proof' than you can give arguments," and "no one in their right mind would try as they might well be categorized in some unacceptable class as well." He had seen for himself how argumentativeness and behaviour perceived as interfering had led to the designation of "witch." As with the woman who spied on courting couples, there were no tales of spells, requests, or revenge: pure social offensiveness indicted this woman. It is fitting that it should happen in the institutional school setting, where socialization is a major goal.

The second teacher to write about Barrenville, Margaret Foster, taught in St John's but went exploring in her hometown with the aid of her wary parents (79/9). "When I mentioned to my dad that I should talk to so-and-so whose grandmother was supposed to be a witch, he was shocked to hear that I would even consider such a thing, it was strictly taboo," she wrote. "I thought it was interesting that my parents refrained from naming the witches. When I was a child I knew of several women who were supposed to be witches. But we never discussed them directly or dared to use their names."

Just as in Egg Cove, a spell between women was often literally a matter of ill feeling. Foster's mother gave a virtual textbook example of the somatic effect of belief.

> Someone had a spell on Mary Howard, she was sick all the time. She wasn't able to get out of bed, she was so sick. She filled up the bottle and had it put in her outdoor toilet. A certain woman came to her house one day. She was there so long and then she said, "Oh my, I've got to go out to your toilet, why don't you get up and get me a cup of tea now, while I'm gone?" Mary said, "Sure I haven't made a cup of tea for my husband this three month." The witch said, "Well, you get up and make me a cup of tea now." The woman went out to the toilet, found the bottle and empt [emptied] it. When she went back in, Mary got the tea for her. That's true. Mary told me that herself. Sure Dr Farber was driven off his head with people coming to him to be tapped.

A medical diagnosis offered no comfort for some sufferers. "I knew a woman in her thirties who had been confined to a wheelchair for years with what was diagnosed as a tubercular leg," Foster wrote. "However this woman insisted that it was all because of her mother-in-law. She believed that her mother-in-law was a witch and had placed a spell on her ... Interestingly enough, when this woman was in her late forties she was able to walk around everywhere. I presume the mother-in-law was dead by then."

Doing interviews proved harder than Foster had imagined it would be. Lack of time hampered her making the connective tissue of talk. For one thing, she found that "you might not be told the story if you don't know the person involved," and for another, that people were uncomfortable telling the stories "in isolation" from related events.

Foster's description of older women's work and visiting patterns gives a rare child's-eye view of how the topic of witchcraft might be spun in the context of everyday conversation, circa 1950:

> After the older women had tidied up after dinner, their
> daughters-in-law had gone down to the flakes, they would go
> visiting in the afternoon … It was always permissible for the
> female children to tag along. The older women sat around the
> table in the big kitchen while the children would sit in the
> background, huddled together on the couch. We were supposed
> to be seen but not heard … There was a great belief in the
> supernatural: in witches, tokens and spirits. The women would
> tell of things they had heard or seen that were bad signs. They
> would tell of things that happened long ago. They told stories of
> visits from the "old hag" and of how they had had to push her
> off to avoid stifling. Most times, unless someone was telling of a
> new experience, these stories were just alluded to. My
> grandmother might ask, "How is Annie?" Aunt Phoebe might
> reply that Annie wasn't very well but that nobody seemed to
> know what was wrong with her. There might be speculation as to
> what was wrong, then someone might hint that perhaps there
> was a spell on her, "'cause look what happened to May." If
> everybody there knew what happened to May then there would
> be nodding and agreement. But if one of the women did not
> know what had happened to May then the story would be told.
> The person that knew May best would tell the story, others might
> interrupt to provide evidence or to reinforce what was being said.
> At the end most people would have some additional comments
> to make. Interruptions would be welcomed since in most cases
> they would confirm and strengthen what the storyteller was
> saying and encourage elaboration.

With their appetite for narrative and news, these women appreci-ated a good storyteller. "The women never pre-planned where to go, it usually depended on one woman. This woman was a great talker, extremely funny, a singer of ditties and was apt to make a few off-colour remarks. Since the others lived in close proximity to her, I'm sure they watched to see where she went. If we were out playing, she might say to a child, 'Tell your grandmother I'm gone into so and so's house.' A few minutes later three or four other women would arrive."

That these women were just of an age to become candidates for witches didn't stop them from making witches of one another. On the one hand this can be seen as the acceptance by a lower-status group of a negative stereotype of itself, turned by some in the group on others in order to exempt themselves. On the other hand, some may have liked the idea of being thought capable, by virtue of age, of casting spells on disagreeable people – not such a bad thing for anyone heading toward a less mobile, possibly dependent stage of life. And what about the girls, sitting silent on the sofa taking it all in? Did they "internalize" the female image of the witch, or wonder whether it might ever be applied to themselves? For the boys playing outdoors, the witch would always be "other" – someone who might affect them but not *be* them. The spells they heard about on the stages or in lofts did not originate in that domain, but in the "female" precincts of home.

The hidden stoppered bottle (besides its straightforward representation as the witch) conveys the interior, claustrophobic sense of spells; the witch's desperate search for it (a marked motif in Barrenville), "outing" her and forcing her to show her hand. "That Farmer crowd are killing me," complained a woman who was unable to urinate after the Farmers hid a bottle in their outhouse. "They are killing me." At this point Foster's parents' stories diverged: her father thought that John Farmer caught her coming out of the outhouse with the bottle "and grabbed it from her and broke it"; but her mother said that he was thinking of someone else, and that John Farmer had left a leak in his bottle. "John said that if he had sealed it, he would have killed her." The purchase of the pins required for these bottles amounted to a public declaration that one was bewitched. Urine and stopper in place, Foster's mother said, "you had to count out nine lots of pins. You'd take a pin from each lot and put them in the cork in the shape of a cross, and you'd say, in the name of the Father, and of the Son and of the Holy Ghost." With this blessing, one could throw the bottle in the ocean to kill the witch.

Foster concluded her essay with remarks on the state of witch lore:

> When I asked several people if they thought there were witches in Barrenville today, all thought that there were and several people said, "They say so and so is a witch, her grandmother used to be one, you know." There was this general feeling about it being passed on from the older generation, but one man told me that it was easy to become a witch. His formula was that all you had to do was to go down to the salt water nine mornings in a row and confess to the devil.

I met with Margaret Foster before I went to Barrenville, and she told me that a witch was simply someone you had to be careful around; there was nothing devilish or satanic associated with them, but nothing good either. They were always older women, although Foster recollected that once as a teenager she was with a group of girls when one of them, the daughter of a reputed witch, announced that she could sink a boat by knocking two pieces of hard bread together. Foster couldn't suggest anyone I might speak with, given the delicacy of the subject, which was in any case (she claimed) almost extinct.

Archive versus Reality: Julia Short

After reading Bannock's and Foster's essays, and hearing Foster's discouragement, I briefly wondered whether I should bother going to Barrenville myself. Would a visitor with no friends or relations there learn anything but more of the same? The archive was already full of Barrenville tales. But the archive is also a miscellany, a sea flinging up not just riches but flotsam and mirage, hieroglyphic messages in bottles. Consider the report about Julia Short, written by a student who lived in a nearby community and had only glimpsed her a few times:

> In Barrenville there is a certain woman, Julia Short, who is supposed to be a witch. I have heard stories of how she has made dolls representing certain people, tied a string around the penis of the doll, and that person would not be able to urinate. I have heard it said that people have had to go to the doctor's at Barrenville and get pumped out. There are other stories

circulating about how certain crops would fail, dogs would die, etc., because Julia had a spell on someone who harmed or slighted her. Julia has no hair, or fingernails, or toenails ... She was a widow and had a son who died young. (68/10/FSC)

The real story of Julia, as I pieced it together from various conversations, is that of someone so unkindly treated by life that any desire she might have to strike back would be more than understandable. A doll-like figure herself, she was less than five feet tall and wore children's clothes and a bright knitted cap; apparently she had always been bald and without fingernails due to a genetic condition – her brother was the same. She had had a daughter, not a son, who died at about the age of ten – an only child who, ironically, had an exceptionally beautiful head of hair. Some say it was her loss that made Julia strange, while others say that she was strange all along. No one seemed to know exactly what the daughter died of – most suggest tuberculosis or malnutrition, for Julia and her husband (who didn't work and was seldom seen) were poor. But Julia blamed Dr Farber, who, according to Ann Williams, my landlady, was brilliant but alcoholic; he might deliver a baby, for instance, and remember nothing about it when the husband came to pay him several days later. Jane Barnes, who taught in Barrenville for a year in the 1960s, heard from her landlady that Julia put a spell on Dr Farber, and that people became afraid of her when he died shortly after that. She recalls that Julia frequented the town hall office, the snack bar, and such other public places as Barrenville offered, not only for company but in order to stay warm, because her husband was mortally afraid of fire and refused to keep much wood in the house. In the fall, Julia would arrange with Dr Hill (Dr Farber's successor) to spend the winter in the psychiatric hospital in St John's, not for treatment but because the place was heated.[41] Jane Barnes's husband, also a teacher, was a favourite of Julia's because he treated her as an equal and was less patronizing than some in the town; she would give him little gifts of candy.

June Roberts, a neighbour of mine in St John's who had served as a nurse in Barrenville for several years in the 1960s, confirmed Julia's medical attention-seeking.[42] Julia once told a third party that she would put a spell on June after June refused to see her one day because there was nothing wrong with her. She said that sometimes Julia would take the train into St John's and sit outside the General Hospital until she was admitted.

No native Barrenvillian told me about Julia's hospital stays; and some had never even heard of her as a witch. Maise Heywood knew her well and hadn't heard it; nor had Margaret Foster, who recalled her only as a "character" who always had something funny to say, such as "Love is nothing but a tickling sensation between two fools." George Bradwell told me that she was clever but had probably always been "odd."[43] She would tell George that "only geniuses or lunatics" came from Egg Cove, but he didn't know which category she put herself in. He said that her accusations against Dr Farber became so troublesome that the doctor took her to court over it. "Your Honour, you have to excuse this woman, she has water on the brain," the doctor said to the judge. "Your honour, you have to excuse this man, he has beer on the brain," she countered. She actively sought a witchly reputation, according to George. His family was well off and politically connected, and his mother was a generous woman (by all accounts, not just George's) who always gave Julia something when she came to call. But one time Julia was "spelling for something" (hinting that she wanted it) and Mrs Bradwell ignored her. "I'm a witch, you know," Julia announced. "Oh, I know," Mrs Bradwell replied, "I'm one too. In fact I'm on the committee of witches, and it's only through me that you got to be one, because I voted for you. I'm much more powerful than you. I could draw you up in such a crump on that chair that you wouldn't be able to get up until I let you." Julia was trumped by the class card, complete with the language of political influence.

By 1970, when Mary Witford knew her, Julia was a widow and not so badly off. Mary told me that she always paid for her groceries at the store where Mary's fiancé Arch worked, and from where he would give her a ride back to her cat-filled house. Julia was eager to attend Mary and Arch's wedding that year and told Mary so every time she saw her. Mary didn't really want to invite her and tried to put her off by saying the invitations weren't ready, it was only a small party, and it probably wouldn't be a nice day anyway. "You'll have the finest kind of day," Julia assured her, "but you'll only get it if you invite me." Mary conceded, and the day turned out "hot enough to split the rocks." Even more surprising and to Mary's dismay, when the reception photographs were developed, Julia appeared in almost every one. She showed them to me, and in each crowd or corner I could just make out a tiny face topped by a bouffant blond wig which had by then replaced the knitted cap. She died not long after that, though Mary had moved away and didn't know exactly when.

The decision to include Julia was prudent; for weddings were notoriously subject to spells, from France (where a witch might tie knots in a string to prevent consummation)[44] to Russia, where "spoiling" (the Russian term for witchcraft) threatened the whole party,[45] to the north coast of Newfoundland, where a student wrote, "When I was getting married [c. 1968], I noticed the names on the list of those invited. Upon asking my relatives-in-law who they were, since they invited some of them, I discovered one of the names belonged to a woman regarded as a sort of witch throughout the years in the community. I was told she had to be invited because if she wasn't, bad luck would come to the bride and groom" (84/11/FSC). Barrenville was probably always too big and subdivided for the custom of open invitation that was customary in smaller places,[46] but certainly no one expressing a desire to attend a wedding could be comfortably turned away. There could be no worse time to have ill will or envy beaming one's way; best to have everyone at the feast, not hidden at home tying string around doll penises.

Which brings us back to that original archival account of Julia, about which I have had mixed feelings. At first, and as I learned of the tragic circumstances of her life, I felt indignant on her behalf that this ridiculous picture should be the main public record of her life. But on reflection, how many people have even that much? And it does portray a fearsome individual to be reckoned with – something Julia might have liked, for she did seize the few resources available to her, her wit and witch lore, to assert equality. George Bradwell said she used to recite:

> I have no use for scissors or comb,
> And I have no place for a louse to roam.
> My head is my own, and I don't care,
> I'm so good as you with a head of hair.

 ## Empty Nets and Not-So-Empty Threats

When Harry Addams was a boy and his sister was a baby, Birdie Howell came to the house, picked her up, and predicted that she would never be in want – which she never has been. The prophecy must have been welcome to a family of limited means. Harry became its main support at the age of fifteen when his father lost a leg, and he has been fishing ever since except during a stint as a lumber-camp cook (recalled fondly because of the abundant food). He nevertheless considers himself "one of the lucky ones," although he is bitter about the closure of the fishery and worried about the future. He could sell his fishing licence (the government permit to engage in the fishery) but he cannot bear the thought of being idle: "I can't rest, no sir … I'm never used to it, see?" He was in his fifties and paterfamilias of a large clan at the time of our interview.[47]

Taken out of context, some of Harry's commentary on witching sounds unnerving. "The Good Book tells you about wizards and witches, and it tells you what should be done: they should be shot, they shouldn't live, they should be destroyed," he said, and his first tale would seem to bear out the injunction. Some men were fishing on a fine windless day when their boat began rocking so wildly that they were nearly thrown overboard. Somehow one of them determined the cause to be a woman "sat down with a bowl on the table with a piece of wood in the bowl. She was rocking the bowl back and forth." The man went to her house with an old musket. "Now," he said, "next time that happens, you won't be living no more … The next time I got to come to you, I have any trouble, I'm going to blow your brains out."

Yet, as often happens when events concerning unnamed characters are compared with those involving family or friends, a milder picture appears. One day, although it was calm, the bottom was torn out of Harry's grandfather's trap. He had promised but forgotten to bring a salmon to this same bowl-rocking woman; so the next day he took her the fish, then set about mending his trap. He was losing valuable time, but she strolled into the garden where he was working and told him not to worry. "Look here," she said, "you'll get two or three hundred quintal if the rest don't trap one." That summer he got twice as much as anyone else.

An identical contrast between theory and practice occurs in an interview with Charlie Harper conducted by his niece in 1990 (91/12/C, my transcription). She was horrified when he told her, "Say, now, if I know a witch – which I don't know, but say if I did know of one – well, I'd take it down Chafe Cove somewhere, take her down Reef Cove, and make away with it … you'd shoot it, or something, or drown it." "That's murder!" the niece exclaimed, when she figured out that "it" referred to a witch. "Oh, I know that, yeah," he replied, "oh yes, it's murder, yes but sure, the Bible – 'tis in the Bible. Take it to

another place, you know, not in your own place, but take it away." Yet
Mr Harper's only story was a benign domestic drama, a perfect parable
of female hegemony over "her man," as the husband in the story is
called. He was aboard a boat set to leave port. "And they couldn't get
the anchor up ... and he said, 'Oh, I forgot to take the [promised] pork
to me wife'... and he carried it to her. She says, 'Go on now, they'll
have the anchor up waiting for you.'" And so they were, when he
returned to the boat. (I spoke with Charlie Harper myself – his story
about Sarah Haley is quoted earlier – and the mind boggles at the
thought of this mild-mannered gentleman stowing someone in a boat
and speeding to a remote cove to make away with her.)

When I asked Harry Addams if he thought anyone ever physically
attacked a witch, he merely said that in his recollection, "years ago,
people fought and cursed on each other" constantly. At one house
he saw a woman bash her husband with an iron frying pan: "Two
words, and bang on his head." But the next morning, they sat at the
breakfast table eating and talking as if nothing had happened. Men
were brought up to domestic helplessness, he continued. "Now usually ... when a man comes home, it's three o'clock in the morning,
he calls his mother to get him a cup of tea, he wouldn't get a cup of
tea if the world was coming to an end. Mother, everything: 'Mother,
get me stockings, Mother, get me shirt, Mother, get me sweater.'"
This is not to suggest that women were servants; on the contrary,
they were captains of the house. The strict division of labour created
great gender interdependence, and if things weren't right at home,
perhaps they might not go so well at sea either. The storm-stirring
witch suggests that the hand that rocks the cradle can, literally, rock
the world.

Harry did not see anything particularly cosmic or mysterious about
witches, however. For him it boiled down to this: "If a witch – a
woman was professed as a witch – if she come and asked you for
something like a fish and you wouldn't give it to her, they said, she'd
put the spell on you." Birdie Howell (she who predicted his sister's
prosperity) lived by "going around people's houses – you'd give her
something, I'd give her something, someone else would give her
something." Once a man refused her some wood from a cartload he'd
just brought in from the country, because it didn't belong to him.
"That's all right," she said. "You got your load of wood down," she
said, "but you won't be unloading it." He fell and broke his leg the
next day. "That's true," said Harry, having heard it from the man

himself. "People told me she could really do it." There was nothing else remarkable about Birdie except that she kept a house full of cats and dogs. (This was nothing compared to the witch Prudence Parson, who in addition to dogs and cats kept goats indoors.)[48]

Despite a fondness for pets, I have found no trace in Newfoundland of the English animal "familiar" who did the witch's bidding; they seem to have been left behind, along with the "cunning" men or women who diagnosed and cured cases of witchcraft, and replaced with a do-it-yourself approach. If a witch wanted an animal to do an errand, she assumed the form herself. This idea was ideally suited to feed a victim's paranoia, for he could thus see her everywhere. According to Harry, one man who was "tormented" by a witch couldn't sleep and would hear her laughing when no one was there; a crow hovered over his boat all day long. When he finally figured out who it was (I don't know how), he filled a bottle and hid it in a trunk, and a cat came into the house to search for it. She couldn't find it and left, and the woman later called (in normal form) to remove the spell. The crow and the cat weren't sent by the witch – they *were* the witch.[49]

Harry Addams had no personal experience of spells, except that his mother once filled the bottle, though he didn't know "who for" or why. Typically, he cites expert opinion: "Dr Farber said himself, Barrenville was fulled up with nothing only witches. He used to have to tap people, this is how he found out." (Harry lives in Dr Farber's former house, which gave a certain immediacy to his words.) I did get one surprise from Harry. I was so accustomed to hearing people say that they had heard of the black heart book but never seen one that I nearly fell off my chair when he said, "Black art book, I saw one. You sell yourself to the devil, and you'll be possessed by devils. You got to say your prayers nine times backwards. I looked at that, I seen that in it … and I'll tell you, stamped on outside, that's what he was called: Black Art Book." (I didn't question the spelling because I wasn't sure of Harry's literacy level.) The owner was a co-worker in a central Newfoundland lumber camp who told Harry that it was "no trouble to sell yourself to the devil" and showed him a "common exercise book" with the Lord's Prayer pencilled in backwards (starting with "Amen"). After Harry saw eight pages, the owner took it back and locked it in his suitcase. This man also claimed to be a seventh son, and Harry said that a worm would turn white in his hand (a standard sign), though he never saw that happen; nor did he hear of his healing anyone as seventh sons are supposed to do. But "you could

get something in your mind and he'd tell it," he was "as good as Kreskin."
The homemade book proves that people really did sometimes try out
magical practices, which presumably could include rocking bowls or
tying off doll penises (although it is hard to see how anyone could be
caught in those acts unless they chose to be).

Certainly they tried anti-witch tactics, at least the magical ones. (Dr
Farber's catheters were displayed in the museum when I was there, but
nary a witch-bottle to hint at the once-storied connection.) Some
allegedly made threats, like the husband of an ailing Barrenville
woman (c. 1964) who went to another woman's house with a knife and
said, "If she's sick any longer, I'll put that right to the handle."[50] We
may never know whether the violence was ever real, but many stories
certainly express murderous impulse. In a final example recorded in
1990,[51] two brothers from Summer Cove near Barrenville blamed their
poor fishing season on an old woman "rumoured to be a witch" who
would stand on the wharf each day and watch them go out, an apparently innocuous act were staring not considered a form of aggression.[52]
They put a witch-bottle behind the stove at their cabin, but one of
them got impatient and broke it, and when they returned to Summer
Cove they found that the woman had died. "Do the fishermen feel
guilty about her death?" the student asked her friend, from whom she
recorded this. "No," said the friend, who knew the brothers, "because
they felt she was the cause of their bad luck, and they were glad she
was gone." But whatever the brothers chose to believe, they did not in
fact attack or even confront this woman in person. Their violence
amounted to no more in the real world than the Barrenville boys'
chant to make snails put out their antennae: "Old woman, old woman,
stick out your horns, if you don't, I'll kill your mother, your father,
your brother, and your sisters" (89/13/FSC). Perhaps the most notable
fact to be taken from this tale is that right up to the collapse of the
fishery, while arguments raged over foreign overfishing, destruction
by trawlers of spawning grounds, and federal mismanagement of the
fishery, tradition still offered the possibility of blaming a woman.

The fishery crisis and its fallout were what really preoccupied Harry
Addams during our interview, not witches; but for him it is impossible
to talk about the past without talking about the fishery, because his
life revolved around it. He said that it is important to remember, when
talking about fishermen's luck, that some fishermen were better than
others, but even the best couldn't catch what wasn't there. Witch tales,
taken as a whole, are a good reminder that fishing was never a matter

of just going out and setting traps; it was never reliable or simple, and the waters did not uniformly teem, year after year.

Despite the hardships of the past, Harry thinks it was better than the present day; now there is *too* much money, he says, and so people don't help one another as they used to do. As for witches, "there could be thousands now too" but we wouldn't know them because "we don't know our own brothers now."

Exit Barrenville

How did Barrenville become the witch capital of Newfoundland? I think that its size was key: it was big enough to support a pool of tales and motifs and an array of "suspects" to whom they could attach, yet small enough that it was still an intensely interactive society with the kinds of expectations and encounters that led to witch incidents. It was also an oral culture; and the more stories were told, the more power they gained to influence the interpretation of events, to reach a kind of narrative critical mass that illuminated everything in its orbit. Hearing about the old hag, for instance, might not only give people nightmares but put a name and a face to them as well. The simple words "all right" were portentous, coming from someone who had been refused a request.

These appeals denied arose from Barrenville's other great generator of witches: poverty. Without it, there would have been no spells over boots or wood or fish withheld. Not all witching scenarios follow this pattern, but these spells are the bedrock on which the credibility of others rests. For my informants, the habit of asking – avoided by men – was enough to explain why all the reputed witches were women.

Two authorities buttressed the antique patterns and practices of witch tradition: the doctor and the Bible. The burning question about Doctors Farber and Hill, of course, is whether they really said all those things about witches. My guess is that Dr Farber, at least, must have said something gnomic, or his alleged pronouncements would not have become so much quoted. His (supposed) belief would easily be transferred to his successor, Dr Hill, but maybe he too had offered an opinion. The spirit in which any utterances might have been made is anyone's guess (especially given Dr Farber's putative alcohol problems). Perhaps he spoke ironically or bitterly; perhaps, as a native son trained at medical school abroad, he thought it was useful to work with people's beliefs; or perhaps he did believe in witches. Whether he or Dr Hill meant to contribute so much to Barrenville's witch lore must remain a mystery.

As for the Bible's being the last word, this is only to be expected where it was the principal book (often the only book) from earliest days. As one of the province's oldest settlements, Barrenville had some of the first schools, established by missionaries whose first order of business was to bring in Bibles and get them memorized. It is possible, too, that at some point a cleric took a special interest in witches and helped inculcate it in this town. In any case, the Bible is cited not just as proof of the existence of witches but to justify attacking them, although it is not certain that anyone really did. People might laugh at Sarah Haley and even claim that she flew about naked (though invisibly) to hag people, but she lived to an old age apparently untroubled by witch-bashers. The main physical violence seems to have been done by victims to themselves, when they made themselves sick with worry over spells.

So we leave Barrenville with unanswered questions but with a very good picture of how people talk about witches. We got a few clues, mostly from stories about Sarah Haley and Julia Short, as to how a "witch" might speak, conscious of her status; but we cannot know how much is being read into the events even when they are retailed by the witches' interlocutors, or how memories may have altered over time. In the following pages a reputed witch speaks for herself, and we look closely at several more.

PART THREE

Triptych: Three Portraits

The portraits in this chapter are assemblages from sources of the most partial and dubious kind. Yet gossip, legend, and hearsay are the very things that make up a "witch," and they are all that is available to anyone who didn't actually know the person in question. For hearers and readers of the tales, the witch can remain as featureless as a stick figure, so I have tried to add dimension by looking as closely as possible at some reputed witches. The women profiled here were of very different character and lived in very different circumstances in different parts of the province. Their stories show some of the many ways one could acquire the label "witch."

 ## Frances Long (1914–1995)

"A bloody witch, I must be."

The speaker was Frances Long, the only reputed witch I met in the course of my research; the remark was made in such an undertone that I didn't hear it at the time, although it is very clear on the tape. It came at the end of her account of the warning she gave to Len Marden, only a week before our interview, when she looked into his teacup and said, "Look here, Buddy, you're in for it." Two days later he was badly burned. "I can do a lot, you know, but people don't believe me," Frances began without preamble, when I explained that I was interested in people with "special powers." But in fact a lot of people did believe her, and I was just one of hundreds who had beaten a path to her door, wanting something from her. In recent years, it was mostly to have their fortunes told; in earlier times, it was to fetch her to deliver a baby or to lay out the dead. Ushering people through her kitchen door and in and out of the portals of life, she saw deeply into their affairs, and she was famous in Broom Harbour and neighbouring south coast communities for predicting domestic events – marriages, break-ups, deaths. Sometimes she read fate in a cup; sometimes she just *knew*. Were she to explain how she did it, she said, she would lose the power – "And so many people depends on me, my dear."

I learned of Frances through a student of Martin Lovelace's; the student's mother, Laura, took Martin and me to Frances's house in Broom Harbour and helped with the interview.[1] (Broom Harbour, now a day's drive from St John's, was reached only by boat until the 1970s; the idiom of Frances's speech reflects the area's West Country English antecedents. A pre-trip check of the archive turned up no witches in Broom Harbour and only a smattering of spells in general.) For what it's worth, my impression of Frances was of an extraordinarily warm and open person. Her words were often harsh, bitter, and downright scary, yet Frances herself did not seem that way at all. I can't be the only one who thought so, or people would not have flocked to her as they did. She was by no means universally popular, however; Laura said that some people referred to her as "that old witch" (though never to her face), and by Frances's own admission her predictions were not always welcome nor aimed to please.

A reading she did for Bea Myers was typical. Five relatives would die within the year, she told Bea, including an aunt, grandmother, and her parents (the latter nine months apart). "Go to hell" was Bea's reaction, but there were five funerals within the year. And that was not all that was in store for Bea. She was estranged from her husband, but at one point he returned and she became pregnant with a boy (the sex as predicted by Frances). The reunion wouldn't last, Frances warned: on the second of January the husband would go to a motel, send for his clothes, and Bea would never see him again. All transpired as she said.

Immediately it is clear that Frances was an astute observer of situation and character, aided no doubt by intelligence from her wide network of contacts. It is also easy to see that a degree of "self-fulfilling prophecy" could occur, by which people are influenced (unconsciously or perhaps knowingly) to bring about predicted events. Perhaps Len Marden got nervous and therefore clumsy after Frances's prediction of trouble; or maybe she detected that he was in a distracted state and headed for a fall anyway. Bea's erratic relationship with her husband was probably no secret to anyone; as to the specifics of his departure, one could imagine Bea laughingly telling him what Frances had said and his deciding that it wasn't a bad idea. Her clients were predisposed to acceptance, or they wouldn't have been there to begin with.

Despite her forthrightness, it was not easy piecing together a clear picture of Frances's background and activities, as her answers were sometimes indirect and even contradictory. (Diabetes, she said, affected her memory, as well as making her "contrary.") Her accounts of Len and Bea notwithstanding, she said that she didn't read for men, and that she never told anyone anything bad, especially about death (and for that reason didn't read old people's cups). She told me that she learned how to do it as a young woman from another woman in hospital (Broom Harbour has a small "cottage" hospital with several beds), but she told her granddaughter, in a later interview, that she taught herself. The only explanation she gave as to how she was chosen as a midwife was that she was "just that type" to do things for people, and that her grandmother had done it. Certainly she had no training or formal education.

In contrast to her vagueness about some aspects of her life, Frances was emphatic about her childhood, starting with the death of her mother when she was four years and her brother eight months old. They had a good life with their father until he remarried eight years later: "And that's when the devil come in through the door. Just as well to tell the truth, isn't it?" Truth is a leitmotif in her discourse. The stepmother, who had children from a previous marriage, would lock her and her brother out of the house all day with no food. One incident from this period in particular reveals a bitter sense of betrayal and loss. The stepmother accused Frances of some impertinence, and her father hit her with a rope, something he'd never done before. That night, Frances prayed with all her might that her mother would return. The next morning her father said that her mother had stood by his bed all night, and that he would never strike her again. (Though raised as an Anglican, in our interview she proclaimed independence from any religion.) The appeal to the lost mother is significant in light of the many "mothering" roles Frances assumed in her life, including to young women who were her main fortune-telling constituency. Here, too, was a formative experience with the witching paradigm: intense wishing brings "supernatural" retaliation for injury. Its household crucible of rage, recrimination, and guilt is made plain.

Frances escaped at fifteen to Grey Cove on a small island nearby, where she worked as a servant until she married three years later. Her brother joined the navy at seventeen and she didn't see him for another fifty-six years. She and her husband had two biological children and adopted several more, and she cared for her husband's mentally disabled brother as well. She was not paid, even in gifts, for her work as midwife or undertaker, yet she was not without a sense of professionalism and she guarded her reputation accordingly. Once (not too long ago) she was called at two o'clock in the morning to a house where a baby had died. She tried "blowing breath" into it without success and the next day went to the doctor to find out what had happened (the baby had suffocated when the father rolled over on it in bed). She had the doctor write a notice to put on the door that the death was through no fault of hers.

Frances was the only one who would give board to Tom Sanders, a Mi'kmaq man from Nova Scotia, when he came to sell baskets and other things. "Some people used to hide away from him, but he'd know when they'd hide away," she said. "I wouldn't hide away, I was too afraid of him at first." Once, while staying at her house, he complained that a man charged him too much for a boat trip. "He won't get nothing by it," he said. "Ah, you isn't going to hurt 'en," Frances said, but shortly afterward, the man's wife miscarried; his son shot his arm in a hunting accident; and the man lost his job and never got another: "That's what Sanders done to him."

For her part, Frances treated him "like one of her own." She never charged him for his stay, even when he brought his wife and children along, and sometimes she gave him clothes or shoes. In return, Sanders said, "Frances, you'll always be lucky; you'll never want for money. You might get down low, but you'll never want." And Frances did scrape by, after she moved back to Broom Harbour, through such expedients as taking in laundry and caring for elderly people in their homes. She declined to accommodate Sanders after the move. "He wanted I to take him, I said, 'No sir, I got no room now, I got grandchildren,' I said, 'indeed I can't take you … I had enough of you when I was up in Grey Cove,' I said, 'Go on.'" She no longer feared him because she was accustomed to him, and besides, she had realized, "I can put a spell on he!"

Sanders's stays at Frances's house can only have bolstered her magical reputation. Besides demonstrating her fearlessness (for all anyone knew), his presence might have suggested that she learned spells from him, for spells were sometimes regarded as teachable or transferable devices. Laura knew a Broom Harbour woman, for instance, who was said to have "gotten" a spell from the Mi'kmaq at Conne River; the witch Jane Philpott in nearby Ember Cove was also said to have acquired spells there.[2]

Frances learned a cure for warts from her husband Fred a few months before he died in 1979. She had no premonition at the time, but on the day before it happened, she was reading her friend Mary's cup and casually overturned her own and glanced into it (although she says you're not supposed to read your own). "Oh my Christ, Mary, somebody's going to die belong to I," she said. She thought it might be her husband's brother, but the next day Fred had a heart attack and fell off a wharf and drowned.

The wart cure involved a secret formula, "something you got to say," but Frances knew the importance of suggestion as well. "Now, I'm going to work magic on you this evening," she told a boy whose father had requested the service. The warts were gone within a week. I asked Frances to remove a wart on my index finger and so was able to observe part of the procedure. She cut an onion and rubbed it on the finger in a circle three times; I had to close my eyes then, but Martin and Laura were allowed to watch her put the onion in a bag and hide it away in the living room. She assured me that the wart would be gone soon, but my faith was shaken by her comment, "Bloody fools. Everybody comes to me, I don't know whether it does any good or not." I was impatient in any case and had a doctor burn it off soon after that.

She voiced no such reservations about her prophecies. These were made mostly for young women wanting to know about boyfriends or husbands; Frances would tell them whom they would marry – or not marry, she added, as in the case of Lisa Lake in Salt Cove. Lisa was engaged to Kevin Barter, who (Frances alleged) was "into drugs." It doesn't take a teacup to see that this did not bode well, and notice in the following transcription that Frances did not in fact have a cup when she announced that Lisa would not marry Kevin. Her account gives a good idea of her style and technique. As she said herself, she asked a lot of questions first; she repeated the answers authoritatively back to Lisa, then dropped the bombshell.

I went up Salt Cove one time – I'm going to tell you this 'cause lots of people says it's lies, but I don't tell no lies. And there was a girl there, Lisa Lake, and her boyfriend ... Kevin Barter. So, they was building a house ... I was going up Mother's Day ...

I said, "Lisa, who's building a house out there?"

She said, "I and Kevin."

I said, "You and Kevin."

"Yes," she said.

Now I never had no cup then.

So she said, "I'm going to get the tea leaves."

I said, "Yes, when I'm ready, Lisa, I've got to ask you questions first." 'Cause you got to ask a lot of questions. "You building a house, Lisa?"

"Yes," she said.

I said, "You and Kevin is building the house together?"

I whacked down me fist on the table ... I whacked me fist down on the table like that [bangs the table], I said, "Lisa, you'll never live in that house."

And he [Kevin] was sat down in the chair like you. The words – how he cursed!

I said, "I don't care about that, you can curse all you like, but," I said, "you are not going to live in that house, Lisa."

I said, "Get the cup, Lisa, let I look in there."

And I said [to Kevin], "Look here, Buddy. Did you give that girl any money?"

"Yes," he said.

I said, "Look here. She's going to pass you back all your money."

I took the cup. I could see it without the cup.

And I said, "Where are you going to, Lisa? You're going away."

"Going to Toronto."

"Yes," I said, "You're going to Toronto, Lisa, and," I said, "you're not coming back to Broom Harbour to marry *that.*"

And he said, "Oh, yes, we're gonna –"

And I said, "You're *not*. You're going to Toronto, Lisa, you're going in for [to train as] a hairdresser over there, but there's plenty of them over there. You're going to work in an old people's home."

And I said, "Lisa," – how many times has she thanked me since then – "Look here, you're going over there, you're going to meet with a fellow, he's not Salvation Army ... he's not a Anglican, he's not a Pentecost ... he's a Catholic man. I'm going to tell you now" –

He [Kevin] was there, sat in the chair –

I said, "Before you get married to this man, you go to his priest and explain everything to him. Then you won't have no worries."

But sir, the cursing I heard that day – I never been cursed so much before and I never will no more.

And I said, "Lisa, go on, next year, the twenty-fourth day of August – this was in May, Mother's Day ... Next year, not this year ... you'll be married to this fellow. You'll come back to Salt Cove, get married to the Army, have the wedding in Hart Cove in the Lion's Club."

Well, sir, he [Kevin] almost drove me out through the door. He didn't drive me out, and that was all.

"You kiss my goddamn ass" – that's coming on that [the tape recorder], isn't it? You'll have to excuse me, dear, I got to say what I said – I said, "You kiss my goddamn ass, now go to hell and tell the devil I sent you there. 'Cause you're nothing, only a tramp on the street."

All right. I come out, that was Sunday ... So then, all right, by and by, Lisa went to Toronto, meet up with this fellow, sent back the snaps [photographs], I said, "Ah, Kevin." I haven't seen him since, I never seen him more. So Lisa, next year, got in with this fellow, came back.

I said, "Lisa, did you do what I tell 'ee?"

And she said, "Frances, I listened to you. 'Cause I didn't have nobody else to listen to."

... Help me God, the twenty-fourth of August they come back to Salt Cove, got married at the Army, went down to Hart Cove Lion's Club, had their wedding.

Ostensibly telling a fortune, Frances was really acting as a counsellor or perhaps a mother figure (she even marks the day, twice, as Mother's Day). She doesn't say why Lisa had "no one else to listen to," and it is not clear whether Lisa was involved with drugs along with Kevin or knew that he was, but the proposal of an alternate future – one without Kevin – was obviously sound. The advice that Lisa confide in the priest shows the importance Frances put on unburdening oneself and speaking the truth.

"Oh, a real witch, my lover," she concluded the story about Lisa, "I don't hurt nobody, all the same." Could she if she wanted to? I asked.

"Yes, I have done it. Hmmm, I have it done. I'm gonna tell you something now what I done. I should not tell it, but – you know, 'tis only, I didn't hurt nobody." What follows is her account of the angry prediction she made to a government official who refused and offended her. There were no teacups in sight when she told him his fate.

Some years ago, Frances had to go to hospital in St John's for an operation, and someone told her that she could get a pass for transportation from the Department of Social Services. She was reluctant ("My God, never been to the welfare in me life") but finances were tight, even with her husband working at the fish plant, so she gathered up her receipts and her nerve and went along with a friend. The social services worker, not a native of Broom Harbour, rejected the application.

"No, he said, "I can't give you no check."
"Oh, all right,' I said, "Look here, Buddy" – I hardly knew his name – James? ... I said, "Look here. You gives people welfare," I said, "what goes in St John's and buys clothes for themselves and this and that." I said, "I wouldn't do that, 'cause I ain't got enough money for that."

She left the office, but he called her back.

I got as far as Terry Barter's, and then I see he patting on the window.
I said, "What you want me for?" I said. "You ain't gonna give me no money for to go to St John's." I said, "That's all right."
He said, "I'll give you money to go to Torraville," he said.
I said, "What in Jesus kind of legs you think I got, I got to walk from Torraville to St John's?
I said, "Look here, Buddy, I got something to tell you." I said, "Next year this time," I said, "you'll be dying in cancer. And you'll think about me."
"Ah," he said [dismissively].
I said, "You will." And I said, "Before you dies, let I go across your mind."
"Well," he said, "I'll give you a pass."
But I said, "Look here, what I said to you about the cancer," I said, "you'll be dying of cancer,"
I said, "That's gone through."
"Ah," he said.

I said, "Mark my words," I said, "when I say something," I said, "I means it." But I said, "If you'd have give me the pass when I first came to the office, I wouldn't have told about the cancer."

His face started to look longer then. And I said, "When I goes into St John's, I'm going to the welfare me own self, and I'm going to tell them what you've done to me" ...

So all right, that's all I thought about it. Help me God, that was in May, I think it was; in September, he got sick, he had to go home, he had cancer, died in November with cancer.

At this point Frances abruptly changed the subject. I tried to clarify whether the death was something that had been bound to happen or whether she had caused it: "It was going to happen, yeah, but I knowed about it, I let him know. Seems like I couldn't help it." Yet her words "That's gone through" suggest something put into motion on the spot. (Laura recalled that the man left the community about the time Frances said, but she didn't know why.)

On the surface or in summary form, this account would appear to be a typical "denial narrative," but hearing it from Frances, in the context of how she presented her life, it is clear that it is really a story about pride. However unintentionally, the government official, a stranger to the community, impugned Frances's hard-won respectability. Uncomfortable as she was in the position of supplicant, his dismissal of her claim added insult to injury, and Frances lashed back with the best – the only – weapon she had. In economic terms, the visit to social services reveals a person on edge in more ways than one: a poor person would have gotten assistance automatically, while someone well off would not have gone in the first place. The affront must have been deeply felt to have met with such a ferocious and seemingly disproportionate response.

A conversation with a student who was connected to Frances through marriage encapsulates Frances's prickly pride. He told me that upon meeting her, he politely enquired, "So, you live with your daughter-in-law?" To which Frances, the owner of the house, replied, "No, she lives with me." This student confirmed that Frances was "very well thought of" in the town, and that she did have the reputation of being a witch.[3]

Frances said that she might show me how to read the cup someday: "Probably you'll be back before I dies, I'll show you how to do it." But I never saw her again. She was going to read the cup for Martin's student and her sister and me the next day and let us videotape it, but when I phoned to confirm I was told that she had gone out of town. I assumed that we had gotten our wires crossed, but later I learned from Laura that Frances never went anywhere and was disappointed that we hadn't shown up as arranged. The next summer I visited Broom Harbour again and went straight to Frances's house, where I was told she was in hospital; Laura and I went to the hospital and learned that Frances had been discharged several days earlier. So it seemed, not to put too fine a point on it, that her relatives lied to keep me away from her. Why?

One possible answer comes from an essay written by Frances's granddaughter, Tessa, in 1994, a few years after my visit. "Many of my family members view my grandmother's ability to tell fortunes as nothing but foolishness," she wrote.[4] (Her husband hadn't believed in "they bloody old cups" either, Frances told her.) Frances was not concerned with what I did with the tape recording ("as long as it's not for broadcast in Newfoundland"), but maybe the relatives were. Tessa also said that although Frances was in reasonable health, she had stopped reading the cup for all but close friends because too many people were coming from all around the area. The stream of callers could have been a household nuisance, although it had been going on for years. "I can remember seeing a lot of strange people coming to our house to have their fortunes told but I never actually understood why or what actually went on when my grandmother was telling fortunes," Tessa wrote. "My grandmother always insisted that we leave the room when she was telling someone their fortune to protect their privacy." Frances told Tessa that people had been "hounding her to tell their fortunes" ever since she taught herself how to do it at the age of fifteen; but "I didn't let nobody know it I could read en, not before I got eighteen after I got married ... because everybody was after me," coming from as far away as Sydney, Nova Scotia. (If this chronology is correct, Frances would have been established as a fortune teller while Sanders was at her house.)

Tessa noted that Frances "seemed offended" at the idea of charging for fortune-telling, "but if anybody was good enough give me twenty-five cents or thirty cents I take it." She must have experimented with a fee at some point, because she also said, "If I charged, it wouldn't come true. That's how I found it." Her midwifery and mortuary services probably operated on a similar tacit understanding, although she told me that she never accepted anything. Tessa told me that

Frances was vague with her on certain questions; she was unable to ascertain, for instance, whether Frances predicted things only through tea leaves or by other means as well.

Although it might be expected that Tessa would have the inside track, so to speak, on the story of Frances, her interview garnered less information than mine; the story of the social services official wasn't there, nor any of the casual profanity of her language. I think that Frances was aware of the negative aspects of her activities and was circumspect with her granddaughter, but that this reservation warred with her ethic of full disclosure. As a stranger, I made a good recipient for the full picture, warts and all. To be fair, it is easy to see the trouble-making potential of her fortune-telling and unsolicited prognostication. The druggie Kevin perhaps deserves no sympathy, but the social services worker was only trying to do his job. Some shrugged Frances's predictions off, as Martin's student did when Frances told her she would do better at university if she didn't wear so many rings. Others found it harder to shed her words. By chance, Martin and I met Jeannie Bragg from Broom Harbour, who related several instances of unwelcome commentary. Once Frances told her that she would get pregnant on a trip to St Pierre (which she did); the prediction made her uncomfortable because it was made in the presence of her mother, who was a "great believer" in Frances. Several years later the mother lay dying in hospital, where Frances was also a patient. Jeannie said that the family became upset with Frances's constant advice, but her mother's last words to her and her sister before falling into a coma were, "Shut up, you two, I'm trying to listen to Frances." At one point while she was unconscious, Frances went to the window and announced, "By the time the tide goes out your mother will be gone." She did die, and Jeannie wondered whether her mother could have heard Frances and, because of her faith in her, given up. Certainly Frances's desire to help could have unintended consequences. Laura told us about an emotionally troubled teenager who went to see Frances, and although his problems were of long standing, some people began blaming them on the visit.

In light of such dissension and gossip, Frances's relatives' obstruction of our meeting was perhaps understandable.[5] Still, it should have been Frances's decision to talk with me, not theirs, and I felt that she and I were cheated. When I heard of her death in 1995, I regretted that we had only met once, but I was glad for even that. To conclude on a further personal note, it is hard to convey the enormous strength of personality I sensed in Frances, from which I think much of her "magical" power derived. More tangible sources were her intimate talks with people throughout the area (an excellent line of intelligence) and her work as midwife, healer, and undertaker. Her presence at critical moments in people's lives let her observe raw human nature and physiological processes. I think, too, that her unpaid services to the community gave her a certain moral authority. People trusted her with their bodies and their secrets. Her pride in her power to meet their needs was the matrix for her casting as wise advisor.

As far as I know, my interview with Frances is the only recorded account of a "curse" (complete with denouement) from the "witch" herself. The American researcher Michael Owen Jones recorded a threatening utterance from a healer whom he studied in central Newfoundland in the late 1960s.[6] Uncle Jim Gallagher, a seventh son of a seventh son, healed eczema and other complaints through touch; but many distrusted him and said that he "worked the black heart" against anyone who did anything against him (although no one suggested that he was a witch). Like Frances, he was "cavalier in religious matters" (as Jones put it) and quick-tempered. He told Jones how he swore on a school-teacher who took a rabbit from one of his traps: "If you eats that rabbit tomorrow, by Jesus, you'll die. I hope to Jesus you'll be paralyzed" (and more). He said that he didn't really think the teacher would have died (though the other men thought so), but "I'd a-done somet'ing wit' 'im." That this came from a healer of self-proclaimed altruism shows the flip side of the confidence-inspiring rituals and pronouncements of charming. It proves (along with my conversation with Frances) that people did receive such threats – they are not just the creation of gossip or legend.

Midwives, like healers, needed to inspire trust, but there is nothing magical about childbirth or its practices. Midwife-witches don't appear in the archival data in greater numbers than other women, and Janet McNaughton found no connection in her study of twentieth-century midwives.[7] Faris said that all the midwives but one in Cat Harbour were considered to be witches (the exception being a native of the place) and suggested that their reputations stemmed in part from the duty of midwives in earlier times to euthanize infants with severe birth defects.[8] No doubt the "good nerve" described by McNaughton's midwife-informants as an important qualification for the job could be exploited if they chose (one woman, if unpaid, "would cast a spell on the baby and it would die": 79/1), but to do so was incompatible with the sympathy that clients identified as a midwife's most important attribute. In Frances this quality must have outweighed any others.

Mary Bell and Her Daughter Rachel

"She could do anything in the world, whatever she wanted to do," said a man of Mary Bell in 1966 (66/2/c). Like Frances, Mary Bell issued predictions both with and without teacups; the cups, however, are not mentioned in the archival accounts where I first learned about Mary. I only heard about them when I went to Lone Island, which lies about a kilometre off the north coast, and it wasn't until after my visit that I discovered two archival papers claiming that Mary had passed her powers on to a daughter, Rachel. No one even mentioned Rachel to me; she must have died shortly after these essays were written in the 1980s, because my landlady, Lydia Sparkes, said that Mary had no relations left in the area; and Ruth Bird, who told me about the cups, didn't mention Rachel either.[1] Mary Bell herself died in the 1940s. What was it about her that left such an indelible impression?

Skippers visited her before a voyage, for instance, "to make sure they were all right" – possibly because she could stir up a storm by churning water in a tub, affecting whichever boats she wanted (66/3/c). One woman called her "a born witch" who "used to study the Black Art Book" and told of a luckless Labrador voyage:

> Of course when they didn't get fish, the first thing they said, "You don't want to wonder what's the trouble – that's Mary Bell got us witched." Well now, [the skipper] was a religious man [which on Lone Island meant either Methodist or Salvation Army], and of course he didn't give much heed to it, you know. But he got that discouraged ... and the men were talking about it so much that he decided he'd come home, and the excuse was that salt was scarce; and he came home and he went to see her and have a talk with her and the last words she said to him when he left was, "Mr Perkins, when you goes back you'll get the fish." (79/4)

Another story came from a man who said that he and a friend, as young men, were hunting seals from a small boat when they met Mary and her husband Chester crossing the bay. Mary and Chester gave them some food and Mary said that they would get two seals, which they did: "That's what the missus said" (67/5/c).

Chester, unlike the shadowy husband of many witches, figures prominently in the archival repertoire. He profited from Mary's advice: she might tell him, for instance, when to go hunting for birds or a seal, and since he was "a wonderful gunner," he would succeed (66/6/c). One spring, he decided to stay home from the Labrador because most schooners had left and it would be too late to get a good berth; but Mary said there was "no harm to try it," so he went after all. The earlier schooners got caught in ice and lost their gear, so his was the first to arrive; and his was the only one to get a good load that year (66/7/c).

According to Ruth Bird, Chester was not native to Lantern Cove, one of two communities on the island; being an "outsider" probably helped his inclusion in the witch tales. He may have had a slightly higher status than some fishermen, being a captain of freighters as well as schooners (although Lone Island had a large schooner fleet so he was by no means the only one). On top of this, he encouraged Mary's reputation, as one man recalled. "Mary Bell had a hard name, but she was not, she didn't deserve the name that they give her. They all said that she was a witch and would do everything that was bad [but] I never seen nothing wrong with her, and I was in her house hundreds of times. But you know she used to say stuff, used to tell stories, though. And Chester used to try for to bring out her words true. He was working on that too, see" (66/8/c). It was probably useful to Chester, lacking a web of relations, that people thought of his wife as a witch. "If anybody crossed Chester … do a bad trick to him … they was in for a hard time" (66/9/c). He was killed in an accident at Bayle Isle (66/10/c), a place he was said to have avoided for more than twenty years because Mary said he would die there (66/11/c).

"There wasn't much she said that didn't come true," Ruth Bird told me. In her sixties at the time of our interview, Ruth had grown up in Lantern Cove, and her father was Mary Bell's stepbrother. When Ruth was still living at home, Mary told her father that he and his family would have to move out of the house where they lived with his widowed father. It turned out that Ruth's grandfather had been seeing someone (presumably Mary's mother) and without warning asked the family to leave. I didn't ask Mary's age at the time because I didn't quite follow who was who, but she would have been a young woman at most and already an outspoken observer of situation and psychology.

Eventually, too, she had a wide network of acquaintances, since her fortune-telling put her in great demand. Clients who did not like her forecast would come back again and again, trying to get her to say something different, but she never would. The worst prediction Ruth could recall was that a certain boat under construction would never leave the slip. People scoffed because the builder had made many good boats before, but this one never did sail. According to Ruth, Mary was well liked and her house was a popular gathering place where pots of soup were kept cooking for company day or night. This chimes with what Lydia Sparkes heard from a woman who was once engaged to Mary's son, and who said that Mary was an exceptionally kind woman. Ruth laughed at the idea that anyone might be afraid of her, acknowledging only that she did resemble a "storybook" witch – bent and misshapen, but not ugly or old.

So I left Lone Island with a rosy image of Mary Bell stirring soup, not storms. Then I found two accounts that blew any airbrushed romanticism out of the water with their depiction of witch lore in all its seamy and slanderous ill will. The students, cousins whom I'll call Jennifer (83/12/c) and Jason (87/13/c), recorded some of the same stories from their relatives. (Jennifer's aunt is Jason's mother.)[2] Jason's brother, a lawyer, said:

> There was an old lady here in Lantern Cove back in the twenties, I guess, her name was Mary Bell. And her husband was a sea captain on one of the freight boats. And the story is that he got the black art book on one of his trips to India, and he brought it back and gave it to his wife Mary. She subsequently used the book to cast her spells and I guess influence people. And I've heard Mom and Dad and a number of the old people home talk about some of the instances where they swear that she used that book and had spells placed on people.
>
> Mary passed this black art book down to her daughter Rachel; and Rachel lives out here just across the point from us there, next-door neighbors. And when I was growing up here in Lantern Cove, she was in her late sixties, early seventies, I think, and a lot of us were scared of her and considered her to be a witch. And not only the kids, but a lot of the grownups in Lantern Cove considered her to be a witch. Anyway, we had a

dispute – my family, my dad – with her family over exactly where the fence should go that separated the two properties. Anyway, that created a lot of animosity during that whole summer, lots of verbal abuse and verbal attacks going back and forth the whole summer. That summer we were painting the house ... and we had the scaffolding all built up ... My brothers Fred and Carl were up on the top part ... and all of a sudden, for no bloody reason, the whole thing collapsed ... We firmly believed it was the fault of Rachel, she had placed a spell on us, and that was our way of explaining why a supposedly solid scaffold should fall down for no reason. (My transcription)

Jennifer's aunt (the young men's mother), told her about the scaffold incident and the property dispute: "I want to tell you here too that during the summer there was a lot of tension between our family and this old lady over my land." The aunt painted Mary as a grasping witch as well, with a story about her prediction that a young man would die at sea when something on the boat fell on his neck; it turned out to be her own son, and "rumour went out" that she could have prevented the death but didn't because she wanted his life insurance money. Despite these tales – or maybe *because* of them – the family maintained a semblance of normal neighbourly relations with Rachel. When Jennifer declined to do some painting for her, pleading lack of time, her aunt was shocked. "I asked her why," Jennifer wrote. "She stated, 'My dear, my husband wouldn't dare refuse to do anything for her. There's bound to be something go wrong if he doesn't do what she wants. You should have done the painting, my dear, even if it meant missing university.' Since that day I sure as hell had bad luck. Subconsciously I relate it to this book."

Ruth Bird told me that Mary eventually went to live with a son in St John's; she didn't mention a son who died, but then she didn't mention Rachel either. Possibly Rachel's identity as a witch was solely the invention of the family with whom she argued over land. They did not seem to have had trouble with Mary; in fact they even had one good story about her. When Jennifer's aunt's father was unable to work one winter, Mary reassured him, "Mr Drew, the wolf will not always be at your door." In May he got a job as a lumber camp foreman "and from then on prospered." But most of her predictions were dire. A skipper who "said something" (i.e., something offensive) about her was told that he'd return from Labrador "with not a fish and lousy as a goat"; of a man "in the bloom of life" with whom she fell out she said, "He'll die, and die a hard death," and his perishing screams soon rang over Lantern Cove; a merchant was warned that before he died he'd come to her for a cake of hard bread – his property burned and he died with a house empty of food (all these stories from Jennifer).

Nowhere in these or older archival accounts do teacups appear. At first I thought this might be because the earlier accounts were recorded by men from men, and tea leaf reading is largely a female affair; it might explain why none of the reported predictions (or curses) involved women – perhaps Mary's forecasts for women were safely contained by the cup, so to speak, and not poured out in anger. But then Jennifer's aunt/Jason's mother, who was so full of tales about Mary, didn't mention tea leaves; in her understanding, it was the Black Heart Book, brought from the West Indies by Chester (or India, as Jason heard it), that gave Mary power: "She used this book to forecast the future, cast spells, and to make life miserable for those people who did her wrong in any way," according to Jennifer. Teacups seem to have played a negligible part in the making of her reputation, to judge by their absence from the record.

In the winter semester of 2006, a Lone Island student in a class I was teaching enlisted his mother to conduct interviews with several older residents of the island.[3] All of them recalled Mary Bell's reputation and alleged possession of a black heart book, and none mentioned fortune-telling. Chester was once again shown as an agent in promoting her reputation, having told a story about "shooting" her himself (according to the informant). After an unsuccessful morning of hunting, Chester had the men land on an island where he "shot the shotbag" (the bag containing shot or gunpowder) because he knew Mary had put a spell on them. When he got home (as he subsequently told the others), Mary slapped him across the mouth because she knew he had "shot" her, for at that moment she had "come right off her feet."

A woman in this group said that Mary was "nothing but an evil spirit" as well as "a very, very rude woman"; another told about her having a washtub on the kitchen floor with a little boat in it, making waves until the boat went over. "They're gone," she said, at exactly the same time that the real boat capsized. Another witch, Elizabeth Brock, who kept a store, sometimes clashed with Mary, "tit-for-tat, spell after spell" – "They used to be into it, the two families," but Mary was the stronger. Other witches were mentioned as well, but Rachel was not among them.

The sharply divided opinions about Mary suggest that she aroused considerable feeling in people one way or another, but perhaps unanimity would be a bigger surprise. Caroline Pin, a native of Lesser Bight, Lone Island's second community, described the female rivalries on the island (75/14). Due to the long absences of the men, she wrote, women were in charge of almost everything; most of them even managed to stay on the island when they married, with the result that they had "closer relationships with other women than the men do with other men … and frequently have closer relationships with friends than with their own husbands." However, Pin continued, "Whereas strong ties exist among the women, the strongest and most intense rivalries exist also. They will never see a friend in trouble without doing the utmost to help, but will deliberately and intentionally hurt a rival." This would seem to be a recipe for witching among women, but Pin doesn't mention it even though she discusses the subject in some detail. She divides the women of the island into seven types, one of which she calls "strange" or "cold":

> These women are avoided either because of strange features or strange behavior. One such woman was Aunt Pauline (the woman my mother first went to work for). She was thought to be a witch but still was a rather nice woman. She was kind and seldom harmed anyone but was avoided socially. It was said she could cure illness and take away warts. The fishermen feared her visits. My grandfather used to say that Aunt Pauline would often visit him just before he went fishing to warn him that he wouldn't catch any. It usually happened that he didn't catch any so he would draw a picture of her and shoot at the picture. Back in her home, Aunt Pauline would become ill and remain so for several days but she never resented it for she felt it was something she had to do.

A similar sense of duty seemed to compel Mary Bell, Jennifer recounted, one night during a storm when it was feared that some seal hunters were lost, to go to every house to assure people that they were safe; she knew because she had met them on the ice in a dream. They returned the next day.

A man interviewed by my student's mother recalled that Patience Welland was supposed to have a black book and "could put a spell on you, working this witchcraft," but when pressed for detail he said, "It's a job to explain ... She had a family of boys, and it seemed like she turned out to be boss, and the boys more or less followed her, more so than their father." Lone Island's strong female culture, as described by Pin, seems to have made some men nervous, even of their own relations. One claimed to have given his aunt headaches for weeks by shooting a drawing of her in the head because he blamed her for his bad luck fishing in Labrador (85/15/FSC); another allegedly killed his sister-in-law for the same reason, by holding a corked bottle of urine over his head (85/16/FSC). Two brothers took a more scattershot approach, according to one man: "Just about every old woman that was in here, they'd mark out and shoot at them, shoot silver at them. Yes, they'd even mark out their own mother, my son, and shoot at her ... They'd aim right for her heart, right for the breast ... I never looked at it much because it was too silly a thing for me to look at" (66/17/C).

"The witch's heart is burning today, isn't it?" Jennifer heard Fred say, after he fell off the scaffold. The boundary feud between Rachel and her neighbours exposes property rights as a very material issue that can lurk behind a murky façade of "witchcraft." What better way to vilify an opponent than to call her a witch? It worked in New England, as Carol F. Karlsen has shown. She unravelled the intricacies of a number of cases to reveal that women who were in a position to control or inherit property, whatever their economic status, were particularly vulnerable to accusations of witchcraft by those who hoped to get hold of the property.[4] In Newfoundland, inheritance and land division practices favoured men by custom and law, though often without documentation. To this day, land ownership can present legal labyrinths, and "quieting of titles" is big business for lawyers who must sometimes trace potential inheritors all over the globe. Discrediting a rival claimant as a witch would not have worked in court (unless perhaps it was a Lone Island lawyer) but it might have influenced local informal decisions, such as whether to give depositions as to the history of usage of a property in the process of title clearance.[5]

Unlike earlier "witches" in other places, Newfoundland women did not have to worry about legal prosecution, so some women seized the idea of witching in an effort to protect their land; cases from Conception Bay[6] and the Southern Shore[7] show a wide distribution of the idea and that sometimes it worked. In the Conception Bay case, a poor widow cursed a family business and land (according to a member of the cursed family). In some recent interviews, Kristian Crummey, a student and native of the town, and I heard three different reasons proposed for the curse: the family took her land; someone laughed at her; and someone had refused her something. Property was right up there with the classic dual motives of refusal and respect.[8]

 ## Janie Smith (c. 1890–1960)

The case of Janie Smith shows how far the violation of social convention can go toward building the legend of a "witch." Almost none of the stories about her concern spells; rather, the set of tales recorded by Sharon Sanderson in 1974 revolve around behaviour that was bizarre by the standards of a small Northern Peninsula town. Sanderson wrote:

> When I was a child, I used to visit my grandparents in Apple Cove every summer. One of the houses there was deserted. It had belonged to an old woman named Janie Smith, who had died a few years before I began visiting there. My cousins and I were afraid to pass her house because we thought that she had been a witch, and that now she haunted the house … My grandfather had often told me that when she was alive, a lot of people thought she was a witch, and that when something went wrong, it was sometimes said that Janie had put a spell on it. (74/18/FSC)

Sanderson's mother described an eccentric individual: "Janie was considered 'odd' because, 'for one thing, she ate mushrooms that grew in the woods.' So I asked her to explain further: 'When I was growing up, nobody'd eat the mushrooms that grew in the woods because the fairies used them for making bread. If you ate them, something bad would happen. Janie Smith was the only one in Apple Cove who'd eat them at the time'" (74/19/FSC). Wanting to know more, Sanderson interviewed ten Apple Cove residents, whose collective testimony suggests that Janie's reputation was a collaborative effort between her and her more conventional neighbours (74/20).

Janie was born on the Northern Peninsula to a Mi'kmaq mother and an English fisherman father. At fifteen she married Charles Smith, her senior by almost twenty years; they had five children before moving to a small island where they were the only inhabitants, and where they subsisted for eight years mostly on what they could catch and grow. Charles would periodically go to the mainland for supplies, but Janie and the children never left the island. If a boat came near, they would pelt it with stones and shout for it to turn away.

Around 1920 they moved to Apple Cove where Charles soon declined with the unspecified illness that made him an invalid until his death almost twenty years later. To support the family, Janie took on odd jobs, such as becoming the local barber. People treated her with reserve; as one informant said, they expected her to be "uncivilized," and she seemed to oblige with displays of outlandish behaviour. Most people, for instance, would kill their Sunday dinner rooster by chopping off its head, but Janie would stand in her yard and slowly squeeze it to death. Besides mushrooms, she would eat crow, which others considered unfit for human consumption.

Most tales about Janie involve similarly antisocial acts. She had a long-standing feud with her nearest neighbour, who claimed that she poured roofing tar on his prize bull so that it had to be destroyed, and that her daughters smashed his windows with sticks. He took his complaints to a visiting magistrate, who dismissed them for lack of evidence, after which Janie escalated her alleged mischief against him.

Several informants, however, said that Janie was often blamed for things she didn't do. A fur trapper, for instance, decided he was having a poor winter because Janie didn't like him and had put a spell on his traps to keep the animals away. His wife forbade him to do as some of their neighbours did, which was to set a wooden cross outside their house facing hers. She was friends with Janie, who often called at the house. One day while she was there, he said, the Anglican minister was seen to approach, so his wife warned Janie to be careful of her words. At first Janie was polite, inquiring only why the minister had not come to see her poor sick husband. The minister replied that as Charles belonged to a different church, he did not wish to intrude, but he would come and pray for him if she liked; to which Janie replied that the damn old fool might go to his reward any time now, and if he didn't, she would take the axe and send him herself.

Janie's husband died around 1940, and not a moment too soon for Janie, if there is anything to the tales. One evening she told the shopkeeper that she was cooking Charles's favourite meal since he might not last until the morning, adding, "I hope to God the old fool is dead when I get back, I'll have a swinging eight [dance] of it tonight." She tried to send the daughters a telegram announcing his death the night before he actually died. No sooner had he drawn his last breath than Janie was said to have been "on him with a razor" to shave and prepare him for burial. Normally men did this for other men, but she insisted on helping, all the while scolding the corpse for being difficult to dress. At the wake, she had the men place chairs alongside the body before the minister arrived. She lay on the chairs and told the minister that she was having "her last lie-down with Charles," then jumped up and announced, "Now it's time to bury the old fool."

There is no need to pity Charles, if there is any truth to Janie's story about how she "got her husband." According to one informant, she told anyone who would listen how she had "[for]'bid the banns" when Charles stood at the altar ready to wed the local schoolteacher. The pregnant Janie stepped forward to announce that he was the father of the child, and he had to marry her on the spot instead. "He thought he could fool a poor little Indian girl," she concluded. Charles was apparently no paragon of normalcy himself. The move to the island reveals a lack of the typical male engagement in community or patriarchal family work structures; before that move, they had lived with Janie's family, another unusual set-up.[1] In the semiseclusion of his illness he had no defence against tales about his wife or himself.

After he was gone, Janie ran a boarding house, which thrived in the local lumber economy and became another major locus of tales. A former boarder said that lodgers were treated well as long as they were wary of Janie's quick temper and shifting moods, and also of her cooking. One man distrusted the mystery meat on the table after Janie got him to shoot a crow for her own dinner. A man who was caught pocketing inedible cookies made with tea leaves was refused food for a week. Still, the house must have been reasonably comfortable to have lasted for fifteen years, and the outlandish landlady was perhaps even an attraction, as fodder for lumber-camp lore.

The only description of Janie's appearance occurs in a report of how, when a new wharf was being built, she visited the site each day all dressed up, complete with silk stockings, "looking just like someone from Corner Brook" (i.e., the big city). The informant said that she was out either to create gossip or to "seduce" men (whether for fun or profit is not clear). No one knew what went on in her house at that point because she had painted the windowpanes green.

The house became a fearsome landmark for the children of Apple Cove, who dared each other to walk past it. The bravest boys would get within hearing distance and chant:

Janie Smith, the mean old witch,
She lives in a ditch
And combs her hair with a hickory switch.[2]

Sometimes Janie emerged to chase them with a broom, vowing to kill anyone she caught.

Janie's name lived on in the threat "Janie will get you!" issued to misbehaving children, and as a byword for strange or obnoxious behaviour: "That's like something Janie would do," or "That's just like Janie's crew" (i.e., her children). Sanderson noted that even though Janie had been dead for more than a decade at the time of her research, a third of her information came from people under twenty-five. Those who had actually known her, however, had higher storytelling status. They insisted that Janie enjoyed having people see her as a witch and had deliberately antagonized her neighbours to promote that image.

Where did this sense of opposition come from? Did it start with her or with them, or as mutual suspicion? Would people have treated her differently if she had behaved more conventionally, or was she marked from the start as an outsider, by virtue of her island life or her Mi'kmaq ethnicity? Mixed aboriginal ancestry is common in the area and not stigmatized; but as we have seen, it would help if one wanted to be thought of as a witch, or to think of someone else as a witch. Yet "magical" power is all but absent from Sanderson's collection. Only one person, the trapper, told of a spell, and it was a thin story at that. No black heart book, no fortune-telling, no haggish appearance; also, no requests for goods or favours, and no veiled threats – only outrageous words and deeds that lived up to a town's expectations.

In 2006 I met Warren Yates, who was born in Apple Cove in 1924, and who had mentioned Janie Smith (in passing) in a memoir printed in a local paper.[3] Mr Yates acknowledged that some people called Janie a witch, but he was quick to dismiss the idea that she was "at that" (i.e., witching). She was a "character" all right, he said, but she had "a heart of gold." In fact, she saved his wife in childbirth, when the cord was wrapped around the baby's neck. The midwife had given up and dropped to her knees to pray, but Janie, who was also in attendance, said, "This is no time to pray." She took over and got the baby safely out. Her only training was having delivered one or two of her own children, but "nothing bothered her." She was "full of fun," he said, but he believes it was her rough prankish sense of humour that led some people to call her a witch. She would wait for courting couples to pass by, for instance, and pitch out the dirty household water to splash them. A teacher who stayed at her boarding house was often in a hurry, so one morning Janie nailed her shoes to the floor. Although she took good care of her invalid husband, if someone was around she might shove a spoonful of food roughly into his mouth and make him choke. (Mr Yates did not know what Charles's illness was; when he was well he had been an ordinary man who worked in the lumber woods in winters and fished in the summer.) Once Janie walked ten miles into a woods camp to visit a man with whom she was reputedly involved (in our first conversation Mr Yates said it was while Charles was still alive, in our second conversation he said it was after he had died). She was "not very fancy-looking," Mr Yates said, although her daughters were. There was also a son, Stevie, who "was a hard ticket but not entirely foolish." Once, as boys, Mr Yates and his brother and Stevie Smith were fishing together in a pond when Stevie (who was a few years older than Mr Yates) got mad because Mr Yates was catching more fish than he was, so he picked Mr Yates up and threw him headfirst into the frigid water. His brother pulled him out and they had to run home to keep from freezing.

Mr Yates said that if anyone made anything of Janie's Indianness, it was herself, because many people in the area had Mi'kmaq ancestry and there was no prejudice against it. She was exactly like everyone else except for her odd idea of fun – the sole reason, in his view, why some people called her "an idle woman," not in the sense of being lazy, because she worked hard and everyone respected that about her, but because of her undeveloped sense of propriety. Eventually the entire family moved away, Janie into St John's with one of the daughters, leaving the empty house to the imagination of children like Sanderson and her cousins. When Janie lived there, Mr Yates said, it was surrounded by beautiful flowers. It became run down with the passage of time, as the legend of Janie blossomed.

Framing Three Witches

Even given the disparities in available information about Frances Long, Mary Bell, and Janie Smith, their histories offer broad points of comparison. Most obvious is the fortune-telling of Frances and Mary but not Janie. Second is their place in the community: Frances and Mary well inside, Janie further out (though not an outcast). As to their economic situation, Mary seems to have been the most comfortable, Frances marginal, and Janie closest to the edge, their degree of prosperity reflecting the working status of their husbands (skipper; fisherman/fishplant worker; invalid). Frances's husband was negligible in her reputation, whereas Mary's actively helped to foster his wife's; Janie's bore the brunt of her acerbic humour. The latter two husbands could not have been more different: Chester an active man in pursuit of a living (and with whom Mary seems to have had an unusually close relationship); Charles a backroom invalid (whom Janie apparently despised). All three women were hard-working and enterprising, with Frances (midwife/mortician/personal care provider) and Janie (barber/boarding-house keeper) in occupations that brought them into more than usual social contact, as did Mary Bell's teacup reading and virtual open house. All three were outspoken, sometimes to the point of aggression or offence; their words, even when benign, broke the bounds of ordinary discourse.

If these "portraits" I have presented were paintings, perhaps they would be cubist: fragmented planes of a subject showing many angles at once, but hardly realistic (and some would say distorted). I prefer to think of them as "found objects" rather than artful compositions, a bricolage of artifacts that singly and in juxtaposition can help us see the person behind the "witch's" façade and understand the construction of that identity.

Coda

The sense that menace can emanate from a person who is wishing one ill, rather than from circumstance or chance, is the quintessence of witch tradition. Although many witch dramas are coproductions between "victim" and "witch," the bewitched are the more important actors because a spell cannot go ahead unless they decide that they are suffering its effects. They are the ones who fulfill a witch's prediction; they are the ones who connect the dots in a series of events, drawing a line between discrete points to reveal a hidden picture of witching. Family or community members may help with this, even sceptics, because disagreement can elicit more tales. And narrative, above all, propagates witch lore. Social values and conditions (neighbourly aid, poverty, risk) must intersect with individual psychology to create witching incidents, but if no one tells of them, they will wither away. Storytelling is the only "craft" involved; the assembly of Newfoundland witches was no circle of crones dancing on a midnight beach but a process of social construction. People forged witches from moulds supplied by tradition but fit the product to their own ends.

Notes

INTRODUCTION

1 Colonial Records. Thanks to Ingeborg Marshall for this reference.
2 Lancre, *Tableau de l'Inconstance des mauvais Anges et Demons*, 91–5.
  The notorious lawyer Lancre noted (p.71) that some people fled to
  Newfoundland when they heard he was on his way from Bordeaux to
  persecute witches – a little-known reason for emigration.
3 Interview with Earle Mackay, Conception Bay, 31 March 1985.
4 Story, "Newfoundland," 33. In the House of Commons in 1793,
  Newfoundland was described as "a great ship moored near the Banks
  during the fishing season, for the convenience of English fishermen"
  (ibid., 13). In 1824 Britain grudgingly granted representational status
  but with minimal institutional apparatus.
5 Wilson, *Newfoundland and Its Missionaries*, 354.
6 According to Statistics Canada, Newfoundland and Labrador was the per
  capita leader of donations to registered charities in 1995 and 1996; it then
  lost its lead to Prince Edward Island, and in 2000 both provinces fell
  behind Nunavut (Canada, Statistics Canada, "The Daily," October 2000).
  That order held for highest median donation through 2006. In 2006
  the number of donors fell for all provinces and territories except
  Newfoundland and Labrador, which was also a leader in increased
  amounts of donations ("The Daily," November 2007).
7 Defede, *The Day the World Came to Town*, 5.
8 Thomas, *Religion and the Decline of Magic*, 661.
9 Both by Peggy Martin: "'Drop Dead': Witchcraft Images and Ambiguities
  in Newfoundland Society" (1977), and "Micmac Indians as Witches
  in the Newfoundland Tradition" (1979).

10 Rieti, *Strange Terrain: The Fairy World in Newfoundland.*

11 Demos, *Entertaining Satan*, viii.

12 Interview with Fred Earle in Lewisporte, 29 August 1991. There is more about Agnes in Part Two.

13 Cohn, *Europe's Inner Demons*, 259.

WITCHFUL THINKING

1 The case recalls a "beggar's curse" laid by a poor man in England in the year 606, when he asked some sailors for alms and was told, "We have nothing on board but stones." The man pronounced, "Let everything turn to stone then," and the ship's food was duly petrified. According to Kittredge, the tale entered the English chronicles and became a standard medieval exemplum (*Witchcraft in Old and New England*, 132). A student report confirmed Willy's reputation: "It is said that when someone goes to see him, they must give him a few dollars before leaving or he will put a curse or some kind of spell on that person and they will have trouble afterward" (66/12/FSC).

2 England, *The Greatest Hunt in the World*, 269.

3 Story, "Newfoundland," 22.

4 Representative government was gained in 1832, so this was a retrograde move to colonial status. It was taken because Newfoundland was not allowed to default on or defer debts, although larger countries were. Patrick O'Flaherty gives a detailed history in *Lost Country*, 404–5.

5 Interview with May and Douglas Nolan, Conception Bay (North Shore), 14 March 1985.

6 Interview with Enoch Riall, Port Antler, 28 August 1990. Also present was Martin Lovelace.

7 Interview with Martin Everly, Lewisporte, 23 August 1990. Also present was Martin Lovelace.

8 Interview with Jim Weller, St John's, 6 November 1991.

SEEING THE SEERS

1 The mill referred to was the sawmill established by the medical doctor, Wilfred Grenfell, along with a hospital and other projects that supplied work for people in the area.

2 Student essay submitted to Martin Lovelace, Winter 1984 (not deposited in MUNFLA).

3 Interview with Millicent and Ray Kelly, 22 September 1990. Also present were the late folklorists David Buchan and Reimund Kvideland; they had just examined my doctoral thesis and I took them to meet some of my informants.

4 *Dr. Chase's Almanac* of 1952, for instance, carried a sidebar in each issue that assigned meaning to various shapes of leaves in the cup (a dog is a faithful friend, a boat is a journey, and so on); a "Special Newfoundland Edition" printed in 1963 included "teacup reading tips" on every page. Chase's *The Mystic Palmist and Fortune Teller* of 1922 was an earlier offering. (Several editions of *Dr. Chase's Almanac* are in the Centre for Newfoundland Studies but I have not seen the *Mystic Palmist*, which is mentioned by Mercer in his *Newfoundland Songs and Ballads*, 35.) The distributor of the almanacs, the Doyle Company, had a huge influence on Newfoundland culture not only as the purveyor of patent medicines such as Dr. Chase's Nerve Food, called by one student "the paramount remedy for all nervous ills in the 1959 outport community of Fogwell" (66/24/FSC), but through its promotional media as well. The "Doyle Bulletin" was heard nightly on the radio for decades, carrying personal messages across the island; and the "Newfoundland Songbooks" (in four editions) were prized items.

5 Porter, *Below the Bridge*, 55–6. Interview in St John's, 26 January 2004 (for which I am very grateful).

6 Pocius, *A Place to Belong*, 184. Visiting patterns in this community were an important determinant in the placement and structure of houses (ibid., 178–96).

7 Rutherford, "Newfoundland Log Book," 25–6.

8 Conversation with the student following a talk on witches for Melissa Ladenheim's Folklore class, 26 February 1993.

9 Buchan, *Folk Tradition and Folk Medicine in Scotland*, 177.

10 Valenze, *Prophetic Sons and Daughters*, 271.

11 "How the Fish Came to Hant's Harbour Sixty Years Ago" was first printed in forty thousand tracts, according to the Reverend Charles Lench, a Methodist who republished it as a ten-cent tract in 1926. "Nothing that Dr Harvey published caused a greater sensation," he wrote. Non-literacy was no bar to hearing the story, for reading aloud was a regular pastime. An unattributed version appeared in "The Treasury of Newfoundland Stories," published by the distributors of Cream of the West flour in 1961 (edited by L.W. Janes and reproduced at the Newfoundland Grand Banks Genealogy Web site, ngb.chebucto.org). Kielly recycled it in 2005 in *Angels*

and Miracles, 61–6; she got it from Cranford and Janes, who give the background and the text of the prayer (128–9).

12 Wilson, *Newfoundland and Its Missionaries*, 276. According to Wilson, "the swearing, Sabbath-breaking, drinking, and general profanity, in the sealing-vessels are truly fearful."

13 Malinowski, *Magic, Science and Religion*, 30–1. Malinowski in fact promulgated the theory (in 1925) with reference to fishers in the Trobriand Islands, among whom lagoon fishing (easy, reliable) required no magic, whereas ocean fishing (dangerous, unpredictable) was full of it.

14 For the history and description of sealing, see Ryan's *Ice Hunters*.

15 Paper by Janna Drover submitted to Newfoundland Folklore, Winter 2006.

JINKERS AND MALE WITCHERY

1 Patterson, "Folk-Lore in Newfoundland," 214–15. Patterson also noted that boiling one's shot (ammunition) in water would cause an enemy's ill will to recoil upon him.

2 England, *Greatest Hunt*, 276.

3 Conversation with Bill Crummey, Western Bay, 7 October 2006. Also present was Kristian Crummey, who led our weekend field trip; thanks to them both.

4 *The Shortis Papers*, vol. 3, pt. 1.

5 Barbour, *Forty-Eight Days Adrift*, 5–7.

6 Ashton, "Hunters, Jinkers, Sealers and Squealers," 51.

7 Faris, *Cat Harbour*, 136.

8 Bovet, *Pandaemonium*, 51.

WITCHING AS EQUAL PARTICIPATION

1 Barbour, *Forty-Eight Days Adrift*, 7.

2 Murray's *More Than Fifty Percent* gives a detailed account of women's work in the traditional economy of Elliston, Bonavista Bay.

3 Neis, "Familial and Social Patriarchy," 43.

4 Harris, *Growing Up with Verse*, 18.

5 Cranford and Janes explain how the switch to a lottery system was made in Hant's Harbour after the rivalries of the old system engendered too much bad feeling (*Cod to Crab*, 30–3). Pocius describes the inception of the lottery system in a Southern Shore community in 1919, as well as some of the trickery that went on before it came into effect – keeping traps in the water all winter, setting them at night, and so on (*A Place to Belong*, 144–6).

6 Faris, *Cat Harbour*, 135.

7 Murray, *Fifty Percent*, 78.
8 Interview with Ellen Martin, Dorothy Wise, and Bob Martin, Nettle Cove, 21 August 1990. Also present was Martin Lovelace.
9 Davis, "'Shore Skippers and Grass Widows,'" 218.

THE VICTIM STRIKES BACK

1 According to this student, both fish hearts and "fish doctors" could be worn in a bag around the neck or carried in a pocket to alleviate rheumatism. Fish doctors are shrimplike orange crustacean parasites about an inch long that are found on injured cod. "The old timers say that the wound heals quickly if a doctor can get to it, whereas a fish with a similar serious wound and having no doctor will surely die." The doctors were also kept for good luck, especially in fishing, and they and the hearts could be stored away in bottles or boxes when not in use.
2 Interview with Paul and Susan Pinter, Chart Island, 25 August 1990.
3 Favret-Saada, *Deadly Words*, 115. She quotes an informant: "Every time he looked, I would say to myself: another misfortune is on the way."
4 McMillen, *Currents of Malice*.
5 Interviews with Flora and Pierce Parsons, 2 and 3 September 1992, in St John's. They live on the Northern Peninsula, where as a girl Flora knew Aggie Tackell. Also present was Martin Lovelace.
6 I examine the phallic associations of counterspells in "Guns and Bottles"; I looked at the counterattacks in a more general way in "Riddling the Witch."
7 Dundes, "Wet and Dry, the Evil Eye."
8 Tausiet, "Witchcraft as Metaphor," 191. Infanticide was at the centre of the trial involving the Parsons family of New England. The mother was convicted, while the father's apparent lack of grief was taken as a sign of witchcraft. Hall, *Witch-Hunting*, 29–60.
9 Roper, *Oedipus and the Devil*, 214.
10 Henningsen, "Witch Persecution," 130.
11 Conversation with Dr Shawn Flynn, St John's, 15 July 2006.
12 Among others, Owen Davies (*Witchcraft, Magic and Culture*, 41) mentions twenty-three-year-old John Bird of Dorset, who was tried in 1871 for beating eighty-five-year-old Charlotte Griffin for "hag-riding" him at night. Earlier in the 1800s, the *North Devon Journal* reported that an Appledore man cut a fourteen-year-old boy who he thought had "witched" his daughter into fits, then dragged him to his house to have the daughter cut him. Christie, "Folklore in North Devon," 139–54.
13 Demos, *Entertaining Satan*, 196.

INDIAN WITCHES

1 A short examination of this idea can be found in my paper "Aboriginal/ Anglo Relations."

2 Mi'kmaq entrepreneurs had travelled the eastern seaboard since the late 1700s to places as diverse as Philadelphia and Newfoundland, making goods on the spot and selling or bartering them door to door. See Upton, *Micmacs and Colonists*, 129. A Methodist missionary who met a group encamped near Bonavista in 1822 noted that "they had been in different parts of Newfoundland for a considerable time, and subsist partly by mendicity, and partly by making small trinkets which people purchase of them" (letter by John Walsh quoted in Winsor, *Hearts Strangely Warmed*, 79). The Anglican bishop Edward Feild wrote of fourteen or fifteen "swarthy Indians" who came to meet him and the new minister when he visited Burgeo in 1848, although he declined to talk with them: "They speak English imperfectly; and I did not hold much conversation with them as they are notorious beggars. They are, I believe, Micmas" (Feild, *Journal of the Bishop of Newfoundland's Voyage*, entry for 22 July). His disdain may have been due to the Mi'kmaqs' being Catholic; he did not like the Acadians at Sandy Point either. They "are of the most idle, loose, and dishonest habits," he wrote, and in the previous winter had "subsisted by begging and thieving" (Feild, *A Journal of a Visitation*, entry for 28 July).

3 For Beothuk history see Marshall, *A History and Ethnography of the Beothuk*; Howley, *The Beothucks or Red Indians*; Speck, *Beothuk and Micmac*; and Pastore, *Newfoundland Micmacs*. Although the death of Shanawdithit in 1829 marked the end of the Beothuk's distinct culture, oral tradition holds that there were Beothuk-Mi'kmaq marriages and children (Marshall, *History and Ethnography*, 156–7; Speck, *Beothuk and Micmac*). The European murder of Beothuk is well known, but there is some debate as to whether the Mi'kmaq killed them as well. Pastore (*Newfoundland Micmacs*) and Jackson ("On the Country," 33–42) suggest that this is a canard arising from white guilt about the Beothuks' demise. Marshall (*History and Ethnography*, 42–5, 154–6) acknowledges the Mi'kmaqs' contention that they never harmed the Beothuk, but she presents the case that they did, motivated in part by rewards from the French (who also supported their killing of the English).

4 Lench, "Life in an Outport," 4. Folklore interviews in central Newfoundland in the 1960s, housed in MUNFLA, contain many accounts of Europeans benefiting from Mi'kmaq healing.

5 Power, "The Micmacs," 1–3.

6 Millais, *Newfoundland*, 300.

7 MacGregor, *Report by the Governor*.

8 Jackson, "*On the Country*."

9 Ibid., 103–6.

10 See Anger, "Putting It Back Together." Self-image improved, too. Edwina Wetzel, a native of Conne River, told a 1993 Memorial University convocation assembly that in her experience, until the 1970s "people were ashamed to be identified as Micmac." See her "Address to Convocation."

11 Jackson, "*On the Country*," 160.

12 Ibid., 147.

13 McGee, "Ethnic Boundaries," 101. His sources are the Wallises and Bock; see next note.

14 The version with the refusal of water is in Bock, *The Micmac Indians*, 93. The Scots merchant and other legends of both fires are in Wallis and Wallis, *The Micmac Indians*, 476–80.

15 Bock, *The Micmac Indians*, 84.

16 Conversation with Gerald Penney, St John's, August 1994.

17 Ruth Holmes Whitehead discusses bones and power acquisition in *Stories from the Six Worlds*, 13.

18 Pattison, "Adult Education and Folklore," 25. Ralph Whitlock also describes the toadman's secret initiation with screaming floating bones in his *Wiltshire Folklore*, 96.

19 Hand et al., *Popular Beliefs*, vol. 2, 1,085.

20 Aubrey, *Three Prose Works*, 236–7.

21 Martin, "Micmac Indians as Witches in the Newfoundland Tradition." Ella Mary Leather describes the English fear of Gypsies in *The Folk-Lore of Herefordshire*, 51. Occasionally, Leather notes, the idea is reversed: "They can't put a spell on you if you *don't* buy anything from them" (emphasis mine).

22 When I first read this I thought that it might mean real Gypsies, but Dorothy Anger told me it probably did refer to the Mi'kmaq, as some of her informants used the term. Conversation with Dorothy Anger, April 1992.

23 With a tragic history of dispossession, the Nova Scotia Mi'kmaq were arguably worse off than those of Newfoundland. The government's "centralization" movement in the 1940s corralled them into reserves and burnt their former homes, at which point over half left Nova Scotia for good. Paul, *We Were Not the Savages*, 290. Paul has an interesting discussion of the importance of sharing in Mi'kmaq culture, and the scorn felt for those who do not (ibid., 40).

24 Interviews with Arnold Vallent and Laura Richards on the south coast, 11 November 1992 and 21 August 1992. Also present was Martin Lovelace.

25 Interview with Lydia and Gordon Sparkes, August 1990. Also present was Martin Lovelace.

26 Galgay and McCarthy, *Shipwrecks of Newfoundland and Labrador*, vol. 2, 89–98.

27 Conversation with Ronald Poole, St John's, June 2005. The subject arose when I learned that he was a retired CN employee, originally from the west coast, who has some Mi'kmaq ancestry. He had never heard the story (nor had he heard of Mi'kmaq curses) but subsequently got this information from a friend (in her thirties, not Mi'kmaq herself). She also told Ronald that the travelling Mi'kmaq sometimes sold medicine, which no one mentioned to me.

MAGICAL JERSEYMEN

1 Chappell, *Voyage*, 110. Thanks to archaeologist Marianne Stopp for unearthing this reference.

2 The bishop deplored the clause in the Jerseyans' contracts requiring them to work on Sundays if necessary. Lacking religious services, he said, that day was spent in "worse than idleness" with activities such as singing and dancing. Feild, *Journal of the Bishop of Newfoundland's Voyage*, entry for 29 July; on the Web at the Project Canterbury Web site *http://justus.anglican.org*.

3 Ommer, *From Outpost to Outport*, 30, and "The Cod Trade," 262.

4 Ebbitt Cutler, in the preface to England, *Greatest Hunt*, 10.

5 Ommer, *From Outpost to Outport*, 19; Le Messurier, *Old-Time Newfoundland*, 7.

6 "Legends in Upper Island Cove," student paper submitted to Martin Lovelace, Winter 1984. An English would-be cabbage thief was similarly affixed (Leather, *The Folk-Lore of Herefordshire*, 60).

7 Planetta, "Sorcery Beliefs," chapters 3 and 4. If people were ready to believe anything of the *Jersais*, Planetta suggests, it was partly because their English language and Anglican religion were "seen as deviant characteristics" among the French-speaking Catholics of the area.

8 Chiasson, *Chéticamp*, 72–3.

9 Lovelace, "Merchantable Magic," 47.

10 English, "The Jersey Men," 17–20.

11 Ommer, *From Outpost to Outport*, 30–2.

12 Jean, *Jersey Sailing Ships*, 44. No source but "folklore" is given for the item. I hoped to find in this book a clue to the "cabble," but none of the names

of boat types sound like that, at least in English; Jersey-built boats included barques, barquentines, brigs, brigantines, schooners (three-masted and topsail), ketches, and cutters. The riggings also had names, and Jean notes that the rig of a "Chasse maree" was unique to the Channel Islands (ibid., 74).

13 Literary versions are discussed by Purkhardt, *La chasse-galerie*. The best known was probably LeRossignol's *The Flying Canoe (La Chasse-Galerie)*, published in 1929 by McClelland and Stewart, discussed in Purkhardt, pp. 11–36. Another version, "The Witch Canoe," can be found in Aubry, *The Magic Fiddler*, 59–69. Celtic saints also whizzed about on things like wicker boats or millstones (Borlase, *The Age of Saints*).

14 He was taken to a place where there were "a lot of people" but he refused to eat the proffered food and was returned after four or five days aboard the birch rind.

15 Crowley, "The Fairyman of Chapel's Cove," submitted to my Newfoundland Folklore class, Winter 2006, deposited in MUNFLA.

16 MacCulloch, *Guernsey Folk Lore*, 297, 338, 357, 368, 332; Marie DeGaris, *Folklore of Guernsey*, 268–9. The tradition is memorialized in "witch's steps" on houses – exterior stone fireplace supports said to be launching pads (Dewar, *Witchcraft*, 9) or resting places to prevent them from going down the chimney to rest inside (Lemprière, *Buildings and Memorials*, 166).

17 Hunt, *Popular Romances*, 88.

18 Henderson and Cowan, *Scottish Fairy Belief*, 37. John Aubrey had some letters from Scotland in 1695 concerning a man who was instantly trans-ported with the fairies to the wine cellars of the king of France when he repeated their cry of "Horse and hattock!" (Henderson and Cowan, *Scottish Fairy Belief*, 38; also in Aubrey, *Three Prose Works*, 95).

19 Watson, *Somerset Life*, 67.

20 Owen Davies notes that household conveyances feature more in nineteenth-century lore than in earlier trial records (*Witchcraft*, 188). Their antiquity on the Continent is shown by the 1539 confession (extracted by torture) of a Geneva woman that the devil gave her a white stick so that she could travel to gatherings by rubbing it with grease and saying, "White stick, black stick, carry me where you should; go, in the Devil's name, go!" (Monter, *Witchcraft in France and S witzerland*, 57.)

21 The 1617 trial of three Guernsey witches shows how secondary all the demonic trappings were to "ordinary" witching. At first the accused women confessed to the usual injury of people and animals, but when tortured (as was not allowed in England) they produced the full panoply

of aerial travel to the *sabbat*, copulation with the devil, and so on. Levack, "The Confessions," 184–9.

22 L'Amy, *Jersey Folk Lore*, 72–3; Pitts, *Witchcraft and Devil Lore*. Dewar (*Witchcraft*, 6–7) notes that not only were there were more trials, there were *many* more when the bailiff was a Jerseyman.

23 Norton, *In the Devil's Snare*, 140–6; 173. English's wife, a wealthy heiress, was also accused, as her mother once had been (ibid., 137).

24 Sullivan, *Newfoundland*, 11–12. Located in the Centre for Newfoundland Studies, photocopied from a document in the British Museum. Quoted passage credited to the *Gazette de l'Isle de Jersey*, 18 November 1786.

25 English, "The Jersey Men," 17.

THE BLACK HEART BOOK

1 Roger Knox (d. 1892) of Houlton, Maine, near the New Brunswick border, was a famous demon-possessed trickster described by Roger E. Mitchell in "George Knox: From Man to Legend." Knox did tricks, produced illusions, cut unnatural quantities of wood, and drew liquor from trees; he owned a book (interestingly named by one informant as the Black Panther book) but only rarely did he curse something (ibid., 22–3; 38–49).

2 Desplanques, "Women, Folklore and Communication," 165.

3 The alphabet book was reproduced in a display mounted in 2005 and still there in 2007, at the Memorial University Education building; the illustration is a woodblock-print heart motif.

4 Christiansen, *The Migratory Legends*, 28–35; Anderson, *Fairytale*, 103–5. "Raising spirits through reading black book" is G297 in Baughman, *Type and Motif-Index of the Folktales of England and North America*, 281; "Black book in the hands of the uninitiated" is D81 in Jauhiainen, *The Type and Motif Index of Finnish Belief Legends and Memorates*, 137. Further analogues may be found in Thompson, *Motif-Index of Folk-Literature*, and Hand et al., *Popular Beliefs and Superstitions*, vol 2.

5 The magician Jack of Kent chanted, "Nobble, stick, nobble, play, fiddle, play," and the corn would thresh itself while he played. He had a little black stick with a fly inside that was really an imp (Leather, *Folk-Lore of Herefordshire* 165). Leather also mentions a charmer who had a black stick with which he could "do anything," for example, make chickens jump onto the table (ibid., 60).

6 An account of "the black stick men" in the same area appears in Lannon and McCarthy, *Fables*, 47–9. One student described a charmer as "this man what was called a black stick" (69/102). An English woman was "held

NOTES TO PAGES 66–7

responsible for using the black stick and foretelling the future." Knott, *Witches of Dorset*, 40.

7 Aspiring sorcerers had been consulting magical manuscripts at least since medieval times (Kittredge, *Witchcraft*, 38, 58, 65, 80–3, 187, 207–9, 228) but by the 1600s everyman could find books of tricks and spells. The best-known prototype is Reginald Scot's *Discoverie of Witchcraft* (1584), which illustrated the mechanics of various illusions as part of an effort to discredit the idea of witchcraft. The strategy backfired, for *Discoverie* was reprinted and imitated well into the 1800s with titles like *The Art of Conjuring; or, Legerdemain made Easy, Exhibiting the Manner of Performing all the Ingenious and Remarkable Tricks of the Most Celebrated Masters in the Black Art* (c. 1815). These titles crossbred with books of "occult" spells, resulting in publications like *The New Conjuror's Museum and Magical Magazine* of 1803, with its sections on legerdemain, astrology, dream interpretation, apparitions, and witchcraft. See Trevor Hall, *Old Conjuring Books*, 206, 196. A bibliographic history of the *grimoire*, or book of black magic, may be found in Summers, *A Popular History of Witchcraft*, 77–98.

8 Weiss, *A Book about Chapbooks*, 105.

9 Jantz, "German Thought and Literature," 15.

10 Mitchell, *George Knox*, 38.

11 Here I must sound like one of my informants when I say that I have not actually seen Dr Earle's book but only read about it on the Internet where it is referenced on many UFO-related Web sites because of the Ohio incident.

12 For a history of this item, see Brown, "The Long Hidden Friend," 89–152; and Yoder, "Hohman and Romanus," 235–48. The Lucky Mojo Curio Company of California Web site gives some good background on what they call Hohman's "cross-over hit," including its popularity in African-American culture; although they offered it for sale it was always sold out when I checked, so I have not seen it myself.

13 I am grateful to Jim Overton for sending me copies of this remarkable correspondence. The investigating ranger (who carried the booklet with him) found the letter-writer away from home but was able to determine from conversations with others (including the local doctor) that the man was not quite normal.

14 The "black psalm" might have been Psalm 109, called "The Cursing Psalm" as recited in parody by an unjustly condemned sailor in 1707, resulting in shipwreck (Brown, *Phantoms, Legends, Customs*, 173), or Psalm 69, verses 20 to 28, which according to Ralph Whitlock ("Fast and Furious") was read in some English churches on Ash Wednesday, which became known

as "Cussing Day" because the "Amen" pronounced by the congregation after each verse was an opportunity for "cussing your neighbor."

15 Ferguson, "The Book of Black Hearts," 107–21. I thank Mark for the loan of his field recording and permission to quote from it here.

16 The Labrador Inuit shamans, or *angakut*, who could be men or women, operated into the twentieth century. The Moravian minister F.W. Peacock described a generalized "séance" held in a semidarkened house, with strange noises interpreted by the *angakok* for the audience, along with a prognosis for the hunt; Peacock, *Labrador Inuit Lore*, 39–40. It is uncertain how long Sedna, the sea goddess, survived in oral tradition. The (German) Moravian missionaries arrived early in Labrador with replacement deities, but they didn't erase the language, so even when Sedna disappeared in name, associated stories and motifs remained. A forty-nine-year-old Labrador artist who made a painting of Sedna in 1996 had a grandfather who was a shaman, although it is not clear whether her inspiration came from him or wider Inuit tradition (*First: Aboriginal Artists of Newfoundland and Labrador*, 146). A good account of the Mother of the Sea (and at least ten of her names) is given by Peter Irnig, the commissioner of Nunavut whose seal hunter father was a shaman who would have to make peace with Nuliajuk if she was angry and withholding seals (in Irnig's foreword to Pelly, *Sacred Hunt*, ix). The pages of the Book of Black Hearts also recall Upton's description (*Micmacs and Colonists*, 12) of the bark kept in the medicine bags of some Mi'kmaq *buoin*, which were decorated with pictures of children, bears, beavers, moose, wolverine, and other creatures. When I described the story to the anthropologist Adrian Tanner, he said it reminded him of "scrying" among the Cree hunters of Quebec, which could involve foretelling the future by staring into a bowl of water or mirror: personal communication, June 2005; see chapter 6, "Rites of Hunting Divination," in Tanner's *Bringing Home Animals*. The self-boiling kettle in the Labrador woman's house is reminiscent of a boiling kettle of seals that a central Inuit *angakok* once had to get past in order to visit Sedna; Boas, *The Central Eskimo*, 179.

17 Millais, *Untrodden Ways*, 48. The guides were not Mi'kmaq but there may have been native influence, for "hunting dreams were almost a necessity of life," according to Upton (*Micmacs and Colonists*, 11).

RELIGION

1 Wilson, *Newfoundland and Its Missionaries*, 144–6.
2 Ibid., 217.

3 The letter in which Wilson defends himself is published on the Internet by David Pike at *www.mun.ca.math~da.pike*. The originals (Pike notes) are held by the Methodist Missionary Society in London, England, with copies in the United Church Archives in Toronto, location #87.225c.

4 Devine, *Good Old Days*, 72–3.

5 A precedent was set when Bishop Carfagnini, an Italian, cursed the town of Harbour Grace in 1880. Rollman, "A Tale of Two Bishops"; Lannon and McCarthy, *Fables*, 57–9.

6 Interview with Margaret Flight, St John's, 26 August 2005. She has no doubt that the priest really said that.

7 Martin Lovelace analyzed some of these legends as part of a proposed project to investigate the social roots of the widespread abuse of children by priests and brothers that was revealed in the 1990s. He observed that many of the stories involve being struck dumb or paralyzed for having defied a priest – much like the social paralysis that struck officialdom when the allegations first came out (personal communication, unpublished project research).

8 Letter to the Society for the Propagation of the Gospel in London. A copy of this document was sent to Martin Lovelace by Edward-Vincent Chafe of Gull Island in Conception Bay. I have not seen the original.

9 Mrs Maloney and Mrs Hayes were interviewed in Bay Bulls, August 1991, and Frances Kavanagh in Clarke's Beach, 1 August 1990. They are all profiled in my book, *Strange Terrain*.

10 Fitzhenry, "The Widow's Curse" (the author says he heard the tale as a boy); Lannon and McCarthy, *Fables*, 54–6.

11 Ó Súilleabháin, *A Handbook of Irish Folklore*, 388, 417–18. The woman might let down her hair and kneel, for instance, as she gives utterance.

12 Cadigan, "Economic and Social Relations," 197.

13 Ibid., *Hope and Deception*, 67.

14 Quoted in Macfarlane, *Witchcraft*, 196.

15 Wix, *Six Months*, 81, 53, 136, 147. No admirer of outport women, Wix pontificated, "I met with more feminine delicacy, I must own, in the wig-wams of the Micmac and Conokok Indians than in the tilts of many of our own people" (ibid., 173). At Isle of Valen in Placentia Bay, he observed that "some married females in one house were literally almost in a state of nudity," but he was later confirmed in his suspicion that their poverty and "manifest want of cleanliness" were due to "mismanagement" (ibid., 53).

16 Winsor, *Building on a Firm Foundation*. The minister at Brigus in 1832 complained there were "none but females" to carry out prayer meetings (ibid., 13).

17 Newfoundland exerted a reciprocal influence on European Methodism, for one of Coughlan's converts helped introduce Wesleyanism to Jersey, and it was the Anglican church's refusal in 1780 to ordain John Hoskins of Trinity that led Wesley to conduct his own ordinations and to recommend that the overseas posts do the same. Rollman, "John Wesley."

18 Wesley, *Works*, 135.

19 Quoted in Ankarloo and Clark, eds., *Witchcraft*, 239.

20 Winsor, *Hearts Strangely Warmed*, 6.

21 "The Methodists' fixation upon the demonic became notorious," according to Roy Porter, *The Athlone History of Witchcraft and Magic*, 240. Also making the point are St Leger-Gordon, *Witchcraft and Folklore of Dartmoor*, 132; and Tongue, "Some Notes on Modern Somerset Witch-Lore," 321–5. R. Trevor Davies discusses the possible vitalising effects of Wesley's "robust credulity" on West Country tradition in *Four Centuries*, 190–8, and includes some West Country newspaper accounts from the late 1800s.

22 Owen Davies, "Methodism, the Clergy, and the Popular Belief," 252–66; and *Witchcraft, Magic and Culture*.

23 Valenze, *Prophetic Sons and Daughters*, 138.

24 Wesley was not the first clerical fan of witch tales, he just hung on longer than most. Joseph Glanvil (*Sadducismus Triumphatus*, 213) made the same complaint in the early sixteenth century with a stout defence of oral tradition: "I know it is a Matter of very little Credit to be a Relator of Stories … But of all Relations of Fact, there are none like to give a Man such Trouble and Disreputation, as those that related to Witchcraft and Apparitions, which so great a Party of Men (in this Age especially) do so rally and laugh at, and without more ado, are resolved to explode and despise, as meer Winter Tales and old Wives Fables; such they will call and account them, be their Truth and Evidence what it will." Notice how an idea discarded (or perceived to be discarded) by elite men is reassigned to women, as in Wesley's complaint that "the English in general, and indeed, most of the men of learning in Europe, have given up all accounts of witches and apparitions as mere old wives' fables. I am sorry for it" (Wesley, *Works*, 135). Another zealous West Country compiler of witch tales was Richard Bovet, whose *Pandaemonium* of 1684 includes some interesting parallels to Newfoundland tradition.

25 Wilson, *Newfoundland and Its Missionaries*, 359.

26 Winsor, *Resounding God's Praises*, 112.

27 Barrett, "Revivalism," 33.

28 Murray, *More Than 50 Percent*, 145–6. The name change was instigated in the early 1900s by the Methodist minister Charles Lench to commemorate the first visit by an Irish Methodist missionary named Ellis in 1814.

29 Interview with Naboth Winsor in Wesleyville, 21 August 1990. Also present was Martin Lovelace.

30 Conversation with Fred and Stella Kirby, 20 August 1990. Also present was Martin Lovelace.

31 Gough, *David Blackwood*, 7.

HAGRIDDEN BARRENVILLE

1 Interviewed in Barrenville, 23 October 1992.

2 First interviewed in Barrenville, 16 July 1992.

3 The late Fred Earle (his real name) was one of the first folklore field researchers in Newfoundland; as liaison for the Memorial University extension service, he toured with the folklorist John Widdowson in central Newfoundland in 1966 and made some of the earliest records of witch lore. I interviewed him in Lewisporte, August 1990. Also present was Martin Lovelace.

4 Interview with Frank and Hannah Tibbert in Barrenville, 7 December 1993.

5 Interview with Charlie Harper (b. 1931) in Barrenville, 17 July 1992. Also present was Gill Williams.

6 I was introduced to Philomena by June Roberts, a neighbour of mine, and interviewed her in St John's, 23 October 1998.

7 Willis, *Malevolent Nurture*, 6–14.

8 Interview with Lorna and Howard Snowdon in Barrenville, 16 July 1992.

9 I first met the Heywoods in October 1992, when I made the tape recording quoted here. But I have stayed in touch with them and heard the stories several more times over the years (December 1994, January 1999, July 2006), as have Martin Lovelace and the folklorist Mark Ferguson. The version with "you dirt!" was given to Ferguson; there is probably a difference in the way men talk to other men about witches that could benefit from male investigation.

10 Ann Williams vaguely recalls something about the brother finding Sarah "coiled up like a puppy," the idea being that she was in a trance.

11 Witchcraft was often thought of as hereditary along the female line in West Country England, and as Janet A. Thompson notes, an accused man was usually related to a woman who had already been accused; see *Wives, Widows, Witches & Bitches*, 109.

12 Three Newfoundland-based studies include international comparisons: Ness, "The Old Hag Phenomenon"; Hufford, *The Terror That Comes in the Night*; and Firestone, "The 'Old Hag.'"

13 To cite just one example, nocturnal "pressing" witches were the main defendants in sixteenth-century Hungarian witch trials, and the Hungarian term for witches comes from the experience; see Klaniczay, "Hungary: The Accusations." In Dorset, being "hagrod" (their term too) was so directly equated with bewitchment that it needn't include a nightmare attack at all. See Lea, "Wessex Witches."

14 The foot-to-neck ascent is a common physical progression; a fictionalized version from Japan can be found in the short story "Sleep," by Haruki Murakami.

15 Coxhead, *Legends of Devon*, 135.

16 Richard Coman, for instance, testified that he woke one night to see Bridget Bishop and two other women enter the room; she sat on his chest so that he "could not speak nor stir." Five others with whom she quarrelled were similarly afflicted. Gragg, *The Salem Witch Crisis*, 93. For more examples see Rosenthal, *Salem Story*, 96–9. Mary Beth Norton (*In the Devil's Snare*, 213–16) notes that some judges did have qualms about spectral evidence, their argument being that Satan or demons could assume the shape of an innocent person.

17 Ness, "*The Old Hag Phenomenon*," 17.

18 Firestone, "'*The Old Hag*,'" 58.

19 Thomas, *Religion and the Decline of Magic*, 669.

20 Larner, *Witchcraft and Religion*, 86.

21 Davies, "Hag-riding," 36.

22 Interview with Cecil and Agnes Sheldon (the parents of Mary Witford, quoted below and present at the interview), Barrenville, 6 December 1993. It was not clear whether the victim was a man or woman.

23 McPhee, *Stop Sleeping through Your Dreams*, 155–7.

24 Hufford, *The Terror*, 3–6.

25 Several more in the class knew people who had had the experience or had even had it themselves. All but one of the essays have been deposited in MUNFLA with 2007 accession numbers.

26 Essay submitted to my introductory Folklore class, Fall 1994. I should note that I did not teach during the twelve years between the two classes mentioned here.

27 Thomas, *Religion and the Decline of Magic*, 673.

28 Macfarlane, *Witchcraft*, 150–5; 205–6. As evidence that poverty alone cannot explain witch persecutions, he notes that there is no correlation

between the poorest areas of England and the rate of accusations (ibid., 155).

29 Thomas, *Religion and the Decline of Magic*, 662, 673–4.

30 Gibson, *Reading Witchcraft*, 81, 92. Malcolm Gaskill makes the related point that witnesses in witch trials were storytellers who consciously or unconsciously shaped their testimony "according to fictive motifs." See his "Witches and Witnesses," 58. There are some good examples of "apparitions" (hags) in this article, and a discussion of "spectral evidence."

31 Gibson, *Reading Witchcraft*, 84.

32 Briggs, *Witches and Neighbours*, chapter 4.

33 Passin, "Sorcery," 11–15.

34 Interview with John Kane (b. 1942), Barrenville, 19 August 1992.

35 Interview with George Bradwell, Barrenville, 19 August 1992. Also present was Gill Williams, who introduced me to him.

36 Once I noticed this pattern I began to see it everywhere. A Devon man who was usually liberal with money to a witch got fed up and refused; he was cursed and died within weeks. Karkeet, "A Budget of Witch Stories," 388.

37 Dalton's *The Country Justice*, quoted in R. Davies, *Four Centuries of Witch-Beliefs*, 106; and Bernard's *Guide to Grand-Jury Men*, quoted in Macfarlane, *Witchcraft*, 172. Macfarlane adds that a gift from the witch could also lead to bewitchment, as by an Essex suspect who was notorious for giving children gifts of apples or bread or complimenting or kissing them, which gestures were always followed by disaster. Mrs Burge's restless pacing was like that of a New England witch who arrived at a victim's home where a bottle was locked in a cupboard and "did not seace walking to and fro, about the House" until it was uncorked. Cotton Mather explained that "in undertaking the Traditional Experiment of Botteling Urine, the Urine must be bottled with Nails and Pinns, and such Instruments in it as carry a Shew of Torture with them, if it is to attain its end." Both quoted in Godbeer, *The Devil's Dominion*, 44–6. Ralph Merrifield (*The Archaeology of Ritual*, 163–75) thinks that the witch-bottle began in England with the sixteenth-century bellarmine, or "greybeard," jugs, which bore human faces; they have been dug up in numerous areas (especially East Anglia) and contained pins, cut-out cloth hearts, and traces of what was probably urine. Today, specimen bellarmine jugs (as well as reproductions for purchase) can be found at the Ferryland archaeological dig on the Southern Shore of Newfoundland.

38 Quoted in Kors and Peters, *Witchcraft in Europe*, 361.

39 One wore pants, for example, and rowed her own boat, the informant's daughter told me. She was an acquaintance of mine whom I approached

about possible contacts before I went to Egg Cove; but her father assured her that everyone who knew anything about it was dead.

40 Lamb, "Ask the Doctor," *Evening Telegram* (St John's), 14 June 1993, 15.

41 Interview with Jane Barnes, St John's, 6 December 1994.

42 Conversation with June Roberts, St John's, 27 February 2005. It was Mrs Barnes who introduced me to Philomena Abbinott.

43 Interview with George Bradwell, Barrenville, 19 August 1992.

44 Kors and Peters, *Witchcraft in Europe*, 367–8.

45 Ivanits, *Russian Folk Belief*. The best defence was not only to invite the sorcerer but give him a place of honour, thus enlisting his aid against rival sorcerers (ibid., 105).

46 Wilfred Grenfell (*Labrador Days*, 105) wrote of a Labrador wedding, "Everyone from far and near was present, quite without the formality of an invitation. It would, indeed, be an ill omen for the future if anyone were omitted through the miscarriage of an invitation."

47 Interview with Harry Addams, Barrenville, 17 July 1992. Also present was Gill Williams.

48 I heard about Prudence not from Harry but from John Kane (19 August 1992).

49 Animals could be witches in their own right, according to the famous navigator Bob Bartlett (*The Log of "Bob" Bartlett*," 111). He relates the story of a man who threw a black cat overboard on a voyage out of Brigus because he thought it was a witch causing bad weather. "Come back to haunt me!" he shouted when he pulled the body up in a net. "That summer Tom died and all hands swear to this day it was the cat's revenge." Another instance was cited by James Murphy (*Customs of the Past in Newfoundland*, n.p.), concerning a long-bedridden man who saw a deer run into one side of his house and out through the other. "It was said that the deer was the witch come to take the spirit out of the man."

50 The story was told by a nephew of the afflicted woman in an essay submitted to Elke Dettmer's Folklore class, Winter 1994. Thanks to Elke for showing it to me.

51 Paper submitted to Melissa Ladenheim's Folklore class, Winter 1990. Thanks to Melissa for showing it to me.

52 A Seattle shopping mall, for instance, posted a thirteen-point code of conduct that prohibited "unnecessary staring" (giving one to wonder what would constitute necessary staring). *The Globe and Mail* (Toronto), 13 December 1999, A16. The same article cites university studies documenting the common belief (among more than ninety percent of university

students, in one case) that a person can sense an unseen person staring at them.

FRANCES LONG (1914–1995)

1 Interview, 28 August 1991.
2 Interview with Delores Petty, Ember Cove, 11 November 1992. Also present was Martin Lovelace.
3 Conversation with Daryl Hanes, 26 February 1993, following a guest lecture to Melissa Ladenheim's introductory Folklore class.
4 Essay by Tessa Long, submitted to Elke Dettmer's introductory Folklore course December 1994. Elke put Tessa in touch with me (not knowing of the Frances connection) and we exchanged papers and comments.
5 Laura said that she learned the hard way not to take the word of younger relations but to consult older people directly. Several years ago, she was hired by a government agency to assess interest in a seniors' housing project. In a few instances, she accepted the assurance of younger family members that older relatives living with them – or with whom they lived – would not be interested. Later some of these old people told her that they would love a place of their own. The fact is that some households depend on the seniors' pension checks. I am not suggesting that this was the case with Frances, only that there can be issues of finance and control in multi-generational households.
6 Jones, *Why Faith Healing?*, 17–19.
7 McNaughton, "The Role of the Newfoundland Midwife," 287; 265; 250–1 and personal communication. Nor was there any connection in New England, according to Demos, *Entertaining Satan*, 80.
8 Faris, *Cat Harbour*, 136.

MARY BELL AND HER DAUGHTER RACHEL

1 Conversation with Lydia Sparkes, a native of Lantern Cove (not exactly a landlady but proprietor of a bed-and-breakfast place where I stayed); also present was Martin Lovelace. Interview with Ruth Bird on Lone Island, 30 August 1991.
2 Jennifer doesn't name Mary Bell or Rachel, but Jason does – and since they both have one informant in common (as noted, Jennifer's aunt is Jason's mother) who talks about the same women, the identity is clear.
3 Newfoundland Folklore, Winter 2006 (not deposited in MUNFLA).

4 Karlsen, *The Devil in the Shape of a Woman*, 84–116.

5 I discovered this process of deposition when buying a house near St John's in 1986. There was no dispute as to ownership, but in order to prepare the deed to present standards, the lawyer required interviews from area residents that amounted to an oral history of the property.

6 Kennedy, *History and Folklore*, 57–8.

7 Keough, "The 'Old Hag,'" 13.

8 After a guest lecture I gave to a folklore class, Kristian told me that the land is still considered an unlucky site. We did our interviews on 7–8 October 2006, with George Slade and the late Bill Kennedy. I am much indebted to Kristian and her uncle, Bill Crummey.

JANIE SMITH (C. 1890–1960)

1 For an ethnography of male working relationships on the Northern Peninsula see Firestone, *Brothers and Rivals*.

2 Helen Porter gave me this version: "Old Mother Witch couldn't sew a stitch / picked up a penny and thought she was rich." She added, "Witches, I would say, would be assumed to be bad housekeepers: not being able to sew would be "very demeaning, because all women were supposed to be able to sew, whether anyone taught them or not." Interviewed in St John's, 26 January 2004.

3 Telephone conversation, 14 March 2006; interview in Paradise, April 2006.

Bibliography

Anderson, Graham. *Fairytale in the Ancient World.* London and New York: Routledge, 2000.

Anger, Dorothy. "Putting It Back Together: Micmac Political Identity in Newfoundland." MA thesis, St John's: Memorial University of Newfoundland, 1983.

Ankarloo, Bengt, and Stuart Clark, eds. *Witchcraft and Magic in Europe: The Eighteenth and Nineteenth Centuries.* Philadelphia, PA: University of Pennsylvania Press, 1999.

Ashton, John. "Hunters, Jinkers, Sealers and Squealers: Cultural Values and Local Songmaking in Newfoundland." In *Bean Blossom to Bannerman, Odyssey of a Folklorist: A Festschrift for Neil V. Rosenberg,* edited by Martin Lovelace, Peter Narvàez, and Diane Tye, 41–54. St John's, NF: Memorial University of Newfoundland Folklore and Language Publications, 2005.

Aubrey, John. *Three Prose Works.* Edited by John Buchanan-Brown. Carbondale, IL: Southern Illinois University Press, 1972.

Aubry, Claude. *The Magic Fiddler and Other Legends of French Canada.* Translated by Alice E. Kane. Toronto, ON: Peter Martin, 1968.

Barbour, Job. *Forty-Eight Days Adrift: The Voyage of the "Neptune II" from Newfoundland to Scotland.* 1932. St John's, NF: Breakwater, 1981.

Barrett, S. Dawn. "Revivalism and the Origins of Newfoundland Methodism: 1766–1774." MA thesis, St John's, Memorial University of Newfoundland, 1993.

Bartlett, Robert A. *The Log of "Bob" Bartlett: The True Story of Forty Years of Seafaring and Exploration.* New York, NY: Blue Ribbon Books, 1928.

Baughman, Ernest W. *Type and Motif-Index of the Folktales of England and North America.* The Hague: Mouton, 1966.

Boas, Franz. *The Central Eskimo*. 1888. Lincoln, NE: University of Nebraska Press, 1964.

Bock, Philip K. *The Micmac Indians of Restigouche: History and Contemporary Description*. Ottawa, ON: National Museum of Canada, 1966.

Borlase, William Copeland. *The Age of the Saints: A Monograph of Early Christianity in Cornwall with the Legends of the Cornish Saints*. Truro, UK: Joseph Pollard, 1895.

Bovet, Richard. *Pandaemonium, or the Devil's Cloyster*. 1684. Aldington, Kent, UK: Hand and Flower Press, 1951.

Bradwell, Stephen. "Mary Glovers Late Woeful Case." Reproduced in *Witchcraft and Hysteria in Elizabethan London: Edward Jordan and the Mary Glover Case*, edited by Michael MacDonald, 3–25. London and New York: Tavistock/Routledge, 1991.

Briggs, Robin. *Witches and Neighbours: The Social and Cultural Context of European Witchcraft*. London, UK: HarperCollins, 1996.

Brown, Carleton F. "The Long Hidden Friend." *Journal of American Folklore* 17 (1904):89–152.

Brown, Raymond Lamont. *Phantoms, Legends, Customs and Superstitions of the Sea*. London, UK: Patrick Stephens, 1972.

Buchan, David, ed. *Folk Tradition and Folk Medicine in Scotland: The Writings of David Rorie*. Edinburgh, UK: Canongate Academic, 1994.

Cadigan, Sean T. "Economic and Social Relations of Production on the Northeast-Coast of Newfoundland, with Special Reference to Conception Bay, 1785–1855." PhD thesis, St John's, Memorial University of Newfoundland, 1991.

– *Hope and Deception in Conception Bay: Merchant-Settler Relations in Newfoundland, 1785–1855*. Toronto, ON: University of Toronto Press, 1995.

Canada. Statistics Canada. "The Daily," 23/11/06;1/11/05;4/11/04; 24/10/2000; 25/11/99. Online at *www.statcan.ca*.

Chappell, Edward. *Voyage of His Majesty's Ship Rosamund to Newfoundland and the South Coast of Labrador*. London, UK: J. Mawman, 1818.

Chiasson, Anselme. *Chéticamp: Histoire et Traditions Acadiennes*. Moncton, NB: Editions des Aboiteaux, 1972.

Christiansen, Reidar Th. *The Migratory Legends*. Folklore Fellows Communications No. 239. Helsinki: Academia Scientiarum Fennica, 1958.

Christie, Peter. "Folklore in North Devon." *Transactions of the Devonshire Association* 128 (1996):139–54.

Colonial Records (CO 194, vol.8, p.228) in the Centre for Newfoundland Studies, St John's, Memorial University of Newfoundland.

Cohn, Norman. *Europe's Inner Demons: An Enquiry Inspired by the Great Witch-Hunt*. New York, NY: Basic Books, 1975.

Coxhead, J.R.W. *Legends of Devon*. Bideford, North Devon, UK: The Western Press, 1954.

Cranford, Garry, and Ed Janes. *From Cod To Crab: Stories and History of Hant's Harbour*. St John's, NF: Flanker Press, 1995.

Davies, Owen. "Hag-riding in Nineteenth-Century West Country England and Modern Newfoundland: An Examination of an Experience-centred Witchcraft Tradition." *Folk-Life* 35 (1996–97):36–53.

– "Methodism, the Clergy, and the Popular Belief in Witchcraft and Magic." *History* 266 (1997):252–66.

– *Witchcraft, Magic and Culture*. Manchester, UK: Manchester University Press, 1999.

Davies, R. Trevor. *Four Centuries of Witch-Beliefs: with Special Reference to the Great Rebellion*. 1947. New York, NY: Benjamin Blom, 1972.

Davis, Dona Lee. "'Shore Skippers and Grass Widows': Active and Passive Women's Roles in a Newfoundland Fishery." In *To Work and To Weep: Women in Fishing Economies*, edited by J.N. Klein and D.L. Davis, 211–29. St John's, NY: ISER Books, 1988.

Defede, Jim. *The Day the World Came to Town: 9/11 in Gander, Newfoundland*. New York, NY: ReganBooks/HarperCollins, 2002.

DeGaris, Marie. *Folklore of Guernsey*. St Pierre du Bois, Guernsey: The Guernsey Press, 1975.

Demos, John Putnam. *Entertaining Satan: Witchcraft and the Culture of Early New England*. Oxford, UK: Oxford University Press, 1982.

Desplanques, Marie-Annick. "Women, Folklore and Communication in Informal Social Gatherings in a Franco-Newfoundland Context." PhD thesis, St John's, Memorial University of Newfoundland, 1991.

Devine, P.K. *In the Good Old Days! Fishery Customs of the Past*. [ca. 1915]. St John's, NF: Harry Cuff, 1990.

Dewar, Stephen. *Witchcraft and the Evil Eye in Guernsey*. St Peter Port, Guernsey: The Toucan Press, 1970.

Dundes, Alan. "Wet and Dry, the Evil Eye: An Essay in Indo-European and Semitic Worldview." In *The Evil Eye: A Folklore Casebook*, edited by Alan Dundes, 257–312. New York and London: Garland, 1981.

England, George Allan. *The Greatest Hunt in the World*. [Published as *Vikings of the Ice*, 1925]. Montreal, QC: Tundra Books, 1969.

English, L.E.F. "The Jersey Men." *The Newfoundland Quarterly* 50 (1950): 17–20.

Faris, James C. *Cat Harbour: A Newfoundland Fishing Settlement*. St John's, NF: ISER Books, 1972.

Favret-Saada, Jeanne. *Deadly Words: Witchcraft in the Bocage*. Translated by Catherine Cullen. Cambridge and Paris: Cambridge University Press, 1980.

Feild, Edward. *Journal of the Bishop of Newfoundland's Voyage of Visitation and Discovery on the South and West Coasts of Newfoundland and on the Labrador, in the Church Ship "Hawk" in the Year 1848*. Entry for 22 July. London: Society for the Propagation of the Gospel in Foreign Parts, 1851. Published on the Internet at the Project Canterbury Web site, *http:// justus.anglican.org*.

– *A Journal of a Visitation in the "Hawk" Church Ship, On the Coast of Labrador, and Round the Whole Island of Newfoundland, in the Year 1849*. Entry for 28 July. London: The Society for the Propagation of the Gospel, 1850. Published on the Internet at the Project Canterbury Web site, *http:// justus.anglican.org*.

Ferguson, Mark. "The Book of Black Hearts: Readdressing the Meaning and Relevance of Supernatural Materials." *Journal of Canadian Studies* 29 (1994):107–21.

Firestone, Melvin M. *Brothers and Rivals: Patrilocality in Savage Cove*. St John's, NF: ISER Books, 1967.

– "The 'Old Hag': Sleep Paralysis in Newfoundland." *The Journal of Psycho-analytic Anthropology* 8 (1985):47–66.

First: Aboriginal Artists of Newfoundland and Labrador. St John's, NF: St John's Native Friendship Centre, 1996.

Fitzhenry, Jack. "The Widow's Curse." *The Newfoundland Quarterly* 4454:3 (1945):9–15.

Galgay, Frank, and Michael McCarthy. *Shipwrecks of Newfoundland and Labrador. Vol. 2*. St John's, NF: Harry Cuff, 1990.

Gaskill, Malcolm. "Witches and Witnesses in Old and New England." In *Languages of Witchcraft: Narrative, Ideology and Meaning in Early Modern Culture*, edited by Stuart Clark, 55–80. New York, NY: St Martin's Press, 2001.

Gibson, Marion. *Reading Witchcraft: Stories of Early English Witches*. London and New York: Routledge, 1999.

Gijswijt-Hofstra, Marijke, Brian P. Levack, and Roy Porter, eds. *The Athlone History of Witchcraft and Magic in Europe. Vol. 5: The Eighteenth and Nineteenth Centuries*. London, UK: The Athlone Press, 1999.

Glanvil, Joseph. *Sadducismus Triumphatus: Or, A full and plain Evidence, concerning Witches and Apparitions*. 4th ed. London, UK: A. Bettesworth and J. Batley, 1726.

Godbeer, Richard. *The Devil's Dominion: Magic and Religion in Early New England.* Cambridge, UK: Cambridge University Press, 1992.

Gough, William. *David Blackwood: Master Printmaker.* Vancouver and Toronto: Douglas and McIntyre, 2001.

Gragg, Larry. *The Salem Witch Crisis.* New York, NY: Praeger, 1992.

Grenfell, Wilfred. *Labrador Days: Tales of the Sea Toilers.* London, UK: Hodder and Stoughton, 1919.

Hall, David D. *Witch-Hunting in Seventeenth Century New England: A Documentary History, 1638–1692.* Boston, MA: Northeastern University Press, 1999.

Hall, Trevor. *Old Conjuring Books: A Bibliographical and Historical Study with a Supplementary Check-List.* London, UK: Duckworth, 1972.

Hand, Wayland D., et al. *Popular Beliefs and Superstitions: A Compendium of American Folklore from the Ohio Collection of Newbell Niles Puckett.* Boston, MA: G.K. Hall, 1981.

Handcock, W. Gordon. *Soe longe as there comes noe women: Origins of English Settlement in Newfoundland.* St John's, NF: Breakwater, 1989.

Harris, Leslie. *Growing Up with Verse: A Child's Life in Gallows Harbour.* St John's, NF: Harry Cuff, 2002.

Harvey, Rev. Moses. "How the Fish Came to Hant's Harbor Sixty Years Ago." 1894. Edited by Rev. Charles Lench. St John's, NF: Robinson and Co., 1926.

Henderson, Lizanne, and Edward J. Cowan. *Scottish Fairy Belief: A History.* East Lothian, Scotland: Tuckwell Press, 2001.

Henningsen, Gustav. "Witch Persecution after the Era of the Witch Trials: A Contribution to Danish Ethnohistory." *Arv* 44 (1988):103–53.

Howley, James P. *The Beothucks or Red Indians: The Aboriginal Inhabitants of Newfoundland.* 1915. Toronto, ON: Coles Publishing, 1974.

Hufford, David J. *The Terror That Comes in the Night: An Experience-Centered Study of Supernatural Assault Traditions.* Philadelphia, PA: University of Pennsylvania Press, 1982.

Hunt, Robert. *Popular Romances of the West of England or The Drolls, Traditions and Superstitions of Cornwall.* [1916]. New York and London: Benjamin Blom, 1968.

Ivanits, Linda J. *Russian Folk Belief.* Armonk, New York, and London: M.E. Sharpe, 1989.

Jackson, Doug. *"On the Country": The Micmac of Newfoundland.* Edited by Gerald Penney. St John's, NF: Harry Cuff, 1993.

Jantz, Harold S. "German Thought and Literature in New England, 1620–1820." *Journal of English and Germanic Philology* 41 (1942):1–45.

Jauhiainen, Marjatta. *The Type and Motif Index of Finnish Belief Legends and Memorates*. Folklore Fellows Communications No. 182. Helsinki: Academia Scientiarum Fennica, 1998.

Jean, John. *Jersey Sailing Ships*. Chichester, Sussex, UK: Phillimore, 1982.

Jones, Michael Owen. *Why Faith Healing?* Ottawa, ON: National Museum of Man, 1972.

Karkeet, Paul Q. "A Budget of Witch Stories." *Report and Transactions of the Devonshire Association* 14 (1882):387–94.

Karlsen, Carol F. *The Devil in the Shape of a Woman: Witchcraft in Colonial New England*. New York and London: W.W. Norton, 1987.

Kennedy, Maxwell. *History and Folklore of Western Bay (Conception Bay North Shore, Circa 1930)*. N.p., n.d. [c. 1995].

Keough, Willeen. "The 'Old Hag' Revisits Saint Brigid: Irish Women and the Intersection of Belief Systems on the Southern Avalon, Newfoundland." In *Women in Newfoundland and Labrador: Weather's Edge: A Compendium*, edited by Linda Cullum, Carmelita McGrath, and Marilyn Porter, 11–22. St John's, NF: Killick Press, 2006.

Kielly, Kim. *Angels and Miracles: True Stories*. St John's, NF: Flanker Press, 2005.

Kittredge, George Lyman. *Witchcraft in Old and New England*. 1929. New York, NY: Russell and Russell, 1956.

Klaniczay, Gabor. "Hungary: The Accusations and the Universe of Popular Magic." In *Early Modern European Witchcraft: Centres and Peripheries*, edited by Bengt Ankarloo and Gustav Henningsen, 219–55. Oxford, UK: Clarendon, 1990.

Knott, Olive. *Witches of Dorset*. Milbourne Port, Dorset, UK: Dorset Publishing, 1974.

Kors, Alan C., and Edward Peters. *Witchcraft in Europe 1100–1700: A Documentary History*. 1972. Philadelphia, PA: University of Pennsylvania Press, 1992.

Lamb, Lawrence E. "Ask the Doctor." *Evening Telegram* (St John's), 14 June 1993, p.15.

L'Amy, John H. *Jersey Folk Lore*. Jersey: J.T. Bigwood, 1927.

Lancre, Pierre De. *Tableau de l'Inconstance des mauvais Anges et Demons*. 1613. Facsimile Internet edition: Cornell University Witchcraft Collection, http:// historical.library.cornell.edu.

Lannon, Alice, and Michael McCarthy. *Fables, Fairies and Folklore of Newfoundland*. St John's, NF: Jesperson Press, 1991.

Larner, Cristina. *Witchcraft and Religion: The Politics of Popular Belief*. Oxford and New York: Basil Blackwell, 1984.

Lea, Hermann. "Wessex Witches, Witchery, and Witchcraft." *The Nineteenth Century and After* 58 (1903):1,010–24.

Leather, Ella Mary. *The Folk-Lore of Herefordshire: Collected from Oral and Printed Sources.* [1912]. Facsimile reprint. N.p., n.d.

Le Messurier, H.W. *Old-Time Newfoundland.* Edited by C.R. Fay. St John's, NF: N.p., n.d. [c. 1950s].

Lemprière, Raoul. *Buildings and Memorials of the Channel Islands.* London, UK: Robert Hale, 1980.

Lench, Rev. Charles. "Life in an Outport." *The Newfoundland Quarterly* 3 (1903):4.

Levack, Brian P. "The Confessions of Witches in Guernsey." In *The Witchcraft Sourcebook*, edited by Brian P. Levack, 184–9. New York and London: Routledge, 2004.

Lovelace, Martin. "Merchantable Magic: Interpreting the Jersey-merchant Legends in Newfoundland." In *Telling, Remembering, Interpreting, Guessing: A Festschrift for Prof. Annikki Kaivola-Bregenhoj*, edited by Maria Vasenkari, Pasi Enges, and Anna-Leena Siikala, 344–9. Suomen Kansantietouden Tutkijain Seura: Joensuu, Finland, 2000.

MacCulloch, Edgar A. *Guernsey Folk Lore.* Edited by Edith F. Carey. London, UK: Elliot Stock, 1903.

Macfarlane, Alan. *Witchcraft in Tudor and Stuart England: A Regional and Comparative Study.* London, UK: Routledge and Kegan Paul, 1970.

MacGregor, William. *Report by the Governor on a Visit to the Micmac Indians at Bay d'Espoir.* Colonial Reports, Newfoundland No. 54. London, UK: For His Majesty's Stationery Office, 1908.

Malinowski, Bronislaw. *Magic, Science and Religion and Other Essays.* 1925. New York, NY: Doubleday, 1954.

Marshall, Ingeborg. *A History and Ethnography of the Beothuk.* Montreal and Kingston: McGill-Queen's University Press, 1996.

Martin, Peggy. "'Drop Dead': Witchcraft Images and Ambiguities in Newfoundland Society." *Culture & Tradition* 2 (1977):35–50.

– "Micmac Indians as Witches in the Newfoundland Tradition." *Papers of the Tenth Algonquian Conference*, edited by William Cowan, 173–80. Ottawa, ON: Carleton University, 1979.

McGee, Harold Franklin, Jr. "Ethnic Boundaries and Strategies of Ethnic Interaction: A History of Micmac-White Relations in Nova Scotia." PhD thesis, Carbondale: Southern Illinois University, 1974.

McMillen, Persis W. *Currents of Malice: Mary Towne Esty and Her Family in Salem Witchcraft.* Portsmouth, NH: Peter E. Randall, 1990.

McNaughton, Janet. "The Role of the Newfoundland Midwife in Traditional Health Care, 1900–1970." PhD thesis, St John's: Memorial University of Newfoundland, 1990.

McPhee, Charles. *Stop Sleeping through Your Dreams: A Guide to Awakening Consciousness During Dream Sleep.* New York, NY: Henry Holt, 1995.

Mercer, Paul. *Newfoundland Songs and Ballads in Print 1842–1974.* St John's: Memorial University of Newfoundland Folklore and Language Publications, 1979.

Merrifield, Ralph. *The Archaeology of Ritual and Magic.* London, UK: B.T. Batsford, 1987.

Millais, J.G. *Newfoundland and Its Untrodden Ways.* London, UK: Longmans, Green, 1907.

Mitchell, Roger E. *"George Knox: From Man to Legend." Northeast Folklore* 11, 1969. Orono, ME: University Press, 1970.

Monter, E. William. *Witchcraft in France and Switzerland: The Borderlands during the Reformation.* Ithaca and London: Cornell University Press, 1976.

Murakami, Haruki. "Sleep." Translated by Jay Rubin. In *The Literary Insomniac: Stories and Essays for Sleepless Nights,* edited by Elyse Cheney and Wendy Hubbert, 72–113. New York, NY: Doubleday, 1996.

Murphy, James. *Customs of the Past in Newfoundland.* St John's, NF: N.p., 1918.

Murray, Hilda Chaulk. *More Than Fifty Percent: Woman's Life in a Newfoundland Outport 1900–1950.* St John's, NF: Breakwater Books, 1979.

Neis, Barbara. "Familial and Social Patriarchy in the Newfoundland Fishing Industry." In *Fishing Places, Fishing People: Traditions and Issues in Canadian Small-Scale Fisheries,* edited by Dianne Newell and Rosemary E. Ommer, 32–54. Toronto, ON: University of Toronto Press, 1999.

Ness, Robert C. "The Old Hag Phenomenon as Sleep Paralysis: A Biocultural Interpretation." *Culture, Medicine and Psychiatry* 2 (1978):15–39.

Norton, Mary Beth. *In the Devil's Snare: The Salem Witchcraft Crisis of 1692.* New York, NY: Alfred A. Knopf, 2002.

Ommer, Rosemary E. "The Cod Trade in the New World." In *A People of the Sea: The Maritime History of the Channel Islands,* edited by A.G. Jamieson, 245–68. London and New York: Methuen, 1986.

– *From Outpost to Outport: A Structural Analysis of the Jersey-Gaspé Cod Fishery, 1767–1886.* Montreal and Kingston: McGill-Queen's University Press, 1991.

O'Flaherty, Patrick. *Lost Country: The Rise and Fall of Newfoundland, 1843–1933.* St John's, NF: Long Beach Press, 2005.

Ó Súilleabháin, Seán. *A Handbook of Irish Folklore.* 1942. Detroit, MI: Singing Tree Press, 1970.

Passin, Herbert. "Sorcery as a Phase of Tarahumara Economic Relations." [1911]. *Man* 42 (1942):11–15.

Pastore, Ralph. *Newfoundland Micmacs: A History of Their Traditional Life.* St John's, NF: Newfoundland Historical Society, 1978.

Patterson, George. "Folk-Lore in Newfoundland." *Journal of American Folklore* 19 (1897):214–15.

Pattison, G.W. "Adult Education and Folklore." *Folk-Lore* 64 (1953):424–6.

Paul, Daniel M. *We Were Not the Savages: A Mi'kmaq Perspective on the Collision between European and Native American Civilizations.* Halifax, NS: Fernwood Publishing, 2000.

Peacock, F.W. *Labrador Inuit Lore and Legend.* St John's, NF: Jesperson Press, 1981.

Pelly, David E. *Sacred Hunt: A Portrait of the Relationship between Seals and Inuit.* Seattle, WA: University of Washington Press, 2001.

Pitts, John Linwood. *Witchcraft and Devil Lore in the Channel Islands.* Guernsey: Thomas M. Richard, 1886.

Planetta, Elizabeth Catherine Beaton. "Sorcery Beliefs and Oral Tradition in Chéticamp, Cape Breton." MA thesis, St John's: Memorial University of Newfoundland, 1981.

Pocius, Gerald L. *A Place to Belong: Community Order and Everyday Space in Calvert, Newfoundland.* Athens and London: University of Georgia Press, and Montreal and Kingston: McGill-Queen's University Press, 1991.

Porter, Helen. *Below the Bridge: Memories of the South Side of St. John's.* St John's, NF: Breakwater Books, 1979.

Porter, Roy. *The Athlone History of Witchcraft and Magic in Europe: Vol. 5: The Eighteenth and Nineteenth Centuries,* edited by Marijke Gijswijt-Hofstra, Brian P. Levack, and Roy Porter. London, UK: The Athlone Press, 1999.

Power, Rev. M.F. "The Micmacs." *The Newfoundland Quarterly* 9 (1910): 1–3.

Purkhardt, Brigitte. *La chasse-galerie, de la légende au mythe: La symbolique du vol magique dans les récits québécois de chasse-galerie.* Montreal, QC: XYZ, 1992.

Rieti, Barbara. "Aboriginal/Anglo Relations as Portrayed in the Folklore of Micmac 'Witching' in Newfoundland." *Canadian Folklore Canadien* 17 (1995):21–9.

– "Guns and Bottles: Newfoundland Counterwitchcraft Measures as Assertions of Masculinity." In *Folklore Interpreted: Essays in Honor of Alan Dundes,* edited by Regina Bendix and Rosemary Lévy Zumwalt, 167–82. New York and London: Garland, 1995.

– "Riddling the Witch: Violence against Women in Newfoundland Witch Tradition." In *Undisciplined Women: Tradition and Culture in Canada,* edited by Pauline Greenhill and Diane Tye, 77–86. Montreal and Kingston: McGill-Queen's University Press, 1997.

– *Strange Terrain: The Fairy World in Newfoundland.* St John's, NF: ISER Books, 1991.

Rollman, Hans. "John Wesley and Newfoundland." *The Telegram* (St John's), 15 June 2003.

– "A Tale of Two Bishops." *The Telegram* (St John's), 23 March 2003.

Roper, Lyndal. *Oedipus and the Devil: Witchcraft, Sexuality and Religion in Early Modern Europe.* London and New York: Routledge, 1994.

Rosenthal, Bernard. *Salem Story: Reading the Witch Trials of 1692.* Cambridge and New York: Cambridge University Press, 1993.

Rutherford, Edward Arthur. "Newfoundland Log Book." *The Newfoundland Quarterly* 70 (1973):25–6.

Ryan, Shannon. *The Ice Hunters: A History of Newfoundland Sealing to 1914.* St John's, NF: Breakwater, 1994.

Scot, Reginald. *Discoverie of Witchcraft.* 1584. With an Introduction by Montague Summers. London, UK: J. Rodker, 1930. Reprint. New York, NY: Dover, 1972.

Shortis, H.F. *The Shortis Papers.* Vol. 3. Pt. 1. Collected in the Centre for Newfoundland Studies, St John's, Memorial University of Newfoundland.

Speck, Frank G. *Beothuk and Micmac.* New York, NY: Museum of the American Indian, Heye Foundation, 1922.

St Leger-Gordon, Ruth. *Witchcraft and Folklore of Dartmoor.* 1965. New York, NY: Bell, 1972.

Story, G.M. "Newfoundland: Fishermen, Hunters, Planters, and Merchants." In *Christmas Mumming in Newfoundland: Essays in Anthropology, Folklore and History,* edited by Herbert Halpert and G.M. Story, 7–33. Toronto, ON: University of Toronto Press, 1969.

Sullivan, John. *Newfoundland, Its Origin, Its Rise and Fall, also, An Epitome of the Jersey Crisis.* Jersey: N.p., 1886. (Located in the Centre for Newfoundland Studies).

Summers, Montague. *A Popular History of Witchcraft.* 1937. New York, NY: Causeway Books, 1973.

Tanner, Adrian. *Bringing Home Animals: Religious Ideology and Mode of Production of the Mistassini Cree Hunters.* St John's, NF: ISER Books, 1979.

Tausiet, María. "Witchcraft as Metaphor: Infanticide and Its Translations in Aragón in the Sixteenth and Seventeenth Centuries." In *Languages of Witchcraft: Narrative, Ideology and Meaning in Early Modern Culture,* edited by Stuart Clark, 179–95. New York, NY: St Martin's Press, 2001.

Thomas, Keith. *Religion and the Decline of Magic: Studies in Popular Beliefs in Sixteenth and Seventeenth Century England.* Harmondworth, UK: Penguin, 1971.

Thompson, Janet A. *Wives, Widows, Witches and Bitches: Women in Seventeenth-Century Devon.* New York, NY: Peter Berg, 1993.

Thompson, Stith. *Motif-Index of Folk-Literature.* Bloomington, IN: Indiana University Press, 1955.

Tongue, Ruth. "Some Notes on Modern Somerset Witch-Lore." *Folklore* 74 (1963):321–5.

Upton, L.S. *Micmacs and Colonists: Indian-White Relations in the Maritimes 1713–1867.* Vancouver, BC: University of British Columbia Press, 1979.

Valenze, Deborah M. *Prophetic Sons and Daughters: Female Preaching and Popular Religion in Industrial England.* Princeton, NJ: Princeton University Press, 1985.

Wallis, Wilson D., and Ruth Sawtell Wallis. *The Micmac Indians of Eastern Canada.* Minneapolis, MN: University of Minnesota Press, 1955.

Watson, W.G. Willis. *Somerset Life and Character.* London, UK: Folk Press, 1924.

Weiss, Harry B. *A Book about Chapbooks: The People's Literature of Bygone Times.* 1942. Hatboro, PA: Folklore Associates, 1969.

Wesley, John. *The Works of John Wesley Volume 22: Journals and Diaries v (1765–75).* Edited by W. Reginald Ward and Richard P. Heitzenrater. Nashville, TN: Abingdon Press, 1993.

Wetzel, Edwina. "Address to Convocation." *MUN Gazette* (St John's), 3 June 1993, 21.

Whitehead, Ruth Holmes. *Stories from the Six Worlds: Micmac Legends.* Halifax, NS: Nimbus Publishing, 1988.

Whitlock, Ralph. "Fast and Furious." *Guardian Weekly* (UK), 1 March 1992.

– *Wiltshire Folklore and Legends.* London, UK: Robert Hale, 1992.

Willis, Deborah. *Malevolent Nurture: Witch-Hunting and Maternal Power in Early Modern England.* Ithaca and London: Cornell University Press, 1995.

Wilson, William. *Newfoundland and Its Missionaries.* Cambridge, MA: Dakin and Metcalf, 1866.

Winsor, Naboth. *Hearts Strangely Warmed: A History of Methodism in Newfoundland 1765–1925.* Gander, NF: BSC Printers, 1982.

– *Resounding God's Praises On Islands, In Coves: A History of the Methodist Church, 1862–1925, and the United Church of Canada, 1925–1990, in Settlements from Greenspond to Deadman's Bay, except Wesleyville.* N.p., n.d. [Privately published c. 1990].

Wix, E. *Six Months of a Newfoundland Missionary's Journal, from February to August 1835.* London, UK: Smith, Elder, 1836.

Yoder, Don. "Hohman and Romanus: Origins and Diffusion of the Pennsylvania German Powwow Manual." In *American Folk Medicine: A Symposium*, edited by Wayland D. Hand, 235–48. Berkeley and Los Angeles: University of California Press, 1980.

Index

Printed in the USA
CPSIA information can be obtained
at www.ICGtesting.com
JSHW080151070823
46057JS00001B/61